Progressivism Madness

A SAPIENT Being's Guide to the Idiocracy and Hypocrisy of the 'Regressivism' Movement

By

Corey Lee Wilson

Progressivism Madness

Progressivism Madness

Fratire Publishing books can be purchased in bulk with exclusive discounts for educational purposes, association gifts, sales promotions, and special editions can be created to specifications. All inquiries for such can be made below.

FRATIRE PUBLISHING LLC
4533 Temescal Canyon Rd. # 308
Corona, CA 92883 USA
www.FratirePublishing.com
FratirePublishing@att.net
1+ (951) 638-5502

FratirePublishing
Relevant Books for **SAPIENT** Beings

Fratire Publishing is all about common sense and relevant books for sapient beings. If this sounds like you and you can never have enough common sense, wisdom, and relevancy, then visit us and learn more about the 40 *MADNESS* series of book titles at www.fratirepublishing.com/madnessbooks.

Printed paperback and eBook ePUB by Ingram Spark in La Vergne, Tennessee, USA
Copyright © 2023: First Edition April 18, 2023
ISBN 978-0-9847490-6-5 (Paperback)
ISBN 978-1-953319-37-1 (eBook)
Progressivism Madness-01-PDF (pdf)
LCCN 2023907266

Special thanks for the cover design by Jenny Barroso, J20Graphics, j20graphics@gmail.com and ebook conversion by Redeemer SoftTech, redeemer.softtech@gmail.com.

Contents

Acknowledgements

I owe a debt of gratitude to the following for "heavily" borrowing at times pieces of their and/or outright sections. I do this unashamedly to use the sapient phrase, "if it ain't broke—don't try to fix it." Most of the borrowed works and research cannot be improved upon—so why try? It's better to assemble these meaningful parts, profound messages, and eloquent arguments into a cohesive whole, told with high school and college students in mind, and that's what I've done and where my talent lies.

Below in alphabetical order are the major contributors to The SAPIENT Being that I borrowed verbatim, quoted, and conceptualized much of their content from a little to a lot. Wherever this happened, I did my best to acknowledge my source. If I didn't at times within the 15 chapters, I did so intentionally because doing so would have distracted from their message. Nonetheless, they are more than acknowledged in the References and Index sections of this textbook.

One last note, to keep the Index section manageable in size, in this textbook, it only lists the cities of Seattle and Miami, and the states of California and Florida for comparison purposes. All other cities, states, and countries are not listed.

City Journal: Is a public policy magazine and website, published by the Manhattan Institute for Policy Research, that covers a range of topics on urban affairs, such as policing, education, housing, and other issues. The *City Journal* and its authors were the most widely used resource for *Progressivism Madness.*

Epoch Times, The: Is America's fastest-growing independent news media, founded in 2000, and their mission is to bring readers a truthful view of the world free from the influence of any government, corporation, or political party. Contrary to fake news organizations, their aim is to tell readers what they see, not how to think; and they strive to deliver a factual picture of reality that lets readers form their own opinions.

Hanson, Victor Davis: Is a fifth generation Californian and the Martin and Illie Anderson Senior Fellow in Residence in Classics and Military History at the Hoover Institution, Stanford University, a professor of Classics Emeritus at California State University, Fresno, and a nationally syndicated columnist for Tribune Media Services. Hanson is also the Wayne & Marcia Buske Distinguished Fellow in History, Hillsdale College and is the 2003 author of *Mexifornia: A State of Becoming* plus other books and articles about current events.

Kotkin, Joel: Is the Presidential Fellow in Urban Futures at Chapman University and founder of the Center for Demographics and Policy there. He is also executive director of the Urban Reform Institute in Houston, Texas, and a regular contributor to *The City Journal, The Hill*, Real Clear Politics, the Daily Beast, and Tablet. He is the author of nine books including the recently released *The Coming of Neo-Feudalism: A Warning to the Global Middle Class* (2020).

National Review: Is an American semi-monthly editorial magazine, focusing on news and commentary pieces on political, social, and cultural affairs and its authors contributed a considerable number of articles to this textbook. The magazine was founded by the author William F. Buckley Jr. in 1955 and has played a significant role in the development of conservatism in the United States, and is a leading voice on the American right.

Rufo, Christopher F.: Is leading the fight against critical race theory in American institutions. His research and activism inspired a presidential order and legislation in 15 states, where he has worked closely with lawmakers to craft successful public policy. Rufo is a contributing editor of *City Journal* and director of the Discovery Institute's Center on Wealth & Poverty. He's directed four documentaries for PBS, including his new film, "America Lost," which tells the story of three "forgotten American cities."

Salzman, Philip Carl: Is a professor emeritus of anthropology at McGill University, senior fellow at the Frontier Centre for Public Policy, fellow at the Middle East Forum, and president of Scholars for Peace in the Middle East.

The Heritage Foundation: Is an American conservative think tank that is primarily geared toward public policy and the foundation took a leading role in the conservative movement during the presidency of Ronald Reagan, whose policies were taken from Heritage's policy study Mandate for Leadership. The Heritage Foundation has had a major influence in U.S. public policy making and is among the most influential conservative public policy organizations in America.

A SAPIENT Being's Preface

In the 21st century, Progressives have innovated in ideology, jettisoning the economic class struggle of Marxism and replacing it with identity classes: gender, race, sexuality, religion, nationality, and ableness. Now it's (allegedly) whites (including "white adjacent" Asians and "hyperwhite" Jews), males, and Christians who are oppressors—and people of color, women, LGBTQ++, Muslims, and the disabled who are the oppressed victims.

With the "social justice" trinity of "diversity, equity, and inclusion," Progressives have returned us to the days of deep Jim Crow, with some races seen as virtuous and others as evil, the only difference being that the colors have changed. Progressive "inclusion" means including preferred races and genders, and excluding the others, as we see in hiring, college admissions, funding, promotions, and awards.

Equity, meaning the statistical equivalence of races and genders, in practice means more of the preferred and fewer of the despised. Objective measures, such as standardized tests, and advanced education programs, are cancelled, because they don't produce the desired "equity" results. Now institutionalized DEI racism and discrimination are regarded as desirable by Progressives, as long as preferred categories benefit.

Who are these Progressives? Answer: They are typically very liberal, highly educated, and majority White—and most say U.S. institutions need to be completely rebuilt because of racial bias. What devious force brought all of this cultural destruction into being? Who injected this destructive poison into the Progressivism movement? The source, of course, is our universities where so many academics and college faculty are the post-modernists, pushing "Progressive" activism at a college near you.

Enough! Now is the time to wake up before we do even graver damage—not only to ourselves individually but to our country as a whole. It's a bitter irony that those who want to drive us into this new hysteria often claim to be "woke." But there is no awakening in woke. It's the sleep of reason that produces monsters, and it poses a profound peril to our republic.

Furthermore, it's because of the insidious nature of Progressivism madness that the SAPIENT Being has created the Sapient Conservative Textbooks (SCT) Program so that students, administrators, and professors can fight Progressivism and its inherent illiberalism and see for themselves how the prevailing Marxist, woke, cancel culture is indoctrinating and brainwashing America's 74 million students.

Like all *MADNESS* textbooks, *Progressivism Madness* offers an opportunity to be part of the solution to these many problems. For some of you this *MADNESS* textbook will be a revelation, an epiphany, a sapient being moment. For others, it will be a triggering event, denial of truth, and a painful intervention.

Are you interested in learning all about the hypocrisy and idiocracy of today's illiberal and retrogressive Progressivism movement, destructive DEI policies and programs, the Marxist foundations of Critical Race Theory (CRT), reverse racism, cancel culture, social injustice, and how to work together to defeat this movement before it destroys our republic? If yes, please read on and if you also believe in the message of this textbook and willing to fight for it—please considering joining or participating in one of the three SAPIENT Being programs below.

Sapient Conservative Textbooks (SCT) Program is a relevant and current events textbooks program (published by Fratire Publishing LLC) to help return conservative values, viewpoint diversity, and sapience to high school and college campuses—and enlighten them on the many blessings to humankind that are the direct result of Western European culture, American exceptionalism, and Judeo-Christian values.

Free Speech Alumni Ambassador (FSAA) Program helps create faculty and administrative positions, throughout America's predominantly liberally staffed college campuses, that can serve as much needed conservative club advisors—because conservative students are facing many obstacles when they attempt to start and charter a right-leaning student organization on campus due to faculty members fearful of losing their jobs or tenure for becoming these organization's advisors.

Make Free Speech Again On Campus (MFSAOC) Program is an interactive opportunity and nexus for high school and college students to start SAPIENT Being campus clubs, chapters, and alliances where independent, liberal, and conservative minded students can meet, discuss, and debate important issues by utilizing the sapient principles of viewpoint diversity, freedom of speech, and intellectual humility—and develop sapience in the process.

Are You a Sapient Being or Want to Be One?

Sapience, also known as wisdom, is the ability to think and act using knowledge, experience, understanding, common sense and insight. Sapience is associated with attributes such as intelligence, enlightenment, unbiased judgment, compassion, experiential self-knowledge, self-actualization, and virtues such as ethics and benevolence.

Being a sapient being is not about identity politics, it's about doing what is right and borrows many of the essential qualities of Centrism that supports strength, tradition, open mindedness, and policy based on evidence not ideology.

Sapient beings are independent minded thinkers that achieve common sense solutions that appropriately address America's and the world's most pressing issues. They gauge situations based on context and reason, consideration, and probability. They are open minded and exercise conviction and willing to fight for it on the intellectual battlefield. Sapient beings don't blindly and recklessly follow their feelings or emotions.

Their unifying ideology is based on truth, reason, logic, scientific method, and pragmatism—and not necessarily defined by compromise, moderation, or any particular faith—but is considerate of them.

Most importantly, per a letter written by Princeton professor Robert George in 2017 and endorsed by 28 professors from three Ivy League universities for incoming freshmen, "Think for yourself!"

George's letter continues:

Thinking for yourself means questioning dominant ideas even when others insist on their being treated as unquestionable. It means deciding what one believes not by conforming to fashionable opinions, but by taking the trouble to learn and honestly consider the strongest arguments to be advanced on both or all sides of questions—including arguments for positions that others revile and want to stigmatize and against positions others seek to immunize from critical scrutiny.

The love of truth and the desire to attain it should motivate you to think for yourself. The crucial point of a college education is to seek truth and to learn the skills and acquire the virtues necessary to be a lifelong truth-seeker. Open-mindedness, critical thinking, and debate are essential to discovering the truth. Moreover, they are our best antidotes to bigotry.

Merriam-Webster's first definition of the word "bigot" is a person "who is obstinately or intolerantly devoted to his or her own opinions and prejudices." The only people who need fear open-minded inquiry and robust debate are the actual bigots, including those on campuses or in the broader society who seek to protect the hegemony of their opinions by claiming that to question those opinions is itself bigotry.

So, don't be tyrannized by public opinion. Don't get trapped in an echo chamber. Whether you in the end reject or embrace a view, make sure you decide where you stand by critically assessing the arguments for the competing positions. Think for yourself. Good luck to you in college!

Now, that might sound easy. But you will find—as you may have discovered already in high school—that thinking for yourself can be a challenge. It always demands self-discipline, and these days can require courage.

In today's climate, it's all-too-easy to allow your views and outlook to be shaped by dominant opinion on your campus or in the broader academic culture. The danger any student—or faculty member—faces today is falling into the vice of conformism, yielding to groupthink, the orthodoxy.

At many colleges and universities what John Stuart Mill called "the tyranny of public opinion" does more than merely discourage students from dissenting from prevailing views on moral, political, and other types of questions. It leads them to suppose that dominant views are so obviously correct that only a bigot or a crank could question them.

Since no one wants to be, or be thought of as, a bigot or a crank, the easy, lazy way to proceed is simply by falling into line with campus orthodoxies. Don't do it!

To be sure, our overly-politicized culture has a tough time viewing any "verbal cacophony" as a sign of strength and vibrancy. And perhaps nowhere is this truer than on many college campuses where political correctness is rampant, groupthink is common, and social media "mobs" arise in a flash to intimidate anyone who openly strays from the prevailing orthodoxy.

At the SAPIENT Being we're not intimidated—and our primary purpose is to seek the truth by enhancing viewpoint diversity, promoting intellectual humility, protecting freedom of speech and expression while developing sapience in the process—no matter what the cost on the intellectual battlefield, campus classroom, and marketplace of ideas. This is our ethos! Is it yours?

Best regards and sapiently yours,

Corey Lee Wilson

Corey Lee Wilson

S.A.P.I.E.N.T. Being

1 – What is 21st Century Progressivism & Who Are These So-Called Progressives?

Credit: Chad Crowe.

Historically, the United States has possessed a single dominant ideology of liberalism "classical" liberalism, not to be confused with today's neo-liberalism) that sustained itself from previous ideological challengers. As noted by Bradley A. Thayer's January 2022 "Our 1776 Moment: Either a Liberal or Progressive America" *Epoch Times* article:

Classical Liberalism is a political ideology that promises liberty for the individual. It employs the concept of inalienable rights and individual freedoms. These ideas and principles are expressed in America's founding documents—the Declaration of Independence, the Constitution, and the Bill of Rights—and have been echoed in American political ideas, practices, tradition, and culture since the American Revolution of 1776.

Opposed to classic liberalism, Western leftists like to refer to themselves as "Progressives," and their worldview most closely resembles an evolving fascism, differing only in degree—so far. Their programs include increased government control, the reduction of civil liberties, and the transfer of power from the people, state governments, and Congress to federal bureaucrats, courts, and international institutions. None of these goals, when compared to classical liberalism, are "Progressive" – but "regressive" to the very foundations of the United States of America.

If we take a unbiased look at every major problem or issue facing America in the 21st century, as this textbook will show, each and every one of them, to one degree or another, is being created by Progressive ideology or negatively impacted by Progressive polices, programs, or agenda.

Today's Progressivism in 21st Century America

American leftists like to call themselves "progressive" as a form of self-praise, a state of being, an assertion that their politics represent a higher consciousness than the prejudices of the mob of unthinking deplorables and will lead mankind to a sunny upland where human nature will transcend its baser impulses, and peace and harmony will reign. The hypocrisy of their belief structure will unfold as we learn more about the Progressivism ideology.

Furthermore, Progressivism Isn't progressive—it's recycled and repackaged Marxism for a 21st century audience as you will see as we learn more about it in the following articles.

Conservatives, independents, and sapient beings should not indulge so-called "Progressives" in this self-deception. We should stop using "Progressive" as a synonym for the noun "Left" or the adjective "left-wing" and use "regressive" or "regressivism" instead. At first, you might be wondering why this antonym is being used—but as we move through this textbook, chapter by chapter, it will become clearly evident there is no progress for Americans from Progressivism's regressivism—only an Orwellian *1984* future that will fundamentally change America for the worse.

Make no mistake: This neo-Marxist assault has been planned and coordinated for years to strike America where she is weakest: in her innate sense of rightness and fair play. Under so-called Progressive pedagogy, you'll see how quickly we have moved from Dr. Martin Luther King, Jr.'s plea that we judge a man by "the content of his character" and back to "the color of his skin." It's regressivism madness—and if Dr. King could see what is happening to his dream—he would be rolling in his grave.

Progressivism's Long March Through America's Institutions

As in Karl Marx's older drama, the moral imperative of Progressives is to once again "set things right." In Marx's time this was the task of revolutionaries. Today this task falls to Progressive politicians and activists, social justice reformers, civil rights workers, cultural appropriation enforcers, diversity, and inclusion warriors and the like who have spread into the media, government, college campuses, neighborhood organizations and workplaces.

In the past, Marxist revolutionaries sought to set things right by leading a revolution to overthrow the capitalist system and replace it with a just economic system. Progressives want to set things right through social change in order to create a "just" society. In a just society everyone is equal: men and women, immigrants and native-born, persons of various racial and ethnic groups, heterosexuals, and homosexuals, first and third world people, disabled and able-bodied.

Progressives feel (and "feel" may be a more appropriate verb than "think") that because they want to do something that is so obviously good (i.e., help the poor, fight racism, climate justice, etc.), their policy recommendations must necessarily be the right and best solutions—and that anyone who disagrees with them is, a bad or hateful person.

Thus, for example, these naive U.S. Progressives are convinced that because they have good intentions, they can make Socialism work. They think socialism hasn't succeeded elsewhere because the leaders either didn't implement socialism thoroughly enough or because those leaders weren't good people.

Or, they champion the myth of Scandinavian "democratic socialism" as proof it can work—when in fact, it's a Progressive myth, false narrative, a hypocrisy—because these countries are just as capitalist as the USA but with larger welfare programs paid for by highly progressive tax rates. These Nordic countries are not socialist, but the ones who most certainly are, and have failed miserably across the world stage, are the Soviet Union, Cuba, Mao's China, North Korea, and most recently, Venezuela.

However, what the Soviet Union failed to do economically and militarily during its losing 20th-century confrontation with the West, cultural Marxism, by way of 21st century Progressivism, are coming closer to realizing the collapse of Western Civilization at the hands of young Progressives via the destruction of what the Russian communists used to refer to as the "principal enemy"—the United States.

Revolutionary Justice and the 'Progressive' Terror

Per the Harley Price "From Mao to Now: A 'Progress' Report on the New Millennium" *Epoch Times* December 2020 article:

Having inherited from their Communist totalitarian forbears the self-righteous certitude that they have proprietary rights to virtue and truth, contemporary Progressives continue to occult a Nietzschean will to power behind a nimbus of moral superiority. In the good old days of Lenin, Stalin, and Mao, non-conforming opinion was condemned as "bourgeois," "anti-revolutionary." Today, the enemies of "so-called" progress are denounced as "bigoted," "racist," "sexist," or "homophobic," and thereupon subjected to all the latest instruments of revolutionary justice from Generations X, Y and Z, the overwhelming demographic of Progressivism.

Non-Progressive opinion—i.e., any criticism of homosexuality, transgenderism, radical feminism, or Black Lives Matter—is criminalized as "hate speech;" ideological censorship is now euphemized as academic "trigger warnings," "speech codes," or Big Tech "fact-checking," or effected by political mobs who have exchanged the brown and black shirts of last century's utopian fanatics for the more fashionable hoodies and balaclavas of the millennial social justice movement.

Lenin's and Mao's paranoid loathing of the bourgeoisie, moreover, has once again mutated, as it did a century ago, from class hatred into race hatred, in the post-modernist diabolization of whites as the inheritors of "privilege," and along with it a collective guilt transmitted through the blood, demanding rituals of expiation. Whites are now considered the racial bogeymen responsible for the world's social and economic woes (as the Jews were for the National Socialists {Nazis}, who had learned from their communist tutors the political usefulness of scapegoating a collective enemy).

How America's Progressives Are 'Retrogressive'

As clarified in the Philip Carl Salzman "How America's Progressives Are 'Retrogressive'" *Epoch Times* article in January 2022: We often hear the terms "Liberal" and "progressive" interchangeably when discussing Democrats? In all fairness to Democrats, the meanings of the two terms could not be more different.

As previously noted, "classical" Liberalism as a political philosophy emphasizes individual freedom, agency, and choice. Human nature, in the liberal view, is a mix of qualities: energy and sloth, selfishness and generosity, creativity and habit. Society exists to provide the maximum freedom to individuals, with the constraints necessary to limit the encroachment of one on another. Inequality in a liberal society reflects the differences in capabilities and motivations among individuals. Liberalism favors free elections of public officials and limited government. For liberals, economics should be based on contractual relations freely entered into by producers and consumers, entrepreneurs, and labor as envisioned by our Founding Fathers, Bill of Rights, and Constitution.

Today's Progressivism, the latest iteration of Marxism, emphasizes equality and rights. Human nature, in the Progressive view, is basically good, with vices resulting from imperfect and oppressive social arrangements. Society is perfectible, and the perfect society is one which guarantees equality and equal rights. The economy should be owned and run collectively, by society at large. The government must be strong, able to control all aspects of society. Political parties unjustly divide the society, and are unnecessary when the government represents all of the people.

On the other hand, this liberal vision supports liberal democracy and capitalism, while the Progressive vision supports socialism and government economic planning. It's no accident that some members of the Progressive caucus in the House of Representatives are members of the Democratic Socialists of America. The caucus favors collectivism, as seen in government control of all major institutions and programs, such as welfare support, pre-schools, education, medicine, and the organization of labor. Progressives prefer government monopolies in all of these fields, which is why they oppose school choice, labor choice, and medical choice (except abortion, which they love).

Progressives see liberal democracies as systems of unjust inequalities resulting from inherited privilege and oppression of the weak. Liberals see Progressives as crushing individual liberty by vesting all functions in an all-powerful government, and thus favoring authoritarian rule.

Progressivism rests on the idea of progress advanced by Karl Marx: a movement driven by class conflict from capitalism to socialism and then to communism. In classic Marxism, classes are defined by economic position, by control over the means of production. The bourgeois class are the owners of the means of production, and the propertyless proletariat are the workers who must live on the pay provided by selling their labor.

Progressive 'Regressives' in North America

In the 21st century, Progressives in North America, with the exception of old-line socialists such as Bernie Sanders, have innovated in ideology, jettisoning the economic class struggle and replacing it with identity classes: gender, race, sexuality, religion, nationality, and ableness. Now it's (allegedly) whites (including "white adjacent" Asians and "hyperwhite" Jews), males, and Christians who are oppressors—and people of color, women, LGBTQ++, Muslims, and the disabled who are the oppressed victims.

The Progressives' identity class conflict has not only not led to "progress" in any discernible form, but also has led to social regression, resuscitating ugly forms of prejudice and discrimination while undermining public order and national sovereignty. Fighting this indoctrination head on, Florida Gov. Ron DeSantis signed the Individual Freedom Act—or the Stop WOKE Act—into law in April of 2022.

Why? With the "social justice" trinity of "diversity, equity, and inclusion," Progressives have returned us to the days of deep Jim Crow, with some races seen as virtuous and others as evil, the only difference being that the colors have changed. Progressive "inclusion" means including preferred races and genders, and excluding the others, as we see in hiring, college admissions, funding, promotions, and awards. The latest example is New York State ranking people for COVID-19 medical treatment according to their race.

Equity, meaning the statistical equivalence of races and genders, in practice means more of the preferred and fewer of the despised. Objective measures, such as standardized tests, and advanced education programs, are cancelled, because they don't produce the desired "equity" results. Now institutionalized racism and discrimination are regarded as desirable by Progressives, as long as preferred categories benefit.

Progressivism's Regressivism Examples Threaten America

Because certain racial minorities are heavily overrepresented among criminals (and victims), Progressives have advocated "justice reform" to alleviate the price that minority dominated criminals justly pay. Progressives thus have advocated defunding and disbanding the police, handcuffing police operations, releasing prisoners from incarceration, a halt to holding the dangerous accused prior to trial by means of no-bail release, and district attorneys who refuse to prosecute criminals, because they view criminals as "victims of society" rather than as victims of their own bad choices.

The result, a surprise to Progressives but to no one else, is a major breakdown in public order, with violent and nonviolent crime surging, particularly in Democrat-led cities, due to "defund the police" policies. For Progressives, public safety is systemic racism, so they're happy to do without it. Even though the vast number of victims of violence are racial minorities, the Progressives continue to obsess over the tiny number of police killings rather than the victims of crime. Progressives prefer criminals to victims of crime. They even encourage people to engage in illegal acts, as when they encouraged rioters in 2020 to loot, burn, and assault police, and then bailed them out until Progressive district attorneys refused to prosecute them.

Progressives particularly favor illegal aliens who have, uninvited and against our laws, entered the country. For Progressives, illegal aliens are preferred to citizens, because many are people of color, because the country is "systemically racist," and the racial balance needs to be changed in favor of people of color, and because Progressives think that they can capture illegal aliens as future voters by plying them with privileges paid for by tax-paying citizens. Progressives have coddled illegal aliens with sanctuary states, cities, and universities, thus protecting the criminals among the illegal aliens, a two-for-one benefit for Progressives.

Progressives are not fond of fair elections, which they always have a chance of losing, so they favor "electoral reform," which means a federal takeover of elections, contrary to the

Constitution, and wish to remove all safeguards against illegal voting. They particularly hate the voter ID requirement, which they label "voter suppression," although IDs are heavily supported by the public and in use in most democracies around the world.

In their opinions about race in America, Progressive Left stand out

% who say ...

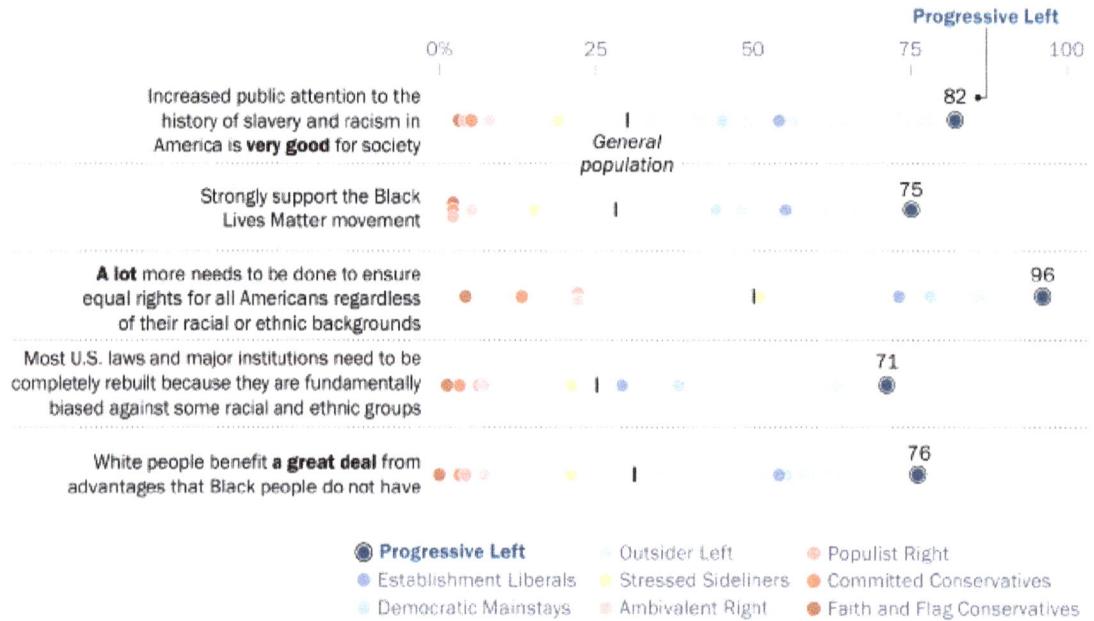

Note: For full question wording and distribution, see detailed tables
Source: Surveys of U.S. adults conducted July 8-18 and Sept. 13-19, 2021

PEW RESEARCH CENTER

When Progressives say, "voter suppression," they mean the suppression of illegal votes, such as those cast by illegal immigrants, or multiple votes by individuals, or votes inscribed by third parties. The manipulation and undermining of voting is another manifestation of Progressives' authoritarian tendencies. Progressives don't really like democracy; they prefer the dictatorship of the proletariat, or, in today's identity politics transformation, dictatorship of the "marginalized and underserved" minorities.

To sum up: Liberals favor individual freedom, limited government, public safety, and national sovereignty. Progressives favor some races and genders over others, criminals over victims, illegal aliens over citizens, and authoritarian rule over democracy. Progressives are about illiberal as they could be—so please don't call them "liberals."

Who Are the Progressive Left?

Who are the Progressive Left? Answer: They are typically very liberal, highly educated, and majority White—and most say U.S. institutions need to be completely rebuilt because of racial bias per the Pew Research Center.

Reflecting their name, Progressive Left have very liberal views across a range of issues — including the size and scope of government, foreign policy, immigration and race. A sizable majority (79%) describe their views as liberal, including 42% who say their views are very liberal—double the share of the next largest group (20% of Outsider Left).

Roughly two-thirds of Progressive Left (68%) are White, non-Hispanic, by far the largest share among Democratic-aligned groups. Progressive Left are the second youngest typology group — 71% are ages 18 to 49, primarily Gens X, Y and Z. Progressive Left are also highly educated, with about half (48%) holding at least a four-year college degree, making it one of the two most highly educated groups overall.

Their liberal outlook is not limited to issues related to the size and scope of government. Their views on race and racial equality also distinguish them from other typology groups: Sizable majorities say White people benefit from societal advantages that Black people do not have and that most U.S. institutions need to be completely rebuilt to ensure equal rights for all Americans regardless of race or ethnicity.

Progressive Left broadly support substantial hikes in tax rates for large corporations and high-income households. They are the only typology group in which a majority express positive views of political leaders who describe themselves as democratic socialists. And Progressive Left are more likely than any other typology group to say there are other countries that are better than the U.S.

Although they are one of the smallest political typology groups, Progressive Left are the most politically engaged group in the Democratic coalition. No other group turned out to vote at a higher rate in the 2020 general election, and those who did nearly unanimously voted for Joe Biden. They donated money to campaigns in 2020 at a higher rate than any other Democratic-oriented group.

Politically, the Progressive Left is overwhelmingly Democratic and nearly unanimous in their support for Joe Biden in 2020. Nearly all Progressive Left (98%) either identify with or lean toward the Democratic Party: 46% say they strongly identify with the party. About a third (32%) are independents who lean toward the Democratic Party.

To Understand and Oppose Progressivism Madness, Their Ideals Must be Clearly Identified

To understand and oppose the post-modernists (i.e., Progressives), the ideas by which they orient themselves must be clearly identified.

First is their new unholy trinity of diversity, equity and inclusion (DEI). Diversity is defined not by opinion, such as viewpoint heterodoxy, but by race, ethnicity or gender identity; equity is no longer the laudable goal of equality of opportunity, but the insistence on equality of outcome; and inclusion is the use of identity-based quotas to attain this misconceived state of equity.

All the classic rights of the West are to be considered secondary to these new values.

Take, for example, freedom of speech—the very pillar of democracy. The post-modernists refuse to believe that people of good will can exchange ideas and reach consensus.

Their world is instead a Hobbesian nightmare of identity groups warring for power. The Hobbesian Nightmare refers to a chaotic, conflict-torn society in which social strata are immersed in a self-centered perpetual antagonism that culminates in widespread violence in which the state apparatus fails to enforce law and order across its territory.

Second is rejection of the free market—of the very idea that free, voluntary trading benefits everyone. They won't acknowledge that capitalism has lifted up hundreds of millions of people so they can for the first time in history afford food, shelter, clothing, transportation—even entertainment and travel. Those classified as poor in the US (and, increasingly, everywhere else) are able to meet their basic needs. Meanwhile, in once-prosperous Venezuela—until recently the poster-child of the campus radicals—the middle class lines up for toilet paper.

Third, and finally, are the politics of identity. Post-modernists don't believe in individuals. You're an exemplar of your race, sex, or sexual preference. You're also either a victim or an oppressor. No wrong can be done by anyone in the former group, and no good by the latter. Such ideas of victimization do nothing but justify the use of power and engender intergroup conflict.

All these concepts originated with Karl Marx, the 19th-century German philosopher. Marx viewed the world as a gigantic class struggle—the bourgeoisie against the proletariat; the grasping rich against the desperate poor. But wherever his ideas were put into practice—in the Soviet Union, Cuba, Mao's China, Vietnam, and Venezuela, to name just a few—whole economies failed, and tens of millions were killed. We fought a decades-long cold war to stop the spread of those murderous notions. But they're back, in the new guise of identity politics.

The corrupt ideas of the post-modern neo-Marxists should be consigned to the dustbin of history. Instead, we underwrite their continuance in the very institutions where the central ideas of the West should be transmitted across the generations. Unless we stop, post-modernism will do to America and the entire Western world what it's already done to its universities.

National Suicide by Education – Care of Progressives

You may not realize it, but you might be currently funding some dangerous people according to the Jordan Peterson "Who Is Teaching Your Kids?" Prager U video: Academia is indoctrinating young minds throughout the West with their resentment-ridden ideology. They have made it their life's mission to undermine Western civilization itself, which they regard as corrupt, oppressive and "patriarchal."

If you're a taxpayer—or paying for your kid's liberal arts degree—you're underwriting this gang of nihilists. Nihilism is a philosophy, or family of views within philosophy, that rejects generally accepted or fundamental aspects of human existence, such as objective truth, knowledge, morality, values, or meaning. Supporting ideologues who claim that all truth is subjective; that all sex differences are socially constructed; and that Western imperialism is the sole source of all Third World problems—is problematic.

Many academics and college faculty are post-modernists, pushing "Progressive" activism at a college near you. They produce the mobs that violently shut down campus speakers; the language police who enshrine into law the use of fabricated gender pronouns; and the deans whose livelihoods depend on madly rooting out discrimination where little or none exists.

Their thinking took hold in Western universities in the '60s and '70s when the true believers of the radical left became the professors of today. And now we rack up education-related debt—not so that our children learn to think critically, write clearly, or speak properly, but so they can model their mentors' destructive agenda.

Academia is Indoctrinating Young Minds With Their Resentment-Ridden Ideology

Per the Philip Carl Salzman "National Suicide by Education" Minding the Campus article in September 2022:

We now teach our children that America is illegitimate, based on genocide and racism, and is systemically evil. Will this lead the next generation to love or despise their country? Who will volunteer for the military, to risk their lives to protect their evil country? When generals assert that the military is racist and sexist, homophobic and transphobic, and harbors white supremacists and domestic terrorists, who will volunteer for the military, to risk their lives to protect their country? Recruitment for the military in both the United States and Canada is severely down, and no one can figure out how to increase it.

We teach our children that our society is divided between helpless victims and cruel oppressors. BIPOC (black, indigenous, people of color) and females are all and everywhere oppressed, and whites and males, Christians and Jews, and (astonishingly) Asians are privileged, evil villains. Children learn to fear and hate their fellow citizens of other races, sexes, religions, and ethnicities. What kind of society will we have when we teach children that race hatred, sexism, and ethno-supremacy are justified and virtuous?

What devious force brought all of this cultural destruction into being? Who injected this destructive poison into our educational system? The source, of course, is our universities. They were taken over by grievance studies advanced by various particular interest groups. First and most decisive were the feminists who established women's and gender studies to advance what they defined as the narrow interests of women.

They adopted the Marxist model of society divided into two warring classes; in place of the proletariat versus the bourgeoisie, they defined the conflicting classes as females versus the patriarchy, all men. The feminists inspired queer studies and LGBTQ+ activism. Black studies, Latinx studies, and Asian studies all championed their races in alleged conflict with the other races. Universities no longer were about what can we learn about the world and its people, but about what you could do through propaganda and activism to advance the narrow interests of your category.

All of these activisms were absorbed in social science and humanities programs, often by joint appointed professors with one or another grievance study. Administrators were either activists themselves or were won over and instituted "social justice" measures of "diversity, equity, and inclusion," hiring "diversity officers" to police the staff and students to ensure that no "wrong think" was allowed to flourish.

Faculties of education, being weak in academic content and lax in pursuing that, adopted grievance theory with a vengeance, and trained their students, the future school administrators and teachers, in the most radical forms of grievance activism. The faculties of education have contaminated our K-12 schools and made them what they are now.

It's true that children are our future, for good or ill, depending on their education. Ill-educate children, as we are doing in the United States and Canada, and the result will be cultural decay, social breakdown, and political decline.

Hate and Fear Are Now Major Motivators on Campus

Also per the Philip Carl Salzman "Hate and Fear Are Now Major Motivators on Campus" *Epoch Times* October 2022 report: Almost every university in North America has committed to what is called "social justice," which is the implementation of identity politics through the mechanisms of "diversity, equity, and inclusion." Identity politics divides everyone into one of two categories: evil oppressor or innocent victim.

Through official mandatory policies, universities have transformed academic culture from a quest to discover truth about the world and its beings, to the indoctrination of identity politics and enforcement of "social justice" policies.

In practice, this means the adoption of identity ideology to the exclusion and suppression of other views. An elaborate bureaucracy of "diversity and inclusion" officers are charged with policing thought, speech, and action. Activists, and those who support them, encourage active hate against their alleged oppressors: males, whites, Christians and Jews, heterosexuals, and cis-normal individuals.

How do we know this? Three ways: First, the vehement rejection of any criticism of or counter-argument to their neo-sexist/racist/bigoted ideological positions, and complete unwillingness to entertain any alternative position to their narratives. Second, the immediate use of the most hateful rhetoric imaginable to designate anyone challenging their position. Third, their immediate and unrestrained demands that the challenger be severely punished and preferably destroyed. Let us take these in order.

In response to any opinion contrary to their own, these activists do not offer counterarguments and contrary evidence. They do not claim that the facts are wrong or the position is untrue. No, they reject the opinion on identity grounds, saying that the challenge denies their existence as people, and that it makes them feel unsafe. Or just that it denies the truth of their sacred narrative, and that the complainant is therefore a heretic, any of whose words must be rejected.

The response on campus to this identity-fueled mob hate and its manifestation in attacks, condemnations, and cancellations is fear. Students fear bad grades if they do not repeat identity politics talking points, and they fear social isolation if they are attacked as enemies of "social justice." Professors fear both students and administrators, especially the "diversity and inclusion" officials whose job it is to weed out dissenters for re-education, punishment, and exile.

Self-censorship by college students is well documented in multiple surveys. A survey by the Foundation for Individual Rights in Education (FIRE) reported that 83 percent engaged in self-censorship.

How far our colleges and universities have come! From open fellowships of research inquiry and intellectual exchange, they have become seminaries of true believers and doctrine enforcers. Identity politics has divided students, professors, and administrators into warring sexes, races, sexualities, genders, ethnicities, and ablenesses, and mandated hate between them. Admission and success, once based on academic achievement, merit, and potential, is now based on one's sex, race, sexuality, etc., and one's devotion to the identity politics "social justice" narrative. We have regressed from Enlightenment openness back to a Medieval religious order.

Safeguarding Our Republic From Progressivism Madness

Furthermore, the Philip Carl Salzman "Safeguarding Our Republic From Progressivism Madness" *Epoch Times* October 2022 article: Radical activists now confront America with a host of unsapient policies, subversive activism, and false narratives like the 1619 Project, Black Lives Matter (BLM), and Critical Race Theory (CRT). The Progressives who champion these false and woke critiques threaten who we are as a nation, accompanied by equally radical proposals to remake our basic institutions.

Furthermore, the Progressive activists who lead these woke movements have targeted America's schools to impose a revolutionary transformation on our country and they also seek to transform the family, work, the marketplace, government, law, religion, entertainment, sports—all of American society with neo-Marxist ideologies. This cannot be allowed to happen and now is the time to wake up to this woke Progressivism madness before it's too late to stop it.

America is exceptional not least because of its long traditions of antislavery, abolition, and dedication to civic equality that transcends race. It is one of the least racist countries in the world and its citizens of all races have achieved extraordinary prosperity and liberty. The peoples of the world seek to become American because our nation offers opportunity to all. Woke radical activists must engage in hallucinatory defamation to erase these facts.

Shall We Surrender to Marxist CRT?

The Progressive activists who lead these movements have targeted America's schools as the means by which to impose a revolutionary transformation on our country. These activists believe not only that our schools are the linchpin of our apparatus of racial injustice and oppression but also the means by which to force their so-called "liberation" on America. They will seize our children's minds to seize America's future.

As previously noted, these radical activists seek to transform the family, work, the marketplace, government, law, religion, entertainment, sports—all of American society with neo-Marxist ideologies. Their proposals to accomplish this are sweeping. They include a call to establish "equity" that requires a quasi-totalitarian imposition of job quotas and the suppression of all opposing speech as part of Diversity, Equity, and Inclusion (DEI) programs.

But every such proposal is ultimately a plan to change the way Americans think. They require a transformation of our schools from places that teach students to seek out truth to places that teach students to seek out power so as to revolutionize America. No free people would accept the radicals' plans, so they wish to teach our children to embrace tyranny, by persuading them that tyranny is actually fairness or justice. How does this happen?

- They abuse the authority delegated to the schools to propagandize and coerce a captive audience, who must assent to indoctrination or risk all the damage to career prospects that follows from poor grades.

- They exploit the innocence and naiveté of the impressionable young Americans who are in no position to recognize the falsehoods and distortions embedded in these appeals.

- The proponents of neo-racism—to give this collection of radical critiques a unifying name—most of all wish to impose their theory as a curriculum.

- They intend to compel every person to study that curriculum, from early childhood education through high school, college, graduate study, vocational training, and on-the-job instruction.

Or Shall We Stand and Fight For Our Republic?

We approve wholeheartedly MLK's equality of opportunity—but oppose emphatically neo-racism's forced equity of outcomes (the "equity" portion of DEI) because we uphold the value of human freedom. Freedom is an intellectual as well as a political virtue: the freedom to think for oneself and the freedom of a people to govern themselves are distinguishable but interdependent. Intellectual freedom allows us to pursue the truth, which entails encountering and weighing the validity of conflicting views.

Political freedom is the attempt to frame laws and reach decisions through orderly and peaceful processes that give due weight to the many and often conflicting judgments of the governed. There can be no political freedom without intellectual freedom.

And yet this is exactly what neo-racism demands—the end of intellectual freedom. The proponents of so-called "Antiracism" state this most explicitly when they assert that anyone who dissents from their view that America is a systemically racist nation perpetuates racism and deserves to be silenced.

Neo-racism's proponents explicitly advocate for censorship. Their doctrines brook no disagreement, dissent, skepticism, or demand for evidence. Their position is that the only allowable intellectual position is enthusiastic assent to their dogma.

This sort of intellectual totalitarianism is not new. Neo-racism imitates the logic of Marxism, which uses opposition to its arguments to confirm them. Only a class traitor would doubt the necessity of the revolution. The same self-confirming circularity always accompanies movements that suppress intellectual and political freedom.

Only witches would doubt the prevalence of witches, and therefore the witch-deniers must be condemned as witches. Neo-racism at its core is yet another of the witchcraft hysterias that chronically afflict society. America has never been immune to these disorders. We feel ashamed when we awake from them, but we forget our better selves while we are in the midst of them.

Now is the time to wake up before we do even graver damage—not only to ourselves individually but to our country as a whole. It is a bitter irony of our moment that those who want to drive us into this new hysteria often claim to be "woke." There is no awakening in woke. It is the sleep of reason that produces monsters, and it poses a profound peril to our republic.

The Increasing Intolerance of the Left Must Stop

In the past decade, the Democratic Party has moved further and further to the Progressive left, while claiming the labels of diversity, inclusion and tolerance per the Bill Connor 'The increasing intolerance of the left must stop" *Charleston Mercury* March 2023 story: Just more than a decade ago, Democratic candidates were not credible without voicing support for traditional marriage, as was the case with both Barack Obama and Hillary Clinton in the 2008 election.

The Democratic Party was solidly against words like "socialism," or of any support for defunding the police. As we have all seen in the recent election cycle, the party has morphed to the far Progressive left, both economically and socially. Although it continues to label itself the party of diversity, inclusion and tolerance, the reality is the opposite and must change. Let me explain.

Despite calls for national unity after many media outlets "called" the 2020 presidential election, Joe Biden's rhetoric was countered by the shrill calls from his party. For example, around the time of Joe Biden's "victory speech" (held before Trump's concession and while votes were being counted and legal challenges made) Rep. Alexandria Ocasio-Cortez tweeted a disturbing question: Whether or not someone was "archiving" Trump supporters to prevent them from being able to "downplay or deny their complicity" of their political support.

Immediately, a group called the "Trump Accountability Project" answering AOC and made clear the blacklisting of Trump supporters was well underway. This is a group, by the way, supported by Buttigieg and Obama aides. CNNs Jake Tapper warned Trump supporters that future "employers" would likely question their "character" for Trump support. "The View's" Sunny Hostin justified the blacklist because "past is prologue" and would not concede the obvious comparison of this to McCarthyism.

The primary means of intolerance of conservatism by the Progressive Left has taken the form of the ultimate stigma in modern America: Racism. Stigmatizing with the charge of racism has become ubiquitous from the Left. As Zachary Leeman has written: "They constantly slam the opposition as white supremacists, misogynists, fascists, etc. Even someone like rapper Ice Cube simply admitting to working with the administration on legislation to help black communities was enough to get him called a racist and labeled a Trump supporter."

Conservatives in Hollywood, like James Woods and others, have expressed how conservative politics have kept them out of certain jobs. As Leeman also wrote: "The president himself accused the industry of blacklisting conservatives after 'Will & Grace' stars Debra Messing and Eric McCormack demanded knowing who was attending a Hollywood fundraiser for the president."

In a twisted irony, the left has even begun to argue that silencing and blacklisting conservative viewpoints is part of creating a more tolerant, diverse and inclusive viewpoint. On our nation's campuses, silencing and ostracism of conservatives is rampant. As published in *Atlantic Magazine* in Feb 2020 (about the University of North Carolina): 68 percent of conservative students self-censor their conservative views due to fear of retribution (compared with under a quarter of liberal students).

More than six times more liberal students than conservative students agreed with shutting down speech students found objectionable. Better than eight times more liberal students than conservative students would refuse to be friends with someone across the political divide. Those numbers are worse at the elite Ivy League schools and across the nation's universities, intolerance of conservatism grown.

The 3 Big Differences Between Conservatives and Progressives

As shown in "The 3 Big Differences Between Conservatives and Progressives" report by The Heritage Foundation: Conservatives say people should have choices. Progressives say one political solution fits all. What's the difference between a conservative and a Progressive? Here are three examples.

No. 1: Conservatives and Progressives have different views about individuals and communities.

Conservatives ask: "What can I do for myself, my family, my community, and my fellow citizens?" Progressives ask: "What is unfair?" "What am I owed?" "What has offended me today?" "What must my country do for me?" The traditional American ethic of achievement gives way to the Progressive ethic of aggrievement.

As opposed to a variety of individuals making up one American community, Progressives seek to place individuals in a variety of competing communities. The first creates unity. The second, identity politics.

No 2.: Conservatives and Progressives have different views about diversity and choice.

For Progressives, different ethnicities and gender identities are welcomed but a variety of opinions and ideas are not.

Just look at two areas of public life dominated by the left. On college campuses free speech is under attack. If you're a conservative working at a social media company or using one of their platforms to share your views, you may find your job eliminated or your account deleted.

And when it comes to choice, Progressives love the word, but they don't want it to apply to our decisions on education, health care, and even how and where we live out our religious faith.

Conservatives take a different approach.

Parents, not the zip code they live in, should choose the school that is best for their child.

We all need health care, but we don't all need the same kind or same amount. And while people should be free to live as they choose, no one should be forced to endorse or celebrate those choices if it violates their religious beliefs.

Conservatives say people should have choices. Progressives say one political solution fits all.

No. 3: Conservatives and Progressives have a different view of "We the People."

Whether it's the Second Amendment, immigration, or putting limits on abortion, if we the people don't pass laws Progressives approve, they turn to judges, executive orders, and government bureaucrats behind closed doors to overturn the will of voters.

Whatever one may think about the wisdom of hiking the minimum wage, banning plastic straws, or removing controversial historical monuments, conservatives believe voters closest to the issues should be the ones making such decisions for their communities—not lawmakers in Washington or a panel of judges five states away.

To sum it up, conservatives believe in individual rights, not special rights. Conservatives believe in allowing Texas to be Texas and Vermont to be Vermont. And conservatives believe we the people can vote with our feet about where we want to live and what laws we want to live under.

2 – Today's Progressives and Their Causes: The Good, Bad, Ugly & Idiotic

Credit: Peace Buttons.

The Congressional Progressive Caucus (CPC), established in 1991, is a congressional caucus affiliated with the Democratic Party and represents the most left-leaning faction of the Democratic Party.

The CPC was established in 1991 by U.S. Representatives Ron Dellums (D-CA), Lane Evans (D-IL), Thomas Andrews (D-ME), Peter DeFazio (D-OR), Maxine Waters (D-CA) and Bernie Sanders (I-VT) and he was the first CPC Chairman. The founding CPC members were concerned about the economic hardship imposed by the deepening recession and the growing inequality brought about by the timidity of the Democratic Party response in the early 1990s.

As of the 118th United States Congress, the CPC has 101 members (99 voting Representatives, 1 non-voting Delegate, and 1 Senator), making it the largest ideological caucus in the Democratic Party (larger than the New Democrat Coalition) and the second largest ideological caucus overall (after the Republican Study Committee). Since, 2021, the CPC has been chaired by U.S. Representative Pramila Jayapal (D-WA).

In the minds of Progressives, their agenda and objectives that follow, taken verbatim from their website—they would no doubt consider them "good." However, as the rest of this textbook clearly demonstrates, that term is highly debatable, and we leave it to sapient minds to decide on their own at the conclusion of Chapter 15 to determine the good, bad, ugly and idiotic of the Progressivism movement.

If this sounds like an overly harsh assessment, turn and read the pages and find out why.

1. **Advancing justice, dignity, and peace for all.**

At the Progressive Caucus, we believe that government must be the great equalizer of opportunity for everyone. We are committed to passing legislation that advances justice, dignity, and peace for all people.

- Realizing the goal of a universal, high-quality, Medicare For All health care system for all.

- Advancing the right of every American to retire with security and dignity.

- Ending poverty and income inequality and securing a living wage for all people.

- Protecting the fundamental right to organize.

- Ending mass incarceration and advancing equal justice under the law.

- Taking urgent, inclusive, and transformative action on climate change.

- Upholding the fundamental reproductive rights of all people.

- Ending our forever wars, cutting the bloated Pentagon budget, and prioritizing diplomacy.

- Advancing humane, fair and just immigration laws.

- Advancing racial justice and equity.

2. **Tackling systems of oppression and dismantling structural racism and discrimination.**

Embedded in our nation's history is a painful legacy of oppression, racism, and genocide. At the Progressive Caucus, we believe that elected leaders have an obligation to confront this legacy and dismantle the systems of oppression and discrimination that allow racism to persist in this nation. In order for any legislation to be truly inclusive and transformative, it must advance the goal of racial justice.

- Advancing racial justice and equity in every policy.

- Supporting a truth commission and reparations to address and repair the continued effects of slavery and discrimination.

- Transforming our budgets and priorities to reinvest in Black, Brown, and indigenous communities and reimagine the role of institutions that exacerbate injustice and inequality.

- Challenging harmful stereotypes and efforts that demonize immigrant, Black, Brown, indigenous, and LGBGTQ communities and actively opposing any legislation or policy that marginalizes those communities.

Taking on systems that privilege the wealthy and powerful to demand a government and economy that works for the people.

We believe elected officials should be beholden to the people, not to wealthy donors and powerful CEOs. At the Progressive Caucus, we reject pay-to-play and revolving door politics and fight for a democracy where the power is in the hands of the people, not concentrated among the rich and well-connected. We reject the failed politics of the past that prioritized the deregulation of financial industries and big polluters and tax breaks for the wealthy and big corporations over the well-being of the public. And we support bold policies to close the gap between the rich and everyday Americans and ensure our government delivers essential services to every person in this country.

- Ensuring regulation of industry with strong consumer protections.

- Strengthening oversight of financial institutions.

- Democratizing our society by getting money out of politics, eliminating political corruption, and protecting and expanding access to the ballot box.

- Ensuring that all of our economic and tax policies address or decrease income inequality.

- Protecting the federal government's role in delivering essential goods, taking on monopolies, and disciplining markets.

3. **A commitment to sweeping, transformative change.**

Recognizing that the problems facing this country are enormous, we are committed to delivering solutions that meet the scale of the crisis. Faced with decades of disinvestment in working class communities, unprecedented income inequality, and a federal budget that fails to meet the needs of millions, we believe that Congress must take sweeping action to deliver the bold policies that this moment demands. The challenges facing this nation are structural -- and Congress must be deliberate and explicit in dismantling these institutional barriers to prosperity, peace, and justice.

- Demanding bold and visionary legislation to address the needs in every community and rejecting incrementalist approaches that fail to deliver urgent transformative change.

- Opposing counterproductive and false narratives on government deficits that have led to decades-long disinvestment in low-income communities, communities of color, families, and working people.

- Reversing decades-long disinvestment in low-income communities, communities of color, families, and working people.

- Delivering structural change that unrigs the rules for working people and forces the wealthy to contribute to our shared prosperity.

The Progressivism Socialism Madness of the Democratic Party (the Bad?)

From *The SAPIENT Being* is the Dr. Raymond M. Berger "Marxism and Progressivism: A Play in Two Acts" article published in June 2018:

The single maddening truth about today's Progressive movement is that it is fundamentally different from the American Progressive movement of the late nineteenth century because it has repackaged Marxist theory into Critical Race Theory (CRT) with new actors and injustices but the same old drama.

The epic struggle between bourgeoisie and proletariat is replaced by the morally laden struggles between privileged and oppressed actors with new names. In this contemporary version of Marxist drama, people of color are pitted against a white male power structure supported by a mysterious but powerful force of institutional racism. Women are pitted against a male patriarchy that invades not only the workplace but intrudes into the very intimacy of the home to wreak injustice.

Progressivism as the New Marxism

As shown in *The SAPIENT Being*, in Marx's older drama, the moral imperative of Progressives is to once again "set things right." In Marx's time this was the task of revolutionaries. Today this task falls to Progressive politicians and activists, social justice reformers, civil rights workers, cultural appropriation enforcers, diversity, and inclusion warriors and the like who have spread into the media, government, college campuses, non-profits, neighborhood organizations and workplaces.

Marxist revolutionaries sought to set things right by leading a revolution to overthrow the capitalist system and replace it with a just economic system. Progressives want to set things right through social change in order to create a just society. In a just society everyone is equal: men and women, immigrants and native-born, persons of various racial and ethnic groups, heterosexuals, and homosexuals, first and third world people, disabled and able-bodied.

This will be a society free from the "isms" of sexism, nativism, racism, heterosexism, colonialism, and ableism.

To the Progressive, the success of the newly liberated oppressed person must not be limited by the extent of their talent or effort. Success is merited by the very existence of their membership in an oppressed group. As in Marxist theory—"from each according to his ability, to each according to his needs"—-even people of lesser abilities and efforts deserve equal outcomes.

The Progressive sees anything less than this as failure. And worst of all, an unsuspecting American audience has not figured this out yet, but the SAPIENT Being has, as well as other sapient journalists, news casts, anti-woke organizations.

How the New Religion of Progressivism Leverages Victimization

As shown in *The SAPIENT Being*, Progressives sees reality entirely within the Marxist framework of oppressor and oppressed. Further, the principal oppressors are white, Christian, or Jewish heterosexual males. They are uniquely oppressive, "white supremacists" who have abused cultural power and privilege at the expense of every other group.

Progressives rank the value of a view not based on the logic or merit of the view but on the level of victimization in American society experienced by the person espousing the view. An LGBT black woman is automatically considered more correct than a straight white male, before any speech exits either of their mouths.

Progressivism Madness by Way of Postmodernism

As shown in *The SAPIENT Being*, the next "core doctrine" of Progressivism builds on the concept of Postmodernism which denies the existence of transcendent, objective truth or morality, so each identity group defines its own reality and morality, not subject to critique by outsiders. This is known as cultural relativism, or multiculturalism.

As an example: If some racial or ethnic groups suffer from higher rates of poverty, unemployment, drug addiction, or divorce, multiculturalism disallows laying blame on the beliefs or actions of those within the group. In keeping with the first "core doctrine" of group identity, individual belief or action isn't available for consideration.

Rather, the blame must, by default, lie in the larger historical, social, or structural forces. This is why Progressives are seemingly obsessed with "systemic or structural" oppression or racism. To attribute negative outcomes to the beliefs or actions of those within the community is "blaming the victim," the cardinal sin for Progressives.

The Three Meta-Errors That Pervade Progressivism

Conservatives have so many policy disagreements with The Progressive Promise that it's hard to keep track of them all (but we will in the next section). However, per the Mark Hendrickson "The Three Meta-Errors That Pervade Progressivism" *Epoch Times* April 2019 report: They all stem from three fundamental errors—the meta-errors of Progressives and Progressivism. And these are: an unjustified faith in government competence, an irrational belief in the power of human will, and what I call "the tyranny of good intentions."

1. Faith in Government Competence

The late historian Clarence Carson correctly identified "meliorism" as a key tenet of Progressive ideology. Adapted from the Latin adjective "melior" ("better"), meliorism is the doctrine that the federal government should intervene in the market economy to improve the economic condition of citizens. That, of course, calls for a far larger role for government than the founders' vision, in which the government's appointed task was to keep us free and let us go about our economic business unmolested.

Progressives' faith in the ability of government to make us more prosperous is unsupported by evidence. In fact, the evidence is that Uncle Sam has proven more accomplished in crippling economic progress than in boosting it.

The poster child for governmental economic incompetence in the United States is the "War on Poverty." After a decades-long trend of the U.S. poverty rate declining (a trend temporarily reversed during the Great Depression, due to unrelenting counterproductive federal intervention), the poverty rate leveled off once the federal War on Poverty was launched in the mid-1960s. Since then, Washington has spent more than $25 trillion in today's dollars, yet the poverty rate has remained stuck in a narrow band (roughly 11 to 15 percent) for more than 50 years.

Other salient examples of government incompetence: the Social Security system is giving workers lower returns than private retirement plans, and it faces severe deficits in the future. Health care expenses, insurance premiums, and deductible payments have soared the more Uncle Sam has intervened. So have the costs of higher education. Yet, despite government's abysmal track record, Progressives propose evermore federal "help."

2. Belief in Human Willpower

Far from abandoning the failed strategy of expanding government to engineer economic progress, American Progressives have doubled down on it. They now want democratic socialism. Progressives believe that the primary reason that government intervention hasn't yet solved all human economic problems is simply an insufficiency of political will: We just haven't tried hard enough.

No amount of real-world evidence—whether the historical failures of socialism in the USSR, People's Republic of China, Cuba, eastern Europe, North Korea, and others, or the current humanitarian disaster in Venezuela, or the grim reality of Native American reservations and Veterans Administration hospitals here at home—can convince them that government economic control isn't the path to prosperity and justice.

The lethal consequences of this mindset are illustrated by an incident that the late Nobel Prize winner Alexander Solzhenitsyn recounted in "The Gulag Archipelago." Soviet officials wanted to transport larger loads of steel by railroad. They took their plan to some railroad engineers. The engineers explained that the request was impossible because the railroad tracks couldn't support more tonnage. The party officials then had the engineers summarily shot as saboteurs of progress. How dare they oppose the political plan! When the officials proceeded to order doubling each train's loads, the tracks broke down, just as the engineers had warned them, and so even less steel reached the desired location.

The lesson here is obvious to anyone with a lick of common sense: The "will of the people" and political mandates are powerless to revise or repeal the laws of physics or the principles of economics. Water boils at 212 degrees Fahrenheit and socialism impoverishes. (If you want to understand why socialism is inherently unviable, read Ludwig von Mises' 1922 book "Socialism: An Economic and Sociological Analysis.")

The Progressives' self-deluded belief that they can bend reality to conform with their will, whims, and wishes can have lethal consequences.

3. The Tyranny of Good Intentions

The "tyranny" here is twofold: It refers both to Progressives being enslaved by their own emotions and their desire to exert power over others.

Progressives feel ("feel" may be a more appropriate verb than "think") that because they want to do something that is so obviously good (e.g., help the poor, preserve a safe climate, etc.), their policy recommendations must necessarily be the right and best solutions—and that anyone who disagrees with them is, a priori, a bad or hateful person.

Thus, for example, these naive U.S. Progressives are convinced that because they have good intentions, they can make socialism work. They think socialism hasn't succeeded elsewhere because the leaders either didn't implement socialism thoroughly enough or because those leaders weren't good people. Read Mises, folks. Even saints with multiple doctorates can't make socialism work.

So besotted are Progressives by their own grandiose visions of their own goodness and rightness that they feel entitled to determine and decree what other citizens must do (not what they must not do, which was the concept of law held by the founders). The fact that their messianic plans, such as the Green New Deal, would make them slave-drivers over their fellow Americans doesn't bother them in the slightest.

Through some warped combination of inflated love for themselves and a corresponding disdain, if not hatred, for others, the tyranny of good intentions turns Progressives into wannabe tyrants.

The seed of tyranny germinates in a colossally self-flattering notion—one that I once held when I was a brainwashed undergraduate bleating for socialism—namely, "The world will be a great place when everyone else accepts the role I have chosen for them."

The great Scottish moral philosopher Adam Smith commented on this syndrome in his 1759 book "The Theory of Moral Sentiments": "The man of system … seems to imagine that he can arrange the different members of a great society with as much ease as the hand arranges the different pieces upon a chess-board."

The arrogance of the social planner (i.e., contemporary Progressives) includes stripping one's fellow man of their basic humanity, their freedom of choice.

We can debate economic theory, the lessons of history, the affordability of various proposals, etc., with Progressives until we are blue in the face. But until we figure out how to correct the three meta-errors underlying their policy proposals, they aren't going to change.

A Country We No Longer Recognize, a Progressive Coup We Never Knew (the Ugly?)

As shown in the Victor Davis Hanson "A Country We No Longer Recognize, a Coup We Never Knew" *Epoch Times* January 2023 article: We are beginning to wake up from a nightmare to a country we no longer recognize, and from a coup we never knew. Welcome to America's Progressivism madness!

In this dystopic reality, the negative impact of Progressivism on America can be seen through the lens of these sapient questions from Hanson as follows:

- Did someone or something seize control of the United States?

- What happened to the U.S. border? Where did it go? Who erased it? Why and how did 5 million people enter our country illegally? Did Congress secretly repeal our immigration laws? Did President Joe Biden issue an executive order allowing foreign nationals to walk across the border and reside in the United States as they pleased?

- Since when did money not have to be paid back? Who insisted that the more dollars the federal government printed, the more prosperity would follow? When did America embrace zero interest? Why do we believe $30 trillion in debt is no big deal?

- When did clean-burning, cheap, and abundant natural gas become the equivalent to dirty coal? How did prized natural gas that had granted America's wishes of energy self-sufficiency, reduced pollution, and inexpensive electricity become almost overnight a pariah fuel whose extraction was a war against nature? Which lawmakers, which laws, which votes of the people declared natural gas development and pipelines near criminal?

- Was it not against federal law to swarm the homes of Supreme Court justices, to picket and to intimidate their households in efforts to affect their rulings? How then with impunity did bullies surround the homes of Justices Brett Kavanaugh, Samuel Alito, Amy Coney Barrett, Neil Gorsuch, John Roberts, and Clarence Thomas—furious over a court decision on abortion? How could these mobs so easily throng our justices' homes, with placards declaring "Off with their d—s"?

- Since when did Americans create a government Ministry of Truth? And on whose orders did the FBI contract private news organizations to censor stories it did not like and writers whom it feared?

- How did we wake up one morning to new customs of impeaching a president over a phone call? Of the speaker of the House tearing up the State of the Union address on national television? Of barring congressional members from serving on their assigned congressional committees?

- When did we assume the FBI had the right to subvert the campaign of a candidate it disliked? Was it suddenly legal for one presidential candidate to hire a foreign ex-spy to subvert the campaign of her rival?

- Was some state or federal law passed that allowed biological males to compete in female sports? Did Congress enact such a law? Did the Supreme Court guarantee that biological male students could shower in gym locker rooms with biological women? Were women ever asked to redefine the very sports they had championed?

- When did the government pass a law depriving Americans of their freedom during a pandemic? In America can health officials simply cancel rental contracts or declare loan payments in suspension? How could it become illegal for mom-and-pop stores to sell flowers or shoes during a quarantine but not so for Walmart or Target?

- Since when did the people decide that 70 percent of voters would not cast their ballots on Election Day? Was this revolutionary change the subject of a national debate, a heated congressional session, or the votes of dozens of state legislatures?

- What happened to election night returns? Did the fact that Americans created more electronic ballots and computerized tallies make it take so much longer to tabulate the votes?

- When did the nation abruptly decide that theft is not a crime, assault not a felony? How can thieves walk out with bags of stolen goods, without the wrath of angry shoppers, much less fear of the law?

- Was there ever a national debate about the terrified flight from Afghanistan? Who planned it and why?

- What happened to the once-trusted FBI? Why almost overnight did its directors decide to mislead Congress, to deceive judges with concocted tales from fake dossiers and with doctored writs? Did Congress pass a law that our federal leaders in the FBI or CIA could lie with impunity under oath?

- Who redefined our military and with whose consent? Who proclaimed that our chairman of the Joint Chiefs of Staff could call his Chinese Communist counterpart to warn him that America's president was supposedly unstable? Was it always true that retired generals routinely libeled their commander-in-chief as a near Nazi, a Mussolini, an adherent of the tools of Auschwitz?

- Were Americans ever asked whether their universities could discriminate against their sons and daughters based on their race? How did it become physically dangerous to speak the truth on a campus? Whose idea was it to reboot racial segregation and bias as "theme houses," "safe spaces," and "diversity"? How did that happen in America?

- How did a virus cancel the Constitution? Did the lockdowns rob of us of our sanity? Or was it the woke hysteria that ignited our collective madness?

Alexandria Ocasio-Cortez: The Dumbest Democrat and the Most Underperforming Congresswoman (the Idiotic?)

As per the Sohil Sinha "Alexandria Ocasio-Cortez: The Dumbest Democrat and the Most Underperforming Congresswoman" TFI Global News story in April 2021: According to a recent report from the nonpartisan Center for Effective Lawmaking—a joint initiative of Vanderbilt University and the University of Virginia—Rep. Alexandria Ocasio-Cortez was among the least effective members of the previous Congress.

AOC proposed a total of 21 bills, all of which were considered "substantive" by the center—but that's where the story ends. According to the center, which uses data from Congress.gov, the official website for US federal legislative information, her bills saw no committee action, no floor votes and none of them ever became law.

Alan Wiseman, a Vanderbilt political scientist and co-director of the center said, "She introduced a lot of bills, but she was not successful at having them receive any sort of action in committee or beyond committee and if they can't get through committee they cannot pass the House."

"It's clear that she was trying to get her legislative agenda moving and engage with the lawmaking process," Wiseman added, "But she wasn't as successful as some other members were—even among [other] freshmen—at getting people to pay attention to her legislation."

When it came to the legislative efficacy of all 240 Democrats in Congress, AOC was ranked 230th out of 240. She came in dead last among the 19 Democratic legislators from New York state.

Federal reform of public housing, a moratorium on fracking and a mandate to offer full federal public benefits to illegal aliens was among the bills that failed. Many of Ocasio-Democratic Cortez's colleagues, according to Democratic House insiders, considered her approach alienating.

"Tweeting is easy, governing is hard. You need to have friends. You need to understand the committee process, you need to be willing to make sacrifices," said one. "Her first day in Congress … she decided to protest outside of Nancy Pelosi's office."

"Legislation was never her focus," according to a second Democratic insider who worked with her in the New York delegation. "It was all about the media and the narrative."

From the Republican stand, Rep. Nicole Malliotakis (R-Brooklyn/Staten Island), told *The Post*, "Her ludicrous policy ideas would destroy our country—Americans should be thankful she's not effective."

Members of AOC's Democratic Socialist "Squad" did better. Rep. Ilhan Omar was ranked 214th after sponsoring 33 bills that never made it out of committee, while Rep. Rashida Tlaib had three substantive bills advanced to the committee, one of which became law. She came in 92nd place.

While the study proves AOC is the most underperforming lawmaker of the current Democrat, her statements will prove that she is one of the dumbest too.

Here Are 8 Stupid Things You Need to Know About the AOC's Green New Deal

This February 2019 article by Courtney Kirchoff titled "Here Are 8 Stupid Things You Need to Know About the Idiotic Green New Deal" at Louder With Crowder is dumbed down to "AOC speak" to drive home the point—but it might also be in language you're most used to. Either way, Alexandria Ocasio-Cortez wants you to know she cares, she has plans, she's, like, totally smart.

But mostly she wants you to know she cares about the planet. As such, she's gifted us the Green New Deal. As Kirchoff explains: "So I poured myself some coffee and slogged through the sludge so you didn't have to. Hint: the Green New Deal is all surface, no substance. Remind you of anyone?

Oh, before we start, as I was working on this, apparently the FAQ about the Green New Deal, which is what I tried reading through, was removed from the Green New Deal website. The blowback was that swift.

If you want to read the full disaster of the FAQ yourself, go here. The 14 page Green New Deal is on NPR's website. It's just as stupid as the FAQ, which was moderately clearer.

Let's get to it, Power Rangers. By the way, this whole bill is a disaster. It eliminates huge swaths of the United States economy with nary a care. That's the biggest problem not numbered here specifically because, well... just look at the sophomoric take in response to AOC's sophomoric take."

1. Not citing sources:

92 percent of Democrats and 64 percent of Republicans support the Green New Deal...even though Ocasio-Cortez just released it today, and all she really released was this FAQ, not the whole bill itself. Also, did you see what's absent from that statement? A source. It's a theme which runs throughout this piece. No sources.

2. Farting cows. Seriously, cow farts.

We set a goal to get to net-zero, rather than zero emissions, in 10 years because we aren't sure that we'll be able to fully get rid of farting cows and airplanes that fast, but we think we can ramp up renewable manufacturing and power production, retrofit every building in America, build the smart grid, overhaul transportation and agriculture, plant lots of trees and restore our ecosystem to get to net-zero.

She wants to get rid of planes and farting cows but isn't sure how to do it in ten years. Ten years, by the way, is, like the inability to cite sources, a theme. All of her plans will happen in ten years. She probably wants to make the 40 Under 4o list is my guess. She won't get there with the disaster that is this FAQ of her bill, but ten years of points for trying.

3. No nukes, they're mean!

Nope, the GND doesn't include nuclear power, in fact, AOC wants to decommission nuclear plants in ten or so years. Ten years is her magical number.

A Green New Deal is a massive investment in renewable energy production and would not include creating new nuclear plants. It's unclear if we will be able to decommission every nuclear plant within 10 years...

Note that she's unclear if she can decommission nuke plants in her magical timeline of ten years, but she does want credit for at least wanting to decommission nuke plants in ten years.

I'm going out on a limb here: she's unclear about a lot of things. A lot.

4. No air travel!

Totally overhaul transportation by massively expanding electric vehicle manufacturing, build charging stations everywhere, build out highspeed rail at a scale where air travel stops becoming necessary, create affordable public transit available to all, with goal to replace every combustion-engine vehicle.

Won't that be nice? We'll all have Teslas and can take trains across the Atlantic Ocean. It's like that joke about the guy who's afraid of flying so he asks God to build a three-lane highway to Hawaii. Maybe that's where AOC got her idea. If what we call this is an idea. Bit of a stretch.

5. Carbon tax? Cap and Trade? Yes, but teeny, "tiny" ones so don't freak out!

So we're not ruling a carbon tax out, but a carbon tax would be a tiny part of a Green New Deal in the face of the gigantic expansion of our productive economy and...

Basically yes there will be a carbon tax, but it's just tiny. If you expect AOC to define tiny, don't. But she does like the word "tiny" so she uses it again for cap and trade:

While cap and trade may be a tiny part of the larger Green New Deal plan to mobilize our economy, any cap and trade legislation will pale in comparison to the size of the mobilization...

See, it's tiny, so don't sweat it. Especially when the mobilization of the Green New Deal, and all which fuels the "GND" is MASSIVE.

6. The mobilization is massive you guys. Like, really big and MASSIVE!

Massive federal investments and assistance to organizations and businesses participating in the green new deal and ensuring the public gets a return on that investment. This is massively expanding existing and building new industries at a rapid pace—growing our economy.

A Green New Deal is a massive investment in renewable energy production and would not include creating new nuclear plants. The Green New Deal is about creating the renewable energy economy through a massive investment in our society and economy.

This is a massive mobilization of all our resources into renewable energies. The level of investment required is massive. The speed of investment required will be massive.

Also, private companies are wary of making massive investments in unproven research and technologies; Massively expand clean manufacturing (like solar panel factories, wind turbine factories, battery and storage manufacturing, energy efficient manufacturing components) and remove pollution and greenhouse gas emissions from manufacturing' Totally overhaul transportation by massively expanding electric vehicle manufacturing. Massive federal investments and assistance to organizations and businesses participating in the green new deal and ensuring the public gets a return on that investment

So is it massive? 13 mentions of massive. If only we could use the word to describe her intelligence. Note to AOC: get a thesaurus. My computer has a dictionary app. Comes with one. Use it, sweet cheeks."

From Kirchoff's analysis: "No surprise that anything government does is MASSIVE but it's never a MASSIVE success. Government initiatives like this end up being a MASSIVE waste of money, a MASSIVE f*ck up, and I'd say a MASSIVE step in the wrong direction."

7. Don't worry about paying for it you guys, we'll find the money! We always find money! American has, like, SOOOOO much money!

The same way we paid for the New Deal, the 2008 bank bailout and extended quantitative easing programs. The same way we paid for World War II and all our current wars. The Federal Reserve can extend credit to power these projects and investments and new public banks can be created to extend credit...so the question isn't how will we pay for it, but what will we do with our new shared prosperity.

The government will pay for it. Taxpayers will pay for it. That means you, the person reading this post right now, will pay for it. But if I had to bet, I'd guess you already knew AOC wanted you to foot the bill for this shitty bill.

But don't worry, you guys, because once the government pays for it, we'll all be so rich, we won't know what to do with all our new shared prosperity! My bet is we'll all snack on our beloved pets, but at least we won't use gasoline in our cars!

8. Eliminating huge sections of the US economy, but... union jobs for all! Rejoice, slackers!

Ensure that all GND jobs are union jobs that pay prevailing wages and hire local. Guarantee a job with family-sustaining wages. Protect right of all workers to unionize and organize. Strengthen and enforce labor, workplace health and safety.

As Kirchoff continues: "YES WE CAN just make wishful statements and make them come true. If you really believe in something, if you clench your eyes and click your heels three times, maybe the Wizard of Oz will give you a brain!

The plan would also call for the elimination of the current energy sector of our economy. But who cares when we can all sustain ourselves on hopes and dreams.

In MASSIVE Summary:

AOC wrote this sucker, possibly from her iPad while watching The Real Housewives of whatever city they're in now. Our researcher described the writing style of this FAQ thusly: It reads more like if you transcribed a podcast or whatever. Long rambling sentences in conversational diction.

This GND is all goals, no plans on how any of it will be executed other than "the government will do all of it." AOC also thinks it'll all happen in ten years. Normally I cringe at vague antecedents, but "it" and "all" here is vague on purpose. Just replace "it" and "all" with Cortez's most hopeful dreams.

The GND eliminates huge sectors of the United States economy. With the idea "green" something or other will replace those industries.

The government can't build a wall in ten years. The Post Office still can't find your package. DMV can't take a photo for your license in under four hours. But the same kind of government lackeys who run the aforementioned institutions are somehow going to make the country completely green in ten years, and also airplane free.

How? With massive mobilization, delusion, and a young woman some New Yorkers thought was bright enough to rep them. Well done, guys."

3 – Progressive Illiberalism, Wokeness, Racism, Cancel Culture & Social Injustice

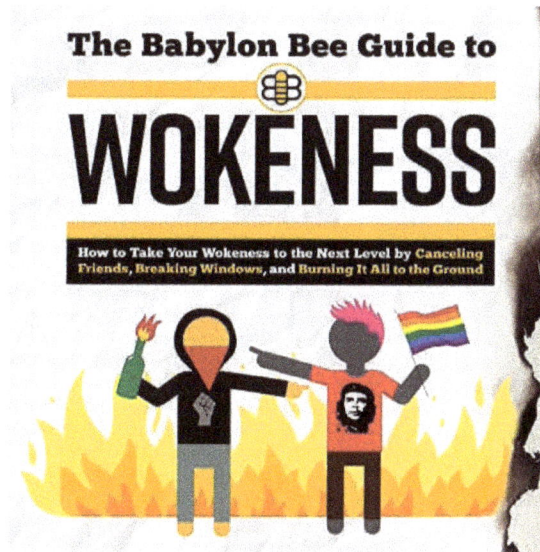

Credit: Babylon Bee.

As noted in the Wilfred Reilly Prager U April 2022 video "The Whiteness of Wokeness:" How do you explain that most people agitating for radical social change on behalf of people of color are not themselves people of color. They are overwhelmingly woke, white leftists.

They use the genuine plight of poor minorities as a wedge, a lever by which to change the basic character of American society—a change that most people of color do not want. Both anecdotal evidence and hard data bear this out.

A good example is the woke left's obsession with politically correct speech. Ostensibly, this is all in the service of protecting the tender feelings of long-suffering minorities. However, according to the best publicly available data, most minority groups dislike PC culture more than whites do.

Eighty-eight percent of Native Americans, 87 percent of Hispanics, 82 percent of Asian Americans, and 75 percent of blacks (vs. 79 percent of whites) call political correctness "a problem." According to multiple studies, only young, white, college-educated liberal and leftist women strongly support speech restrictions.

A Pew poll about the use of the term "Latinx,"—an attempt to remove gender from "Latino" and "Latina,"—makes this point. Only a quarter of all Hispanics and 38 percent of Hispanic college graduates have even heard of the term. What's more, only 3 percent ever opt to use it. Many find it ridiculous. If anything, the pattern here is one of white leftists telling Hispanics to speak in a more woke fashion—and Hispanics refusing to comply. This turns out to be the rule, not the exception.

Defunding the police, a left-wing cause célèbre for much of 2020 and 2021, is another case in point. A study conducted by Gallup found that 81 percent of black Americans want the police presence in their neighborhoods "to either remain the same or increase." Only 19 percent of blacks favored any decrease whatsoever in police presence.

Little wonder. As empirically-minded scholars have long pointed out, anti-police and "soft on crime" policies tend to dramatically increase crime rates in urban minority neighborhoods. In 2021, 12 major cities broke previous homicide records. Meanwhile, the number of arrests nationwide plummeted 24% in 2020, to the lowest in 25 years, according to FBI data.

Then There's Education Policy

On charter schools, labeled racist by many liberals and leftists, data show another significant split: Blacks and Hispanics, especially parents, favoring school choice; white liberals and leftists opposing it. According to recent data from Democrats for Education Reform, 58 percent of black Democrats and 52 percent of Hispanic Democrats have a positive opinion of charter schools. In contrast, just 26 percent of white Democrats favor charters.

Economist Thomas Sowell has observed that in the major American charter networks, among those classrooms in which students of color make up 90 percent or more, kids perform almost exactly on par with the majority-white student population of the nation's public schools. Some do far better. In a misguided effort to increase diversity, white leftists have lobbied to lower educational standards for blacks and Hispanics. Yet, evidence suggests that maintaining traditional standards is a much more effective approach.

The average combined SAT score for the sizable and mostly black senior class at the Success Academy charter-school system in 2019 was 1268; 10 percent of the class scored higher than 1400. Like most charters today, Success Academy is a "pure lottery" school that does not get to pick and choose students. Given that fact and the school's results—we're talking about New York City—it is no surprise that minority parents, unlike white Democrats, strongly support charter schools.

The simple truth is that black and Hispanic citizens do not show much enthusiasm for cancel culture, for pulling good (and mostly minority) cops out of their neighborhoods, or for depriving their kids of a sound education in service to woke white notions of equity. There's an excellent reason for this. The people who suffer from these radical policies are "people of color." And most "people of color" know it.

The obvious question that usually arises when someone makes these points is: "So why do 90 percent or so of black Americans vote for the party that supports all these destructive policies?" The answer is as simple as the query: blacks are constantly told that the only serious alternative to the left is a racist party that wants to put them "back in chains," to quote Joe Biden when he was Vice-President.

This pitch has been very successful. In short, it works. If it ever stops working—as I am hardly the first to note—U.S. politics would change overnight. While we wait and see if this will ever happen, one practical piece of advice remains relevant: If you want to know what individual members of any particular group happen to think, ask them—not those who claim to speak and act in their best interest.

Peak Woke?

It should be clear by now that truth is not a Woke value. Those on the far-left side of the political spectrum have made certain claims in recent years, including: maintaining slavery was the primary reason for the founding of our nation; innocent, unarmed blacks are being shot down by police with impunity in great numbers all across America; because of systemic racism, people of color have little chance of escaping poverty and achieving a middle-class lifestyle in the U.S.; and, because of sexism and glass ceilings, women face limited opportunities in the workplace.

What's becoming obvious to even the casual observer of public life is that the Woke are more than happy to sacrifice the truth on the altar of power. If you can exert inordinate influence in the major institutions of America, including on the President of the United States, why let the facts get in the way? If the main thesis of *The New York Times'* 1619 Project has very little historical support but wins a Pulitzer Prize, then why recant when eminent historians reduce that thesis to rubble?

The ultra-Progressive mindset maintains its grip on institutional power, but in terms of what people actually believe, it's on the downswing as shown in the Oliver Traldi "Peak Woke?" *City Journal* article in July 2022.

About a decade ago, something began building steam in America's elite cultural and intellectual institutions—universities, national newspapers and magazines, museum boards, award committees. Callout culture, cancel culture, identity politics, social justice, critical race theory, postmodern neo-Marxism, wokeness: whatever you want to call it, it was happening. Wokeness developed new and previously extreme ideas around race and gender, and especially around how people ought to conduct themselves in their everyday interactions when race and gender were considered (and race and gender were always to be considered).

America's Great Awokening produced cottage industries and small fortunes. Consultants and trainers peddled odd academic theories to multinational corporations, earning millions; authors such as Ibram X. Kendi won massive grants and intellectual prizes. On the other side, public intellectuals like Jordan Peterson emerged in part as theorists of what was wrong about woke culture; conservatives like Ben Shapiro and liberals like Dave Rubin grew their audiences with an anti-woke message.

It's important to note that wokeness has had this effect in the Progressive world for precisely the same reason that it has exasperated people in academia, journalism, and business. It tears institutions apart from the inside by encouraging people to see minor interactions as conflictual and victimizing, to respond catastrophically to events toward which they should show resilience, and to set up massive bureaucracies to deal with these sorts of disputes.

If anything, wokeness is worse for political organizations, because its adherents see the internal politics of the organization as being as important as, or more so, than any external project. So a Progressive nonprofit might feel internal pressure to conform to woke standards even as a Progressive legislative agenda languishes.

Anatomy of the Woke Madness

Per the Victor Davis Hanson "Anatomy of the Woke Madness" Independent Institute report in June 2021: Wokeism has become our most popular secular religion—at least for a moment dethroning climate change. It reduces all of the past and present into puerile binaries between "whites" and "non-whites."

Its aim is for the present generation to rewrite our history—whether by The 1619 Project and cancel culture or iconoclastic statue-toppling and Trotskyization of names and places. Wokeism becomes a child's morality tale of noble non-white victims versus villainous white victimizers. Erasing the past and its language supposedly fuels a recalibration of the future, all in the here and now, a holy Year Zero

In the process, wokeism has done a lot of damage to America, and will do even more if left unchecked. Here are its chief characteristics.

Elites vs. Elites

First, remember that wokeism is a top-down phenomenon. It started in academia with "critical race theory" and "critical legal theory." These are bastard offshoots of harebrained "critical theory," which arose from a demoralized and adrift Europe after the cataclysms of two devastating European-spawned world wars.

These 'theories' are merely adolescent delusions that norms, customs, traditions, laws, and rules are just arbitrary "constructs." Thus they should have no authority over those whom they "oppress." These relativist props are the tools of the white male hierarchy to gain and consolidate their "power." So they can only be resisted by rejecting all these insidious "norms," whether the canons of physics and math, jurisprudence, standardized test scores, or the idea that police keep the "peace."

Outside of the campus, the media, the entertainment industry, the corporate boardroom, Wall Street, and Silicon Valley, thousands of rank-and-file social justice warrior demonstrators are not demanding, for example, to enroll women in Special Forces combat units. Grassroots America does not insist on subsidized transgendered surgeries.

Instead, leftist Washington politicos and bureaucrats pressure the Pentagon brass, in quid pro quo fashion. The subtext is that those who promote woke policies are assured of promotion and future exemption from audit of lucrative retirement consulting for defense-related corporations.

The people—that is, 51 percent of America—is not organizing for more cancel-culture censorship on Facebook, or even greater percentages of college admissions determined largely by race. Inner-city residents are not clamoring for less police patrolling. Defunding law enforcement is an elite obsession of those who do not live in insecure places.

Whether in the corporate boardroom or in Hollywood casting meetings or in the campus president's office, race-based obsessions mostly reflect intramural wars between elites for the lucrative spoils of the one-percent's news anchorships, roles in TV shows and commercials, diversity deanships, and admissions quotas to the Ivy League.

As a result, class considerations have vanished. They are replaced by absurd racial reductionism. For example, CNN mediocrity Don Lemon, by virtue of his race-mongering, can pose as a multimillionaire victim. The anonymous white deplorables at Walmart, caricatured as smelly in the Lisa Page-Peter Strozk text trove, are his proverbial anonymous oppressors.

Apparently, we can only prevent the tragedy of thousands of young black males killing each other and hundreds of innocent bystanders each year in our major cities—if Oprah, at her $90 million estate, conducts a series of TV interviews with Meghan Markle (denizen of a $15 million mansion) about the psychodramatic slights she feels she received from the Royal Family, or if Black Lives Matter founder and Marxist Patrisse Cullors gets her $35,000 new fence around her new Topanga Canyon home, in an era when "walls don't work."

The elite Woke are now obsessed about race because of leftist failures in the past to galvanize a permanent class of victims of the grasping rich—given the upward mobility and expanding economy of the United States.

Race, in contrast, is deemed immutable. The Left sees it as permanent proof, a stamp of victimization and thus deserving of reparatory government action. LeBron James may be worth $1 billion, but he will always be a needy voice of the helpless given his race. Or so the woke would have us believe.

Performance Virtue Signaling

Second, given its elite origins and spread, it is no surprise that wokeism is a psychological mechanism that exempts the privileged by virtue signaling and performance grievance-mongering in lieu of meaningful real action. Wokeism is neither consistent nor logical. Its self-serving selectivity means Hunter Biden's serial use of the N-word is not inconsistent with his father's lectures that the deplorables pose an existential racist threat to the nation.

America's inner cities are unsafe, violent, often dangerously unclean, and characterized by terrible schools, plagued by terrible municipal administration, and suffering terrible housing. Yet wokeism never holds the mayors, the district attorneys, or the city councils of these urban failures accountable for the misery they inflict on the non-white and poor.

When a shrill Representative Alexandria Ocasio-Cortez (D-N.Y.) produces a selfie video about the planet burning up in 12 years, or claims "racism" explains efforts to ensure that immigrants come in legal fashion, she believes that she is then exempt both from doing anything concrete about urban crises, and from any guilt about living a privileged lifestyle.

Kicking "racist" Donald Trump off social media apparently means Mark Zuckerberg does not feel too bad about building a monstrous 57,0000-square foot mansion on a pristine Hawaiian island site. The social justice warrior and Facebook billionaire might as well have been a 15th -century Florentine Catholic sinner, ponying up 1,000 golden florins to gift a few blocks on the rising

Duomo to ensure he could indulge himself on his $12,000 electric surfboard, and that his future stay in Purgatory would be short, and in Paradise long.

Before being pre-COVID-19 woke, Colin Kaepernick of mixed racial ancestry, was a so-so multimillionaire NFL quarterback. He was known mostly for being suspended for using a racial N-word slur. Kaepernick was raised by white parents and apparently worried whether he was authentically one of the oppressed.

But after joining the church of wokeism, he became an approved voice of the victimized. And so he began lodging collective grievances against the supposed sins of America while building a fortune hawking Chinese-approved products.

So wokeism is so often an empty indulgence for the elite that enjoys exemptions it never extends to others.

When Individuals Disappear

Third, Wokeism destroys individualism. We cease being persons and instead become categorized peoples. What does it matter that Al Sharpton was a racist demagogue, that Jesse Jackson a skilled shakedown artist of corporate America, that Bayard Rustin, in contrast, a brilliant civil rights strategist, or that Martin Luther King, Jr. was an ecumenical believer in the inherent goodness of a flawed America of his times—once they are all to be reduced to being just black, and therefore just equally victims?

In the same manner, did Robert Kennedy, Lester Maddox, Hubert Humphrey, and Bull Connor equally suffer from "whiteness"? Wokeism, then, is a nonstop tribal warfare that reduces everyone on one side into uniform victims, despite their naturally varying morality, and on the other into cookie-cutter victimizers, although some were and most were not.

Racist obsession strangles individual character and renders everything irrelevant in comparison. Are we now to stop watching "Saving Private Ryan" because most of those who died on Normandy Beach were white? Thus what does it matter that some soldiers were braver than others? And what did it matter in a larger sense that a mostly white majority America defeated an all-white Nazi Germany? Were Churchill and Roosevelt, and Stalin and Hitler, just a bunch of old white people, given it was irrelevant that the former were democratic leaders who saved Western civilization and the latter were mass murderers?

Racism Everywhere—and Thus Nowhere

Fourth, race is not unimportant, but it is not the only catalyst of history or arbiter of life in the present. Cancer couldn't care less about the race of the cells it warps. COVID-19 is not a white or black pandemic, for all the efforts to make it so. Google "racism" and learn that everything from gluten allergies to robots are now products of racism.

Segregation of the U.S. military was a travesty during World War II, and had grave implications of abject hypocrisy for a democracy at war, but it was still not the central issue that explained the global conflict, at least not in comparison to the 6 million dead of the Holocaust, or the 20 million killed on the Eastern Front, or the 15 million whom Japan butchered in China. To the extent racism drove the death count of World War II, by the numbers it was mostly a matter of the Japanese intersectionally slaughtering supposedly inferior Asian Chinese and Germans exterminating white, supposedly non-"Aryan" Jews and Russian "Untermenschen."

Pericles' Funeral Oration, the Magna Carta, and the Declaration of Independence can be appreciated apart from race and gender. In contrast, wokeism takes every event of the past and present and warps it into a racial litmus test, and thus a banality of oppressor and oppressed, as if history is always third-grade melodrama rather than complex tragedy.

Merit is Racist

Fifth, wokeism's existential enemy is merit. Critical Race Theory claims that meritocratic criteria are rigged or "constructed" in subtle ways to reflect the dominant hegemonies of the white male heterosexual hierarchy. Thus physics has no innate laws across time and space. There are no race-neutral skills or lack of the same in a United Airlines pilot.

We know the wages of such woke relativism. Indeed, we have seen the pernicious effects when sex or religion or race or ideology in the past has been used to calibrate talent in lieu of merit, whose measurement can transcend how we look or in what faith we believe.

Wokeism dictates that if the "oppressed" are "underrepresented," it is because of society's rigged rules of exploitation. So the woke's remedies trump considerations of quality and excellence. Yet we know what happened when ideologues in 1930s Germany purged university departments, when commissars overruled Soviet officers in World War II, when Jim-Crow white racists found ways to ensure talented blacks could not go to college, or when brilliant female law graduates were offered only secretarial work in prestigious law firms: Society at large suffered from unscientific, crackpot -isms that knowingly warred on talent for purposes of political control.

The ancient American idea is now dead that if a group was collectively underrepresented in particular fields and professions, the remedy was simply twofold: organize to ensure equality of opportunity, and then when a fair shot was guaranteed, prepare, study, and sacrifice to ensure quantifiable excellence to capitalize on the opportunity. All that to the woke is now "racism."

The final irony of wokeism? Its efforts to intrude on private lives come right out of the pages of *1984* and *Animal Farm*. Its racism is a more sophisticated form of Confederate one-drop racial lunacy. Its methodology operates according to the rules of the Spanish Inquisition. And its cancel culture mimics the system of Soviet commissars.

How Did Such Collective Madness Infect a Once Pragmatic and Commonsensical America?

Nascent wokeism went viral during the terror of COVID-19, our first global pandemic in a century, the first ever national quarantine, the first ever self-induced recession, the most destructive riots in U.S. history after the death of George Floyd, and the first ever election where well over 60 percent did not vote on election day. And the country went stark-raving mad in response.

As the virus fades, the lockdown becomes porous, pent-up demand fuels an economic recovery, the absence of law enforcement becomes far more deadly than its omnipresence, violent crime spikes and seeps into the suburbs, and the people resist the Left's unconstitutional hijacking of state protocols of voting, then what happens?

Do we revert to the norms of the civil rights movement where the content of our character alone matters, not the color of our skin?

Or have we sunk so deeply into the woke quicksands, that we cannot thrash our way up to the air, and thus suffocate from the ancient pressures of the bog that have always destroyed civilizations?

My Woke Employees Tried to Cancel Me: Here's How I Fought Back and Saved My Nonprofit

Grace Daniel is the co-founder of a nonprofit that trains care providers to victims of trauma globally. She writes under a pseudonym below for her in depth article titled "My Woke Employees Tried to Cancel Me: Here's How I Fought Back and Saved My Nonprofit" published by The Daily Signal in June 2021:

By now there are enough "cancel culture" stories to fill volumes. After my own story about standing up to a woke mob—and succeeding—went viral on Twitter, I decided to speak out, because I am convinced that Americans need more encouraging stories about standing up to cancel culture, and information on how they can do it themselves.

In order to withstand attacks, you'll need to be armed with an understanding of the ideas in play, and the courage to stand up to bullies. I hope my story can help give you both.

My story began in 2010, when my husband and I founded a nonprofit organization that trains people around the world who are providing care for survivors of trauma. We were pleased with the success of our organization for the first several years, but around 2016, we noticed a change.

My husband, who serves as executive director, eventually found himself uneasy among his staff. The general tone was one of criticism. It wasn't explicitly directed at him at first, but toward "systems," the "hegemony," and "normativity."

We were not acquainted with critical theory at the time, but the common rhetoric about "systems of power and oppression" was an indicator that there was a shared perception of reality among team embers to which we were not privy.

We initiated all-team sessions to hear from our staff and discern what was happening. What usually happened was the staff made vague assertions that the organization was "causing harm" and would present a list of demands. I later came to understand these meetings were essentially "struggle sessions"—an opportunity for our woke employees to shame us into submission, a technique often used in Mao's China.

I decided to do some research into the ideology that was animating the staff to see what my husband and I could do to save our organization and the people we serve. I'm convinced that there's no shortcut around this learning process if you want to successfully make a principled stand. Here are some of the things I learned.

Know What You Are Dealing With

Through my research, I came to realize that our staff were following "critical theory" and its descendant theories, like critical race theory and queer theory.

These theories basically divide society into two groups: oppressor and oppressed. If you are white, straight, male, and/or wealthy, you are an oppressor. If you are a racial minority, gay or trans, a woman or identify as some other gender, and financially not wealthy, you are oppressed. The objective of critical theory is to defeat oppressors and overturn the system that benefits them.

Those who have embraced the tenets of critical theory are colloquially referred to as "social justice warriors," or simply "woke." (It's important to note that most people who have been influenced by critical theory and its descendant theories—like critical race theory and queer theory—most likely wouldn't identify themselves as "critical theorists").

I like the term critical social justice to identify the ideology, because it doesn't have a pejorative connotation and is descriptive of the earnest (though I believe misguided) motivations of many of its adherents.

Whatever they are called or what other people call them, they share the conviction that they have acquired a critical consciousness that enables them to rightly perceive systems of power and oppression unseen by others (hence, being "woke"). This belief governs all of their actions.

Understand How the Battle With the Woke Mob Is Fought

To protect yourself and your organization from becoming subverted by critical social justice ideology and subsequently cancelled, you must understand how the battle is fought.

First, critical social justice is an anti-objectivity ideology: One of its fundamental assertions is that there are no objective truths, only "positional" truths. As explained by Ozlem Sensoy and Robin DiAngelo in their 2017 book "Is Everyone Really Equal?":

One of the key contributions of critical theorists concerns the production of knowledge. ... These scholars argue that a key element of social injustice involves the claim that particular knowledge is objective, neutral, and universal.

An approach based on critical theory calls into question the idea that objectivity is desirable or even possible. The term used to describe this way of thinking about knowledge is that knowledge is socially constructed.

Bearing that in mind, you can throw out your notions of engaging in classical discourse where the best idea will emerge victorious. Your ideas are not on trial: You are.

Shift the Focus From 'Identity'

Your woke assailants will accuse you of ineptitude, the inability to perceive reality, or even immorality based on your identity—by which I mean, the characteristics you can't change about yourself. Your identity can even disqualify you from talking about certain subjects.

For example, they will demand your silence in conversations on race if you are deemed "white" or even "white adjacent." They will suggest you do "harm" or "violence" if you are "cis-gendered" and attempt to engage in conversation on gender identity.

This identity-based gatekeeping is a result of the presupposition in critical social justice that all truth is "positional." Therefore, only those who have a certain "social position" due to their identity can perceive or speak truth on topics related to their identity.

Don't take the bait and engage in self-defense. You will be eviscerated if you let the conversation become about you.

When I realized that an employee was attempting to control my behavior based on my identity, I deflected by using her own woke moral code against her. She told me I couldn't speak on a topic because I'm straight, to which I replied that it was wrong to assume about my sexuality just because I'm married to a man. (She immediately groveled.)

Instead of trying to defend yourself from their attacks on your identity, you must remain fiercely committed to keeping the focus of the conversation on ideas rather than identities. Keep the dialogue on the faultiness of their ideas, not on yourself or them.

Level the Playing Field With Ground Rules

Third, it is by no means a fair fight. Your opponents will cry foul no matter your speech or behavior. Claims of "harm" will be made simply on account of certain ideas being brought into the conversation or sacrosanct commitments of critical social justice being challenged.

This is why you must be "above reproach." Let your interlocutors know you will be recording all organizational conversations. Insist that terms be defined clearly from mutually agreed upon authoritative sources or fruitful engagement will be impossible.

On that last point, definition of organizational terms was a key component of our success. The first term I worked to define was "psychological safety."

This was a necessary first step because even challenging some of our staff's ideas was seen as "violence." Being an organization dedicated to addressing trauma, we were shocked that words like "causing harm" and "unsafe" were used liberally by the clinically trained individuals on our program staff to describe conversations about ideas (a sad result of their education in psychology through a critical theory lens).

I found Greg Lukianoff and Jonathan Haidt's book "The Coddling of the American Mind" and was stunned by the similarity between the behaviors discussed in the book and those exhibited by our staff. Particularly, the description of "emotional reasoning," a cognitive distortion which can be defined as "letting your feelings guide your interpretation of reality," was apt for our staff.

As explained by Haidt and Lukianoff, there are consequences to using emotional reasoning:

A claim that someone's words are 'offensive' is not just an expression of one's own subjective feeling of offendedness. It is, rather, a public charge that the speaker has done something objectively wrong. It is a demand that the speaker apologize or be punished by some authority for committing an offense.

I used the material in "Coddling," the research on psychological safety by Amy Edmondson (who coined the term), and some evidence-based models of organizational psychological safety to craft an organizational definition of the term "psychological safety" our staff were required to read. This would preclude vague definitions of the term and force our staff to recognize when their accusations of "harm" were unsubstantiated.

It was painfully clear that these clinically trained mental health professionals, while purporting to be on a mission to increase safety and reduce harm, were accomplishing the opposite by adhering to a worldview that sees some people as inherently participating in harm and other people as inherently oppressed based solely on their identities.

Another term I defined was "evidence-based." The most disheartening aspect of this whole experience was that individuals who had received advanced degrees in clinical fields had become completely detached from science rooted in observation and verifiable claims. That the assertions of critical social justice could not be falsified was a clear indicator to me that it is ideological in nature rather than scientific.

It was revealing to me that our team members not only resisted the traditional definition of science, but indicated our adherence to it was a symptom of "white supremacy" that contributed to the disenfranchisement and harm of entire groups of people.

Why was it important to define "evidence-based"?

For starters, both the employees and I were motivated to help treat victims of trauma. To do so, our approach must be guided by evidence that is both verifiable (can be objectively confirmed to be true) and therefore falsifiable (can be objectively dismissed as untrue).

"Evidence" that does not meet this criteria is anecdotal and, far from being helpful to trauma-informed methodologies, actually can lead away from accurate conclusions about the nature of and remedies for trauma.

Therefore, if our mission of being truly helpful to address the impact of trauma on human beings is to be effective, we have to avoid theories and ideologies that undermine honest scientific inquiry. Effective, evidence-based treatment of trauma is incompatible with the incoherent and destructive ideology of critical social justice, which is why anyone who is fighting for true justice must expose critical social justice for what it is.

As soon as I insisted that our nonprofit operate based on evidence-based principles, many of the emotional and irrational attacks that the employees were using lost their effect. Unfortunately, even as the incoherence of their ideology was exposed, our staff remained committed to their chosen framework for understanding reality, and insisted that a commitment to objectivity was harmful.

We had to come to terms with the reality that we were at an ideological impasse. The staff members who disagreed with us ultimately left the organization, accusing us of perpetuating ongoing harm.

Why My Husband and I Stayed in the Fight

I hope you can see the urgency that this ideological war necessitates. It's not a matter of "agreeing to disagree." As our cultural and academic institutions are captured by critical social justice ideology, the impacts will be on the most vulnerable.

What will happen in women's prisons, for instance, when "woman" is redefined to be inclusive of biological men who identify as women?

What will happen to children when schools teach some classmates are inherently oppressors and some are inherently oppressed?

Or, as in the case of my own story, what will happen in mental health care when "norms" for health—established by rigorously tested data—are erased in an effort to "increase inclusivity" and "celebrate diversity"?

The truth is that those who had the most to lose if my husband and I had lost the battle for our organization were the people our trainees serve. These are children, women, and men whose lives have been affected by the most egregious abuses and tremendous suffering. They deserve the best care possible.

We Won Our Fight With the Woke Mob and So Can You

You do not have to be an academic, a pundit, or a brilliant orator to join the fight. Wherever you have a sphere of influence, you have an important role to play in combatting the toxic effects of ideological subversion.

You need to spend some time acquainting yourself with the fundamental tenets of critical social justice, then stay courageously committed to addressing the faultiness of these assertions.

I recommend reading Neil Shenvi's book reviews to introduce yourself to critical theory. James Lindsay and Helen Pluckrose's book "Cynical Theories" is a deep dive into critical theory for those interested in gaining a robust understanding of the ideology.

You will need to learn not to be concerned with what people think or say about you, since your character will undoubtedly be called into question and your identity attacked.

Whenever "harms" or "violence" are indicated, require specific words, actions, and incidents be provided as evidence to support these claims. Whenever possible, insist upon shared definitions of key terms before engaging in discussion.

I am convinced that critical social justice can and will be defeated ultimately for the sole reason that it's so fundamentally misaligned with reality. However, the tragic truth is that much collateral damage is being done to individuals and institutions where this ideology has already taken root.

The more people who decide to take a stand courageously against this destructive ideology, the sooner we will usher in a sound and truly helpful discourse around solutions to injustice.

What Does it Mean to be 'Woke?' Majority in the US Have Positive View

Per the Brendan Rascius "What does it mean to be 'woke?' Majority in the US have positive view, study finds" *Kansas City Star* March 2023 article: Seemingly everyone has an opinion on the word "woke," a buzzword that has become thoroughly entrenched in the zeitgeist. But depending on who you ask, it either describes someone who is conscious of social injustices or someone who is excessively politically correct.

The term is often invoked as a pejorative by opinion writers and cable news pundits, and it's even the subject of the Stop W.O.K.E. Act, a law in Florida that says it aims to "put an end to wokeness that is permeating our schools and workforce."

But how do average Americans define "woke?" It turns out, a majority are inclined to use a complimentary definition, according to a USA Today/Ipsos poll published on March 8, 2023 and it included 1,023 participants across the country.

 Fifty-six percent of survey respondents said the term means "to be informed, educated on, and aware of social injustices," while 39% said it "involves being overly politically correct and policing others' words."

Differences in definition largely broke down along party lines and respondents' ages, according to pollsters:

- A vast majority, or 78%, of Democrats surveyed said "woke" describes someone aware of injustices, while 56% of Republicans said it describes someone who is extremely politically correct. Independents were more evenly divided over the term's definition.

- Additionally, nearly half (48%) of survey respondents ages 50-64 defined "woke" as "being overly politically correct," while only 33% of respondents ages 18-34 said the same.

- While there was some agreement on the definition of "woke," Americans are more sharply divided over whether the word is a compliment or an insult, pollsters said. Forty percent said it is an insult and 32% said it was a compliment.

- "While a majority of Republicans (60%) and a plurality of independents (42%) consider "woke" to be an insult, nearly half of Democrats (46%) say they take it as a compliment," pollsters wrote.

- Differences also appeared by age group. Forty-three percent of those ages 18-34 view the word as a positive attribute, while only 19% of those over age 65 said the same.

- Also in terms of age, those over the age of 65 were more likely (38%) to say they don't know what the word is supposed to mean, compared to just 21% those under 35 who claim the same unfamiliarity.

Recently, the term "woke" has been used by Florida Gov. Ron DeSantis, widely seen as a front-runner for the 2024 Republican presidential nomination. He railed against "woke" politicians and policies in a recent speech delivered in California, according to previous reporting from *McClatchy News.*

"I think these liberal states have gotten it wrong and why are they getting it wrong? I think it all goes back to ideology," DeSantis said. "And it goes back to this woke mind virus that's infected the left and all these other institutions. I mean, think about the way they have governed their states."

"It is ideology run amok," DeSantis added, according to CBS News. "That is why the quality of life has declined in places in San Francisco, in New York City, and in Philadelphia and Chicago. It is all rooted in that and that woke ideology rejects the core foundational principles that made this country great," DeSantis said. "We will never surrender to the woke mob."

10 Signs You're as Woke as Hell

Wokeism has been described by its critics as the omnipresent use of race—and to a lesser extent, gender—to replace meritocracy and thus ensure equality of result. Some see it as an update of 1960s cultural Marxism fads. Others scoff that it is just a return to 1980s-style political correctness. Still more see it as the logical successor to 1990s-type race, class, and gender obsessions—albeit with a shriller and more dangerous Jacobin, Soviet, and Maoist twist. Wokeism's hysteria also invites comparisons to the Salem witch trials and McCarthyism. Neither description, nor the ten signs of wokeness listed below are flattering. "Go woke—be joke!"

1. You're quick to lecture strangers about the consequences of white privilege.

2. Your Facebook page is a collection of articles about Progressive causes.

3. Sometimes you're so woke your friends cannot deal with it.

4. A Black Lives Matter T-shirt is your aesthetic fashion statement.

5. You can inaccurately and illiberally defend the Antifa movement.

6. You've participated in several campus protests or shout-downs.

7. You'll only date Democrats, Marxists, or someone as woke as you.

8. You've stood up in class, pointed, and told someone to check their privilege.

9. You made all your friends vote for Biden in the last presidential election.

10. Your Trump Derangement Syndrome (TDS) score is a 5, the highest level.

Unjust: Social Justice and the Unmaking of America

There are just two problems with "social justice": it's not social and it's not just. Rather, it is a toxic ideology that encourages division, anger, and vengeance. In this penetrating work, Commentary editor and MSNBC contributor Noah Rothman uncovers the real motives behind the social justice movement in his 2019 book *Unjust: Social Justice and the Unmaking of America* and explains why, despite its occasionally ludicrous public face, it is a threat to be taken seriously.

American political parties were once defined by their ideals. That idealism, however, is now imperiled by an obsession with the demographic categories of race, sex, ethnicity, and sexual orientation, which supposedly constitute a person's "identity." As interest groups defined by identity alone command the comprehensive allegiance of their members, ordinary politics gives way to "Identitarian" warfare, each group looking for payback and convinced that if it is to rise, another group must fall.

Progressive Left: Very liberal across a broad spectrum of issues

% who say ...

Progressive Left

| | 0% | 25 | 50 | 75 | 100 |

There are other countries that are better than the U.S. — 75

General population

Reduce size of America's military — 65

The U.S. should phase out the use of oil, coal and natural gas completely, relying instead on renewable energy sources only — 78

The fact that there are some people who have personal fortunes of a billion dollars or more is a bad thing for the country — 73

Like a political leader who identifies as a democratic socialist — 60

People who have immigrated to the U.S. illegally generally make the communities they live in better — 86

Success in life is pretty much determined by forces outside of our control — 62

Tax rates on large businesses and corporations should be raised — 98

- ● **Progressive Left**
- ● Establishment Liberals
- ○ Democratic Mainstays
- ○ Outsider Left
- ○ Stressed Sideliners
- ○ Ambivalent Right
- ● Populist Right
- ● Committed Conservatives
- ● Faith and Flag Conservatives

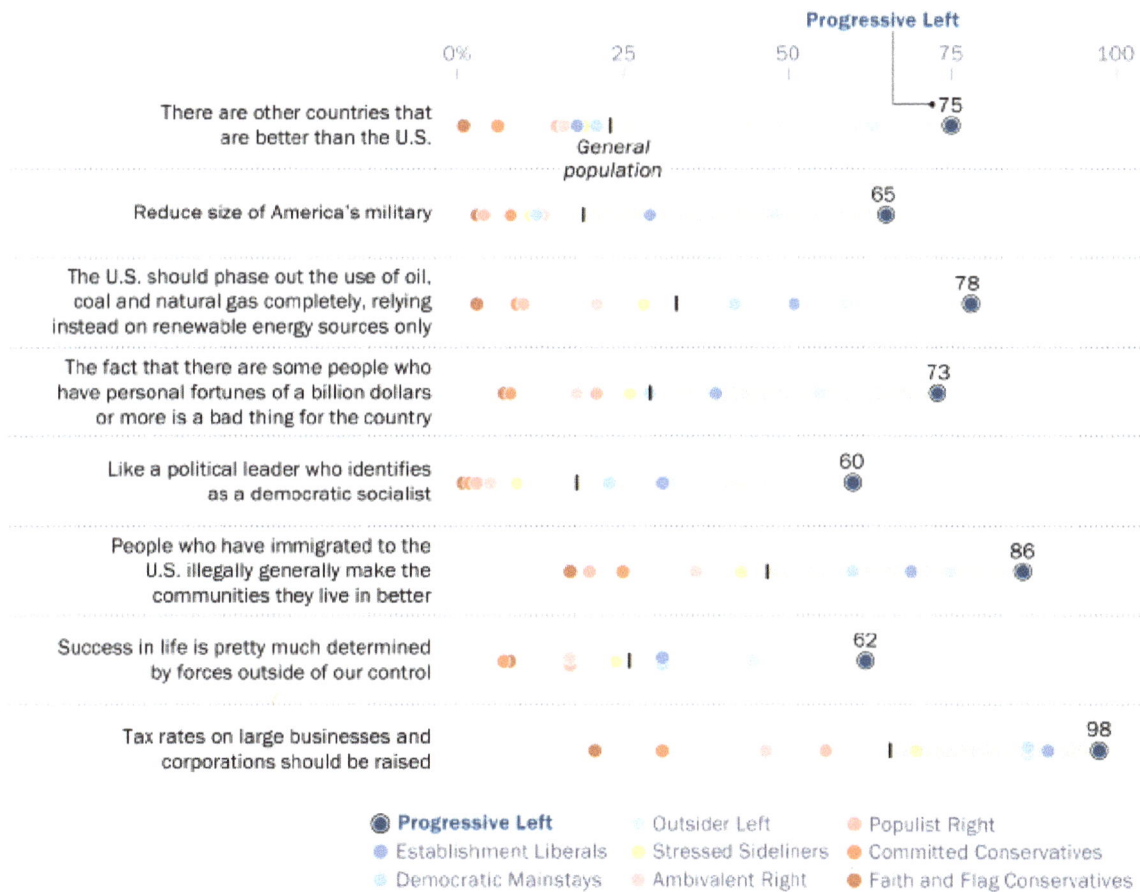

Note: For full question wording and distribution, see detailed tables.
Source: Surveys of U.S. adults conducted April 20-29, July 8-18 and Sept. 13-19, 2021.

PEW RESEARCH CENTER

In a society governed by "social justice," the most coveted status is victimhood, which people will go to absurd lengths to attain. But the real victims in such a regime are blind justice—the standard of impartiality that we once took for granted—and free speech. These hallmarks of

American liberty, already gravely compromised in universities, corporations, and the media, are under attack in our legal and political systems.

4 – Does Orwell's *1984* Live & Breathe Within the Progressivism Movement?

Credit: The Independent.

The totalitarian novel *1984* is a relatively new genre explains Larry P. Arnn in his "Orwell's *1984* and Today" *Imprimis* Volume 49, Issue 12 article in December 2020:

In fact, the word "totalitarian" did not exist before the 20th century. The older word for the worst possible form of government is "tyranny"—a word Aristotle defined as the rule of one person, or of a small group of people, in their own interests and according to their will. Totalitarianism was unknown to Aristotle, because it is a form of government that only became possible after the emergence of modern science and technology.

The protagonist of *1984* is a man named Winston Smith. He works for the state, and his job is to rewrite history. He sits at a table with a telescreen in front of him that watches everything he does. To one side is something called a memory hole—when Winston puts things in it, he assumes they are burned and lost forever. Tasks are delivered to him in cylinders through a pneumatic tube.

Winston's job is to fix every book, periodical, newspaper, etc. that reveals or refers to what used to be the truth, in order that it conform to the new truth and his awareness of this endless, mighty effort to alter reality makes him cynical and disaffected. He comes to see that he knows nothing of the past, of real history: "Every record has been destroyed or falsified," he says at one point, "every book has been rewritten, every picture has been repainted, every statue and street and building has been renamed, every date has been altered. And that process is continuing day by day and minute by minute. . . . Nothing exists except an endless present in which the Party is always right."

Does any of this sound familiar?

Orwell's *1984* and Today's Progressives

There are three stratums in the society of *1984*. There is the Inner Party, whose members hold all the power. There is the Outer Party, to which Winston belongs, whose members work for—and are watched and controlled by—the Inner Party. And there are the proles who live and do blue collar work in a relatively unregulated area.

Winston ventures out into that area from time to time. He finds a little shop there where he buys things. And it is in a room upstairs from this shop where he and Julia, the woman he falls in love with, set up a kind of household as if they are married. They create something like a private world in that room, although it is a world with limitations—they can't even think about having children, for instance, because if they did, they would be discovered and killed.

In the end, it turns out that the shopkeeper, who had seemed to be a kindly old man, is in fact a member of the Thought Police. Winston and Julia's room contained a hidden telescreen all along, so everything they have said and done has been observed. In fact, it emerges that the Thought Police have known that Winston has been having deviant thoughts for twelve years and have been watching him carefully.

When the couple are arrested, they have made pledges that they will never betray each other. They know the authorities will be able to make them say whatever they want them to say—but in their hearts, they pledge, they will be true to their love. It is a promise that neither is finally able to keep.

After months of torture, Winston thinks that what awaits him is a bullet in the back of the head, the preferred method of execution of both the Nazis and the Soviet Communists. He will instead undergo an education, or more accurately a re-education. His final stages of torture are depicted as a kind of totalitarian seminar. The seminar is conducted by a man named O'Brien, who is portrayed marvelously in the film by Richard Burton. As he alternately raises and lowers the level of Winston's pain, O'Brien leads him to knowledge regarding the full meaning of the totalitarian regime.

As the first essential step of his education, Winston has to learn doublethink—a way of thinking that defies the law of contradiction. In Aristotle, the law of contradiction is the basis of all reasoning, the means of making sense of the world. It is the law that says that X and Y cannot be true at the same time if they're mutually exclusive. For instance, if A is taller than B and B is taller than C, C cannot be taller than A. The law of contradiction means things like that. Know of an synonymous ideology?

It would preclude a man from declaring himself a woman, or a woman declaring herself a man, as if one's sex is simply a matter of what one wills it to be—and it would preclude others from viewing such claims as anything other than preposterous.

That's the law of contradiction, which the art of doublethink denies and violates. Doublethink is manifest in the fact that the state ministry in which Winston is tortured is called the Ministry of Love. It is manifest in the three slogans displayed on the state's Ministry of Truth: "War is peace. Freedom is slavery. Ignorance is strength." And as we have seen, the regime in *1984* exists precisely to repeal the past. If the past can be changed, anything can be changed—man can surpass even the power of God. But still, to what end?

There will be no loyalty, except loyalty toward the Party. There will be no love, except the love of Big Brother. There will be no laughter, except the laugh of triumph over a defeated enemy. Does any of this remind you of something?

Nature is ultimately unchangeable, of course, and humans are not God. Totalitarianism, by way of Progressivism, will never win in the end—but it can win long enough to destroy a civilization. That is what is ultimately at stake in the fight we are in. Today we can see the totalitarian impulse among powerful forces in our politics and culture. We can see it in the rise and imposition of doublethink, and we can see it in the increasing attempt to rewrite our history.

Orwell Explains How Socialists Alter Language to Alter History

George Orwell wrote that through altering the past, and by portraying any remembered history as evil, socialist regimes could render classic texts such as the U.S. Declaration of Independence incomprehensible in their original context. People then would be incapable of understanding the original intentions behind them according to the Joshua Philipp "Orwell Explains How Socialists Alter Language to Alter History" *Epoch Times* August 2019 article:

And as if to demonstrate how close today's society has come to what Orwell warned of, the Declaration of Independence has been framed just like this today. Under the new idea of "hate speech," the censors at Facebook flagged the Declaration of Independence as containing offensive language.

To demonstrate the full scale of irony, let's look at what Orwell predicted in his novel *1984*:

"In practice this meant that no book written before approximately 1960 could be translated as a whole. Pre-revolutionary literature could only be subjected to ideological translation—that is, alteration in sense as well as language. Take for example the well-known passage from the Declaration of Independence."

Orwell then quotes the passage: "We hold these truths to be self-evident, that all men are created equal, that they are endowed by their creator with certain inalienable rights, that among these are life, liberty, and the pursuit of happiness.

"That to secure these rights, governments are instituted among men, deriving their powers from the consent of the governed."

With that statement, the Founding Fathers of the United States described truths they believed were self-evident: that the rights of men—and equal opportunities in the world—are given to men by their divine creator. And that among these natural rights are the right to live, the right to liberty, and the right to pursue happiness.

The Founding Fathers state that men institute government to secure these natural rights and that government derives its power from the consent of those it governs. This concept, in and of itself, goes against the totalitarian trinity of socialism, fascism, and communism that took hold of the world in the 20th century.

Subverting Totalitarianism

Under modern totalitarian systems, the people are given their rights by the government—not the other way around. In these systems, there are no natural rights, and there is no creator beyond the halls of government; happiness is in money and immoral indulgence, rather than in virtue; and the average man is seen as too foolish to be given the freedoms of liberty.

Orwell saw this coming. His fictional totalitarian regime was specifically a socialist regime, with "INGSOC" being his acronym for "English Socialism."

Orwell continues his quoting of the Declaration of Independence, noting the next line: "That whenever any form of government becomes destructive to those ends, it is the right of the people to alter or abolish it, and to institute new government."

In other words, if a regime opposes the natural rights it describes, and goes against the idea that government arises from the "consent of the governed," specifically to uphold these natural rights, then the people of that country have the right to alter or abolish that government, and build a new one.

With that idea in force, none of the totalitarian regimes of the 20th century could stand for long.

Newspeak

Understanding this, Orwell imagined how a socialist regime would deal with such subversive values. Orwell's answer was the idea of a government-altered language and a warped system of values that could alter the way people interpret information. And this isn't purely fiction either—as altering the way people interpret information is the goal of psychological warfare.

Orwell called this form of altered language and doctored method of perception "Newspeak."

To illustrate how this system works, Orwell explained how it would be applied by socialism to alter how people interpret the Declaration of Independence. He said that with a document like this, the very concepts would have to be regarded as criminal, and "a full translation could only be an ideological translation, whereby Jefferson's words would be changed into a panegyric on absolute government."

He explained that the phrase "all men are created equal" could be a sentence used by the regime, but it would change it to "all mans [sic] are equal," and its meaning would be interpreted differently to express a "palpable truth" such as the idea that "all men are of equal size, weight, or strength."

In the same way, in our modern systems, the meaning of "all men are created equal" has been changed. Some interpret it through the lens of identity politics, that alleged differences in equality between races should be resolved by government tyranny to manufacture equal outcomes. Rather than have an equal shot at life, the modern totalitarians believe equality should be enforced so that any effort leads to the same equal outcome.

This, of course, deviates from the idea that people are "created" equal by the divine, and that government should not inhibit the liberty, freedom, or "pursuit of happiness" of an individual or group—especially not through mass social engineering that would categorize and regulate people by race.

Black White

Others today try to discredit the Declaration of Independence altogether by attacking the legitimacy of the Founding Fathers and the system of government they created for the United States.

This is based in the idea of criticizing the past, often through a lens of perception that has been altered by socialist politics. The main tool used for this in modern socialist academics is "critical theory," which teaches students to interpret all of history through the Marxist lens of the alleged struggle between the "oppressor" and the "oppressed."

Under this Marxist lens, the Founding Fathers become the "oppressed" fighting against the "oppressors" in Britain, making them communist revolutionary figures in the eyes of people indoctrinated by this ideology. However, they also become "oppressors" because they held slaves, thereby discrediting any of their actions or claims in the eyes of people who use this system of logic. Through this system, the perceptions of the Founding Fathers can be used in different ways, as political interest demands.

Orwell also explained how this would work. He called this concept "BlackWhite." He wrote, "Like so many Newspeak words, this word has two mutually contradictory meanings." Applied to an enemy, "it means the habit of impudently claiming that black is white, in contradiction of the plain facts," and when applied to a Party member, "it means a loyal willingness to say that black is white when Party discipline demands this."

In other words, it means that people can say something is bad when it fits their ideological interest. And say the same thing is good when it fits their ideological interest. The perception of right and wrong is no longer based on a set system of values, but instead on whatever the socialist policy demands at that moment.

This concept is at the heart of today's double standards in Progressive politics—where something is good or excusable if done by their own camp, yet evil and worthy of constant attack if done by their opponents. Yet, as Orwell explained, it's not a conscious system of double standards, but instead an internalized belief: "It means also the ability to BELIEVE that black is white, and more, to KNOW that black is white, and to forget that one has ever believed the contrary."

DoubleThink

"This demands a continuous alteration of the past, made possible by the system of thought which really embraces all the rest, and which is known in Newspeak as DOUBLETHINK," Orwell wrote.

And Orwell explained that altering how the past is perceived is an important part of socialist tyranny. Without real knowledge of the past, a person will tolerate his current conditions "partly because he has no standards of comparison."

As a means of control under socialism, Orwell explained, the citizen must "believe that he is better off than his ancestors and that the average level of material comfort is constantly rising,"

Orwell wrote. "But by far the more important reason for the readjustment of the past is the need to safeguard the infallibility of the Party."

"The mutability of the past is the central tenet of Ingsoc," he wrote. "Past events, it is argued, have no objective existence, but survive only in written records and in human memories. The past is whatever the records and the memories agree upon.

"And since the Party is in full control of all records and in equally full control of the minds of its members, it follows that the past is whatever the Party chooses to make it."

Once again: Does any of this sound familiar? Does any of this remind you of something? Know of a synonymous ideology?

Progressives' Embrace of the 'Brave New World'

Per the John Feehery "Feehery: On the ballot this year: Progressives' embrace of the 'Brave New World'" *The Hill* May 2022 article: From what we've seen so far with how far Progressives have pushed the Biden administration leftward, many of their policies and programs are a referendum of the Democrats' new found embrace of the "Brave New World."

When Aldous Huxley published his dystopian novel *Brave New World* in 1932, the world was convulsed in worldwide depression, the rise of authoritarian regimes in the Soviet Union and Nazi Germany, and the emergence of racial purity movements in America, Europe and Japan.

In Huxley's *Brave New World*, citizens were engineered through artificial wombs, the masses were indoctrinated from childhood about their rightful place in society, the family unit was destroyed so that individuals were better controlled by the state, and the people were constantly barraged by distracting and meaningless popular entertainment and fed a tranquilizer called Soma.

It is not hard to see the connection between Huxley vision and the views of the Progressive left. They embrace critical race theory, discount the value of the two-parent family, promote the mindless values of a vapid Hollywood, and want everybody to get better access to marijuana.

Why Are Progressives So Illiberal?

Victor Davis Hanson explains in his "Why Are Progressives So Illiberal?" Independent Institute February 2021 in-depth report:

One common theme in the abject madness and tragedies of the 21st century is that Progressive ideology now permeates almost all of our major institutions—even as the majority of Americans resist the leftist agenda. Its reach resembles the manner in which the pre-Renaissance church had absorbed the economic, cultural, social, artistic, and political life of Europe, or perhaps how Islamic doctrine was the foundation for all public and private life under the Ottoman Sultanate— or even how all Russian institutions of the 1930s exuded tenets of Soviet Marxism.

Pan-Progressivism

To be a Silicon Valley executive, a prominent Wall Street player, the head of a prestigious publishing house, a university president, a network or PBS anchor, a major Hollywood actress, a retired general or admiral on a corporate board, or a NBA superstar requires either Progressive fides or careful suppression of all political affinities.

According to the Center for Responsive Politics, 98 percent of Big Tech political donations went to Democrats in 2020. Censorship and deplatforming on Twitter, Facebook, and other social media companies is decidedly one-way. When Mark Zuckerberg and others in Silicon Valley donate $500 million to help officials "get out the vote" in particular precincts, it is not to help candidates of both parties.

Google calibrates the order of its search results with a Progressive, not a conservative, bent. Grandees from the Clinton or Obama Administration find sinecures in Silicon Valley, not Republicans or conservatives.

The $4-5 trillion market-capitalized Big Tech cartels, run by self-described Progressives, aimed to extinguish conservative brands like Parler. Ironically, they now apply ideological force multipliers to the very strategies and tactics of 19th-century robber-baron trusts and monopolies. Poor Jack Dorsey has never been able to explain why Twitter deplatforms and cancels conservatives for the same supposed uncouthness that leftists routinely employ.

Silicon Valley apparently does not believe in either the letter or the spirit of the First Amendment.

It exercises a monopoly over the public airwaves, and resists regulations and antitrust legislation of the sort that liberals once championed to break up trusts in the late 19th and early 20th century. As payback, it assumes that Democrats don't see Big Tech in the same manner that they claim to see Big Pharma in their rants against it.

Surveys of "diverse" university faculty show overwhelming left-wing support, reified by asymmetrical contributions of 95-1 to Democratic candidates. The dream of Martin Luther King, Jr. to make race incidental to our characters no longer exists on campuses. Appearance is now essential. More ironic, class considerations are mostly ignored in favor of identity politics. "Equity" applies to race not class.

The general education curricula is one-sided and mostly focused on deductive -studies courses, and in particular race/class/gender zealotry that is anti-Enlightenment in the sense that predetermined conclusions are established and selected evidence is assembled to prove them.

We are also currently witnessing the greatest assault on free speech and expression, and due process, in the last 70 years.

And the challenges to the First and Fifth Amendments are centered on college campuses, where non-Progressive speakers are disinvited, shouted down, and occasionally roughed up for their supposedly reactionary views—and by those who have little fear of punishment.

Students charged with "sexual harassment" or "assault" are routinely denied the right to face their accusers, cross examine witnesses, or bring in counterevidence. They usually find redress for their suspensions or expulsions only in the courts. What was thematic in the Duke Lacrosse fiasco and the University of Virginia sorority rape hoax was the absence of any real individual punishment for those who promulgated the myths.

Indeed in these cases many argued that false allegations in effect were not so important in comparison to bringing attention to supposedly systemic racism and sexism. In Jussie Smollett fashion, what did not happen at least drew attention to what could have happened and thus was valuable. It was as if those who did not commit any actual crime had still committed a thought crime.

Almost all media surveys of the last four years reflect a clear journalistic bias against conservatives in general.

Harvard's liberal Shorenstein Center on Media, Politics and Public Policy famously reported slanted coverage against Trump and his supporters among major television and news outlets at near astronomical rates, in some cases exhibiting over 90 percent negative bias during Trump's first few months in office. Liberal editors can now be routinely fired or forced to retire from major Progressives newspapers if they are not seen as sufficiently woke.

No major journalist or reporter has been reprimanded for promoting the fictional "Russian collusion" hoax—and certainly not in the manner the media has called for punishment, backlisting, and deplatforming for any who championed "stop the steal" protests over the November 2020 elections. The CNN Newsroom put their hands up and chanted "hands up, don't shoot"—a myth surrounding the Michael Brown Ferguson shooting that was thoroughly refuted. Infamous now is the CNN reporter's characterization of arsonist flames shooting up in the background of a BLM/Antifa riot as a "largely peaceful" demonstration. BLM, of course, has been nominated for a Nobel "Peace" Prize. After the summer rioting, one could better cite Tacitus's Calgacus, "Where they make a desert, they call it peace."

A George W. Bush or Donald Trump press conference was often a free-for-all, blood-in-the-water feeding frenzy. A Barack Obama or Joe Biden version devolves into banalities about pets, fashion, and food. The fusion media credo is why embarrass a Progressive government and thus put millions and the planet itself at risk?

Andrew Cuomo's policies of sending COVID-19 patients into rest homes led to thousands of unnecessary deaths. Still, the media gave him an Emmy award for his self-inflated and bombastic press conferences, many of which were little more than unhinged rants against the Trump Administration.

Anthony Fauci's initial pronouncements about the origins of the COVID-19 virus, its risks and severity, travel bans, masks, herd immunity, vaccination rollout dates—and almost everything about the pandemic—were wildly off. Yet he was canonized by the media due to his wink-and-nod assurances that he was the medical adult in the Trump Administration room.

It would be difficult for a prominently conservative actor or actress to win an Oscar these days, or to produce a major conservative-themed film.

Bankable actors/directors/producers like Clint Eastwood or Mel Gibson operate as mavericks, whose films' huge profits win them some exemption. But they came into prominence and power 30 years ago during a different age. And they will likely have no immediate successors.

Ars gratis doctrinae is the new Hollywood and it will continue until it bottoms out in financial nihilism. When such ideological spasms contort a society, the second-rate emerge most prominently as the loudest accusers of the Salem Witches—as if correct zeal can reboot careers stalled in mediocrity. Hollywood's mediocre celebrities from Alec Baldwin to Noah Cyrus have sought attention for their careers by voicing sensational racist, homophobic, and misogynist slurs—on the correct assumption their attention-grabbing left-wing fides prevents career cancellation.

Hollywood, we learn, has been selecting some actors on the basis of lighter skin color to accommodate racist Beijing's demands to distribute widely their films in the enormous Chinese market. Yet note well that Hollywood has recently created racial quotas for particular Oscar categories, even as it reverses its racial obsessions to punish rather than empower people of color on the prompt of Chinese paymasters.

Ditto the political warping in professional sports. Endorsements, media face time, and cultural resonance often hinge on athletes either being woke—or entirely politically somnolent. A few stars may exist as known conservatives, but again they are the rare exceptions. For most athletes, it is wisest to keep mum and either support, condone, or ignore the Black Lives Matter rituals of taking a knee, not standing for the flag, or ritually denouncing conservative politicians. Those who are offended and turn the channel can be replaced by far more new viewers in China, who appreciate such criticism directed at the proper target.

Again, what is common to all the tentacles of this Progressive octopus is illiberalism.

Of course, Progressivism, dating back to late 19th-century advocacy for "updating" the Constitution, always smiled upon authoritarianism. It promoted the "science" of eugenics and forced race-based sterilization, and the messianic idea that enlightened elites can use the increased powers of government to manage better the personal lives of its subjects (enslaved to religious dogma or mired in ignorance), according to supposed pure reason and humanistic intent.

Many Progressives professed early admiration for the supposed efficiency of Benito Mussolini's public works programs spurred on by his Depression-era fascism, and his enlistment of a self-described expert class to implement by fiat what was necessary for "progress."

Even contemporary Progressives have voiced admiration for the communist Chinese ability to override "obstructionists" to create mass transit, high-density urban living, and solar power. Early on in the pandemic Bill Gates defended China's conduct surrounding the COVID-19 disaster. Suggesting the virus did not originate in a "wet" market was "conspiratorial;" travel bans were "racist" and "xenophobic." In contrast, had SARS-CoV-2 possibly escaped by accident from a Russian lab, in our hysterias we might have been on the brink of war.

So it is understandable that Progressivism can end up as an enemy of the First Amendment and intellectual diversity to bulldoze impediments to needed progress. To save us, sometimes leftists must become advocates of monopolies and cartels, of censorship, or of the militarization of our capital.

The new Left sorts, rewards, and punishes people by their race. And some Progressives are the most likely appeasers of a racist and authoritarian Chinese government and advocates of Trotskyizing our past through iconoclasm, erasing, renaming, and cancelling out. San Francisco's school board recently voted to rename over 40 schools, largely due to the pressure of a few poorly educated teachers who claimed on the basis of half-baked Wikipedia research that icons such as Lincoln, Roosevelt, and Washington were unfit for such recognition.

Absolute Power for Absolute Good

There are various explanations for unprogressive Progressivism. None are necessarily mutually exclusive. Much of the latest totalitarianism is simple hula-hoop groupthink, a fad, or even a wise career move. Loud Progressivism has become for some professionals, an insurance policy— or perhaps a deterrent high wall to ensure the mob bypasses one for easier prey elsewhere. Were Hunter Biden and his family grifting cartel not loud liberals and connected to Joe Biden, they all might have ended up like Jack Abramoff.

More commonly, Progressivism offers the elite, the rich, and the well-connected Medieval penance, a vicarious way to alleviate their transitory guilt over privilege such as a $20,000 ice cream freezer or a carbon-spewing Gulfstream by abstract self-indictment of the very system that they have mastered so well.

Progressives also believe in natural hierarchies. They see themselves as an elite certified by their degrees, their resumes, and their correct ideologies, our version of Platonic Guardians, practitioners of the "noble lie" to do us good. In its condescending modern form, the creed is devoted to expanding the administrative state, and the expert class that runs it, and revolves in and out from its government hierarchies to privileged counterparts in the corporate and academic world.

Progressivism patronizes the poor and champions them at a distance, but despises the middle class, the traditionally hated bourgeoise without the romance of the distant impoverished or the taste and culture of the rich. The venom explains the wide array of epithets that Obama, Clinton, and Biden have so casually employed—clingers, deplorables, irredeemables, dregs, ugly folk, chumps, and so on. "Occupy Wall Street" was prepped by the media as a romance. The Tea Party was derided as Klan-like. The rioters who stormed the Capitol were rightly dubbed lawbreakers; those who besieged and torched a Minneapolis federal courthouse were romanticized or contextualized.

Abstract humanitarian Progressives assume that their superior intelligence and training properly should exempt them from the bothersome ramifications of their own ideologies.

They promote high taxes and mock material indulgences. But some have made a science out of tax evasion and embrace the tasteful good life and its material attractions. They prefer private schooling and Ivy League education for their offspring, while opposing charter schools for others.

There is no dichotomy in insisting on more race-based admissions and yet calling a dean or provost to help leverage a now tougher admission for one's gifted daughter. Sometimes the liberal Hollywood celebrity effort to get offspring stamped with the proper university credentials becomes felonious. Walls are retrograde but can be tastefully integrated into a gated estate. They like static class differences and likely resent the middle class for its supposedly grasping effort to become rich—like themselves.

The working classes can always make solar panels, the billionaire John Kerry tells those thousands whom his boss had just thrown out of work by the cancellation of the Keystone XL Pipeline. It is as if the Yale man was back to the old days when the multimillionaire and promoter of higher taxes moved his yacht to avoid sales and excise taxes and lectured JC students, "You study hard, you do your homework and you make an effort to be smart, you can do well. If you don't, you get stuck in Iraq."

There is no such thing as "dark" money or the pernicious role of cash in warping politics when Michael Bloomberg, George Soros, and Mark Zuckerberg, both through direct donations and through various PACs and foundations—channeled nearly $1 billion to left-wing candidates, activists, and political groups throughout the 2020 campaign year.

In sum, the new tribal Progressivism is the career ideology foremost of the wealthy and elite—a truth that many skeptical poor and middle-class minorities are now so often pilloried for pointing out. Progressives have adopted identity politics and rejected class considerations, largely because solidarity with elite minorities of similar tastes and politics excuses them from any concrete concern for, or experience with, the middle classes of all races. The Left finally proved right in its boilerplate warning that the "plutocracy" and the "special interests" run America: "If you can't beat them, outdo them."

Self-righteous Progressives believe they put up with and suffer on behalf of us—and thus their irrational fury and hate for the irredeemables and conservative minorities spring from being utterly unappreciated by clueless serfs who should properly worship their betters.

Joe Biden's 'Ministry of Truth'

The Biden administration's Department of Homeland Security (DHS) announced May 2022 week that it has launched what is being dubbed a Disinformation Governance Board to combat "misinformation."

No, really reports Joe Concha in his "Joe Biden's 'Ministry of Truth'" *The Hill* May 2022 article:

A government agency creating a "ministry of truth" to combat what it deems misinformation? And it's going to fall under the leadership of DHS Secretary Alejandro Mayorkas? The guy presiding over the worst border crisis of our lifetimes, who publicly denies it is a crisis at all while privately admitting it is? Who better to give more responsibility in a democracy that largely rejects government intervention over free speech? What could possibly go wrong?

The person chosen to lead this new "Committee of Public Information" under Mayorkas is Nina Jankowicz, who calls herself "a disinformation fellow" and a Russian disinformation expert.

This is always a fun game to play: Let's say Gov. Ron DeSantis (R) had decided to create a "Disinformation Governance Board" in the state of Florida. And to lead that effort, let's say he chose someone who once openly pushed a partisan conspiracy theory. You can only imagine the exclamations about a "chilling attack on democracy" and totalitarianism rearing its head in the Sunshine State.

Here's what Mayorkas's choice to helm Biden's "Ministry of Truth" once said about Hunter Biden's infamous laptop, which many on the left and in the media dubbed as Russian disinformation in the weeks before the 2020 election.

"We should view it as a Trump campaign product," Jankowicz said of the story at the time. "Not to mention that the emails don't need to be altered to be part of an influence campaign. Voters deserve that context, not a [fairy] tale about a laptop repair shop," she also tweeted in October 2020.

Well, it turns out the laptop from hell really is just that for Hunter Biden and possibly his father, the sitting president. *The New York Times* and *The Washington Post*, which both pushed the same conspiracy theory that the laptop came from Russia to hurt Joe Biden and help Donald Trump, recently confirmed that the laptop and its contents belong to Hunter Biden. A federal investigation into Hunter is expanding, with reports that he may have violated money laundering, tax and foreign lobbying laws.

The new head of the "Ministry of Truth" isn't tweeting much about that investigation these days. Why is that?

Jankowicz was also a big fan of the now-discredited (and laughable) Steele dossier. Here's what she tweeted about a guest appearance that Christopher Steele made on something called the "Infotagion" podcast: "Listened to this last night. Chris Steele (yes THAT Chris Steele) provides some great historical context about the evolution of disinfo. Worth a listen."

Steele's sources have since been proven not to be credible. His allegations of Russian collusion with the Trump campaign, of Russian hookers and "pee tapes"—also not credible. Yet Jankowicz once recommended that we listen to "THAT Chris Steele" when it comes to disinformation.

And here's what she tweeted in recent days about Elon Musk's purchase of Twitter: "Last week I told @NPRMICHEL: I shudder to think about if free speech absolutists were taking over more platforms, what that would look like for the marginalized communities ... which are already shouldering ... disproportionate amounts of this abuse."

This pro-Steele anti-Musker will report to Mayorkas, who said in congressional testimony that he inherited "a broken and dismantled" immigration and border security system from the Trump administration and that "only Congress can fix this." He added, "Yet we have effectively managed an unprecedented number of non-citizens seeking to enter the United States."

Border crossings have skyrocketed under Biden-Mayorkas, surpassing an estimated 2 million each in 2021 and 2022. The numbers weren't remotely near those under Trump. It was the

Biden administration that stopped border wall construction and ended an effective "Remain in Mexico" policy for asylum-seekers. It was Biden who as a presidential candidate urged migrants to "surge the border"—and they listened.

The guy whose agency is launching a Disinformation Governance Board also, without evidence, accused his own Border Patrol agents of whipping migrants, saying that it "painfully conjured up the worst elements of our nation's ongoing battle against systemic racism."

You get the point. Mayorkas and Jankowicz are two of the last people who should be leading any "Ministry of Truth." And the U.S. government shouldn't even have considered creating something like this to be run by partisans with political agendas.

Yet this horrible idea apparently has been in the works for some time among Democrats.

"There's absolutely a commission that's being discussed, but it seems to be more investigating in style rather than truth and reconciliation," Rep. Alexandria Ocasio-Cortez (D-N.Y.) said in an Instagram video in 2018. "I do think that several members of Congress in some of my discussions have brought up media literacy because that is part of what happened here. We're going to have to figure out how we rein in our media environment so you can't just spew disinformation and misinformation."

"Rein in our media environment"—how comforting, coming from AOC. Here's what she said in a 2018 "60 Minutes" interview when asked about how she'd been fact-checked about her dubious public comments:

"People want to really blow up one figure here or one word there. I would argue that they're missing the forest for the trees. I think that there's a lot of people more concerned about being precisely, factually and semantically correct than about being morally right."

What an utterly fascinating way to define truth: Hey, it's not that important to be factually correct, as long as a person is, from their own perspective, morally right.

Maybe Mayorkas can add AOC—who really seemed to care about conditions at border facilities until a Democratic president made her suddenly lose her voice—as an honorary spokesperson for the new "Ministry of Truth."

The Biden administration says it simply wants to battle misinformation. The best way to start might be to purchase a large mirror. When you blame Russian President Vladimir Putin's invasion of Ukraine for inflation that has been rising for well over a year or blame Trump for the current state of the U.S. border or say democracy is at stake if voting rights aren't federalized, then the arbiters-of-truth business isn't one it should be in.

Joe Biden Is the Brezhnev of DEI

From the Rich Lowry "Joe Biden Is the Brezhnev of DEI" *National Review* February 2023 article: In a push for so-called equity so shockingly far-reaching that, not so long ago, a woke diversity officer wouldn't have attempted it at even the most Progressive liberal-arts college, Biden is making the federal government a frank instrument of a racialized radicalism.

Issued in February 2023, Biden's latest executive order will empower ideological shock troops to distort federal policy across the board.

Lest there be any mistake, Section 4 of the order is titled, "Embedding Equity into Government-wide Processes." The administration's policy, according to the order, is "to advance an ambitious, whole-of-government approach to racial equity and support for underserved communities."

Biden already handed down Executive Order 13985, or Advancing Racial Equity and Support for Underserved Communities Through the Federal Government, on his first day in office, but this time he isn't fooling around.

The new order, like so many of the Left's projects in 21st-century America, is equally sinister and parodic.

The heads of federal departments and agencies are commanded to establish Agency Equity Teams within 30 days. This edict runs all the way from the most prestigious and powerful departments, such as Treasury and Defense, to NASA and the National Science Foundation.

The teams will "coordinate the implementation of equity initiatives and ensure that their respective agencies are delivering equitable outcomes for the American people" (although not all of them).

These teams are designed to be robust. They will be led by a senior official and "shall include senior officials from the office of the agency head and the agency's program, policy, civil rights, regulatory, science, technology, service delivery, financial assistance and grants, data, budget, procurement, public engagement, legal, and evaluation offices, as well as the agency's Chief Diversity Officer, to the extent applicable."

Is that all?

The Office of Management and Budget should be consulted to ensure the Agency Equity Teams get the resources they need.

And, of course, the teams should coordinate with the agency's environmental-justice officer (pursuant to Executive Order 14008, Tackling the Climate Crisis at Home and Abroad), and with the senior official who is working with the Gender-Policy Council (pursuant to Executive Order 14020, Establishment of the White House Gender Policy Council).

Among the other executive orders cited, by the way, are Executive Order 13988, Preventing and Combating Discrimination on the Basis of Gender Identity or Sexual Orientation; Executive Order 14031, Advancing Equity, Justice, and Opportunity for Asian Americans, Native Hawaiians, and Pacific Islanders; and Executive Order 14049, White House Initiative on Advancing Educational Equity, Excellence, and Economic Opportunity for Native Americans and Strengthening Tribal Colleges and Universities.

No one can accuse President Biden of being anything but at the top of his game in issuing equity-related EOs.

He does not actually call for Five-Year Plans in his latest order—it's more urgent than that.

Agency heads will have to submit an annual Equity Action Plan to a newly created White House Steering Committee on Equity, which, if we want to continue the Soviet analogy, will be the DEI equivalent of Gosplan.

It is to be led by the assistant to the president for domestic policy, who is none other than Susan Rice.

Her steering committee will include senior officials from various policy councils and offices within the Executive Office of the President, and it will oversee the government-wide equity efforts.

Agency heads, by the way, are ordered to "prioritize and incorporate strategies to advance equity" into "individual performance plans for senior executives."

Indoctrination within the government will continue apace. The Agency Equity Teams "shall support continued equity training and equity leadership development for staff across all levels of the agency's workforce."

There's an amusing Orwellian rhetorical tic in the order's references to "equity for all," as if it weren't an inherently racialist idea opposed to the traditional notion of equality.

At one point the edict says that the "term 'equity' means the consistent and systematic treatment of all individuals in a fair, just, and impartial manner." It then goes on to list all the specific groups who deserve to be treated "equitably," beginning with "Black, Latino, Indigenous and Native American, Asian American, Native Hawaiian, and Pacific Islander persons and other persons of color."

There are a couple of things to be said about all this.

One, if you think the federal government is too incompetent to carry out this project, think again. Anyone who is not on board the Oberlin College–style Jacobinism expressed in the order will be intimidated into staying silent and going along, or will simply leave for another job.

Two, it has to be a priority of every Republican running for president to begin tearing up this ideological infrastructure root and branch on Day One.

Three, and relatedly, it'd be nice if it was only the federal government promoting this poison, but DEI—and an associated gender ideology—is becoming the default setting in American life. The GOP will have to be committed to fighting it, to the extent possible, in all realms. The wishy-washiness of a Larry Hogan won't do.

It's bad enough that the federal government is a blundering behemoth, but if Joe Biden gets his way, Leviathan is about to become thoroughly and determinedly woke.

5 – Universities: Ground Zero for the DEI Metamorphosis of Progressivism

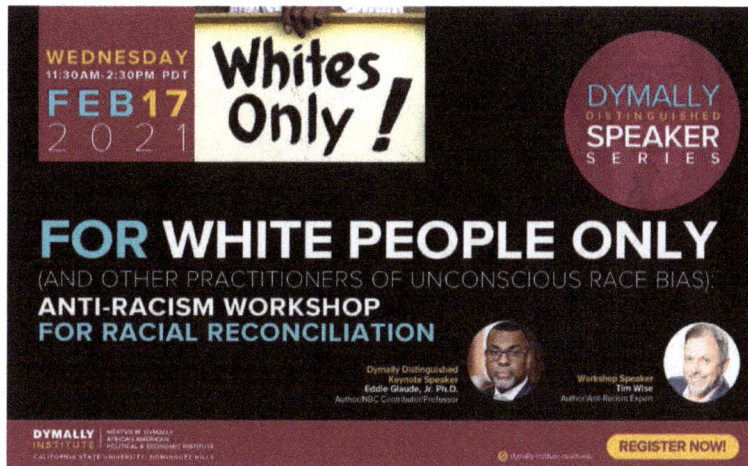

"White People Only: An Anti-Racism Workshop for Racial Reconciliation,"
at California State University, Dominguez Hills (CSUDH).

Social-justice ideology is turning higher education into an engine of Progressive political advocacy, according to a new report by the National Association of Scholars. Left-wing activists, masquerading as professors, are infiltrating traditional academic departments or creating new ones—departments such as "Solidarity and Social Justice"—to advance their cause.

They are entering the highest rung of college administration, from which perch they require students to take social-justice courses, such as "Native Sexualities and Queer Discourse" or "Hip-hop Workshop," and attend social-justice events—such as a Reparations, Repatriation, and Redress Symposium or a Power and Privilege Symposium—in order to graduate. Or, there are elective classes like the one shown in the image above part of the school's controversial Critical Race and Ethnic Studies coursework.

But social-justice education is merely a symptom of an even deeper perversion of academic values: the cult of race and gender victimology, otherwise known as "diversity." The diversity cult is destroying the very foundations of our civilization. It is worth first exploring, however, why social-justice education is an oxymoron.

This new academic state religion combines the ideology of intersectionality with strands of radical feminism, anti-imperialism, and gay and transgender activism as noted in the Howard Gold "Opinion: At America's most 'woke' colleges, extreme liberal politics fails students and free speech" Market Watch article published in January 2020:

But it's really about turning the existing power relationships on their head, so that, say, black lesbians or trans women are now at the top of the inverted pyramid and "cis" white males are at the bottom. "Toxic masculinity" and "white privilege" are the roots of all evil. The last shall be first, and the first last.

It's true that men have dominated the world and women lag behind; gay people have been persecuted, trans people continue to be targets of violence, and African-Americans and other people of color are still victims of systemic racism and discrimination in jobs, housing, and policing. But self-righteous undergraduates, backed by professors and administrators, are turning this new campus orthodoxy into a toxic stew. "Four legs good, two legs bad," the sheep brayed in "Animal Farm." Once again, life imitates Orwell.

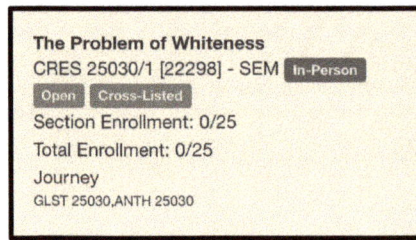

The Problem of Whiteness
CRES 25030/1 [22298] - SEM In-Person
Open Cross-Listed
Section Enrollment: 0/25
Total Enrollment: 0/25
Journey
GLST 25030,ANTH 25030

Credit: University of Chicago "The Problem of Whiteness" Critical Race & Ethnic Studies course.

Why Universities Must Choose One Telos: Truth or Social Justice

Aristotle often evaluated a thing with respect to its "telos"—its purpose, end, or goal. The telos of a knife is to cut. The telos of a physician is health or healing. What is the telos of university? These questions are answered in the Jonathan Haidt "Why Universities Must Choose One Telos: Truth or Social Justice" Heterodox Academy article in October 2017:

The most obvious answer is "truth" — the word appears on so many university crests. But increasingly, many of America's top universities are embracing social justice as their telos, or as a second and equal telos. But can any institution or profession have two teloses (or *teloi*)? What happens if they conflict?

As a social psychologist who studies morality, I have watched these two teloses come into conflict increasingly often during my 30 years in the academy. The conflicts seemed manageable in the 1990s. But the intensity of conflict has grown since then, at the same time as the political diversity of the professoriate was plummeting, and at the same time as American cross-partisan hostility was rising. I believe the conflict reached its boiling point in the fall of 2015 when student protesters at 80 universities demanded that their universities make much greater and more explicit commitments to social justice, often including mandatory courses and training for everyone in social justice perspectives and content.

Now that many university presidents have agreed to implement many of the demands, I believe that the conflict between truth and social justice is likely to become unmanageable. Universities will have to choose, and be explicit about their choice, so that potential students and faculty recruits can make an informed choice. Universities that try to honor both will face increasing incoherence and internal conflict.

[Please note: I am not saying that an individual student cannot pursue both goals. In the talk below I urge students to embrace truth as the only way that they can pursue activism that will effectively enhance social justice. But an institution such as a university must have one and only one highest and inviolable good. I am also not denying that many students encounter indignities, insults, and systemic obstacles because of their race, gender, or sexual identity. They do, and I favor some sort of norm setting or preparation for diversity for incoming students and faculty. But as I have argued elsewhere, many of the most common demands the protesters have made are likely to backfire and make experiences of marginalization more frequent and painful, not less. Why? Because they are not based on evidence of effectiveness; the demands are not constrained by an absolute commitment to truth.]

As I watched events unfold on campus over the past year, I began formulating an account of what has been happening, told from the perspective of moral and social psychology. I was invited to give several talks on campus, and I took those invitations as opportunities to tell the story to current college students, at Wellesley, at SUNY New Paltz, and at Duke. By the time of the Duke talk I think I got the story worked out well enough to send it out into the world, in the hope that it will be shown on many college campuses. It's long (66 minutes). But it is as short as I can make it. There are many pieces to the puzzle, and I had to present each one in order.

Outline of the Talk: Introduction:

We begin with two profound quotations from Dr. Jonathan Haidt:

"The philosophers have only interpreted the world, in various ways; the point is to change it." – Karl Marx, 1845

"He who knows only his own side of the case knows little of that. His reasons may be good, and no one may have been able to refute them. But if he is equally unable to refute the reasons on the opposite side, if he does not so much as know what they are, he has no ground for preferring either opinion..." –John Stuart Mill, 1859

Marx is the patron saint of what I'll call "Social Justice U," which is oriented around changing the world in part by overthrowing power structures and privilege. It sees political diversity as an obstacle to action. Mill is the patron saint of what I'll call "Truth U," which sees truth as a process in which flawed individuals challenge each other's biased and incomplete reasoning. In the process, all become smarter. Truth U dies when it becomes intellectually uniform or politically orthodox.

1. Telos

Each profession or field has a telos. Fields interact constructively when members of one field use their skills to help members of another field achieve their telos. Example: Amazon, Google, and Apple are businesses that I love because they help me achieve my telos (finding truth) as a scholar. But fields can also interact destructively when they inject their telos into other fields.

Example: Business infects medicine when doctors become businesspeople who view patients as opportunities for profit. I will argue that social justice sometimes injects its telos of achieving racial equality (and other kinds) into other professions, and when it does, those professionals betray their telos.

2. Motivated Reasoning

A consistent finding about human reasoning: If we WANT to believe X, we ask ourselves: *"Can-I-Believe-It?"* But when we DON'T want to believe a proposition, we ask: *"Must-I-Believe-It?"* This holds for scholars too, with these results:

- Scholarship undertaken to support a political agenda almost always "succeeds."

- A scholar rarely believes she was biased.

- Motivated scholarship often propagates pleasing falsehoods that cannot be removed from circulation, even after they are debunked.

- Damage is contained if we can count on "institutionalized disconfirmation"—the certainty that other scholars, who do not share our motives, will do us the favor of trying to disconfirm our claims.

But we can't count on "institutionalized disconfirmation" anymore because there are hardly any more conservatives or libertarians in the humanities and social sciences (with the exception of economics, which has merely a 3-to-1 left-right ratio). This is why Heterodox Academy was founded—to call for the kind of diversity that would most improve the quality of scholarship (at least if you embrace Mill rather than Marx).

3. Sacredness

Humanity evolved for tribal conflict. Along the way we evolved a neat trick: Our ability to forge a team by circling around sacred objects & principles. In the academy we traditionally circled around the truth (at least in the 20th century, and not perfectly). But in the 21st century we increasingly circle around a few victim groups. We want to protect them, help them, and wipe out prejudice against them. We want to change the world with our scholarship. This is an admirable goal, but this new secular form of "worship" of victims has intersected with other sociological trends to give rise to a "culture of victimhood" on many campuses, particularly those that are the most egalitarian and politically uniform. Victimhood culture breeds "moral dependency" in the very students it is trying to help—students learn to appeal to 3rd parties (administrators) to resolve their conflicts rather than learning to handle conflicts on their own.

4. Anti-Fragility

"What doesn't kill me makes me stronger." Friedrich Nietzsche was right, and Nasim Taleb's book "Antifragile" explains why. Kids need thousands of hours of unsupervised play and thousands of conflicts and challenges that they resolve without adult help, in order to become independently functioning adults. But because of changes in American childrearing that began in the 1980s, and especially because of the helicopter parenting that took off in the 1990s for middle class and wealthy kids, they no longer get those experiences.

Instead they are enmeshed in a "safety culture" that begins when they are young and that is now carried all the way through college. Books and words and visiting speakers are seen as "dangerous" and even as forms of "violence." Trigger warnings and safe spaces are necessary to protect fragile young people from danger and violence.

But such a culture is incompatible with political diversity since many conservative ideas and speakers are labeled as threatening and banned from campus and the curriculum. Students who question the dominant political ethos are worn down by hostile reactions in the classroom. This is one of the core reasons why universities must choose one telos. Any institution that embraces safety culture cannot have the kind of viewpoint diversity that Mill advocated as essential in the search for truth.

5. Blasphemy

At Truth U, there is no such thing as blasphemy. Bad ideas get refuted, not punished. But at SJU, there are many blasphemy laws—there are ideas, theories, facts, and authors that one cannot use. This makes it difficult to do good social science about politically valenced topics. Social science is hard enough as it is, with big, complicated problems resulting from many interacting causal forces. But at SJU, many of the most powerful explanatory tools are simply banned.

6. Correlation

All social scientists know that correlation does not imply causation. But what if there is a correlation between a demographic category (e.g., race or gender) and a real world outcome (e.g., employment in tech companies, or on the faculty of STEM departments)? At SJU, they teach you to infer causality: systemic racism or sexism. I show an example in which this teaching leads to demonstrably erroneous conclusions.

At Truth U, in contrast, they teach you that "disparate outcomes do not imply disparate treatment." (Disparate outcomes are an invitation to look closely for disparate treatment, which is sometimes the cause of the disparity, sometimes not).

7. Justice

There seem to be two major kinds of justice that activists are seeking: finding and eradicating disparate *treatment* (which is always a good thing to do, and which never conflicts with truth), and finding and eradicating disparate *outcomes*, without regard for disparate inputs or third variables. It is this latter part which causes all of the problems, all of the conflicts with truth. In the real world, there are many disparities of inputs, but anyone who mentions such disparities on campus is guilty of blasphemy and must be punished. I work through an example of how the attempt to eliminate outcome disparities can force people to disregard both truth and justice. This is no way to run a university.

8. Schism

Given the arguments made in sections 1-7, I think it is clear that no university can have Truth and Social Justice as dual teloses. Each university must pick one. I show that Brown University has staked out the leadership position for SJU, and the University of Chicago has staked out the leadership position for Truth U. (This has been confirmed by their rankings in the new Heterodox Academy Guide to Colleges, see the Appendix for the link).

I close by urging students on every campus in America to raise the question among themselves: which way do we want our university to go? I offer a specific tool to raise the question: the Heterodox University Initiative. If students on every campus would propose these three specific resolutions to their student government, perhaps as the basis of a campus-wide referendum, then students could make their choice known to the faculty and administration. The students would send a clear signal as to whether they want more or less viewpoint diversity on campus. At the very least, a campus-wide discussion of Marx versus Mill would be a constructive conversation to have.

Without a "Diversity" Leg to Stand On

Every year since 2013, usually during the first week of September, the *Harvard Crimson* publishes survey results profiling the incoming freshman class, including their political and social orientations. These feature-length reports have consistently shown that a dominant majority of Harvard's incoming students identify as politically and socially Progressive, with ever-fewer students identifying as conservative.

In 2022, however, per the Renu Mukherjee "Without a "Diversity" Leg to Stand On" *City Journal* October 2022 article: The *Crimson* didn't publish the feature and didn't reply to my inquiry about whether they would do so. Harvard may have good reasons for wanting to delay such a report, given an upcoming Supreme Court case.

In *Students for Fair Admissions v. President and Fellows of Harvard College*, the Supreme Court will reexamine a half-century-old justification for race-based university admissions—namely, that racial diversity generates viewpoint diversity on campus and contributes to the lively exchange of ideas. Past results of Harvard's freshman surveys, which detail growing racial diversity but diminishing viewpoint diversity, discredit this justification.

Harvard's own freshman survey data undermine one of its justifications for affirmative action.

Of the Class of 2025, for example, only 1.4 percent identify as very conservative; only 7.2 percent identify as somewhat conservative; and only 18.6 percent identify as moderate. By contrast, 72.4 percent of freshmen identify as predominantly liberal. Yet this class is the "the most diverse class in the history of Harvard," according to William R. Fitzsimmons, dean of admissions and financial aid.

Other survey responses drive the point home. Of members of the Class of 2025 who supported a candidate in the 2020 presidential election, 87 percent backed Joe Biden. Meantime, 82 percent said they supported the Black Lives Matter protests of 2020, which resulted in at least $1 billion in damages and numerous deaths, while nearly half (49.8 percent) said that they supported defunding the police. This doesn't sound like viewpoint diversity to me.

Without viewpoint diversity as a justification, race-based admissions—that is, affirmative action—may not survive.

Since 2014, Students for Fair Admissions (SFFA), a nonprofit group of more than 20,000 students, parents, and others, has argued that affirmative action violates Title VI of the 1964 Civil Rights Act and the Fourteenth Amendment's Equal Protection Clause, which prohibit public and private universities receiving federal funds from discriminating based on race, color, and national origin.

This straightforward legal argument is likely to play well with a Supreme Court that leans toward originalism, but this doesn't mean that the justices' decision will rest on that philosophy alone. In fact, the Court's jurisprudence on race-conscious admissions has centered predominantly not on the legality of the policy but on its implications for higher education.

In his landmark opinion in *Regents of the University of California v. Bakke*, Lewis Powell argued that the use of race as a factor in college admissions ought to be permitted because it would (presumably) lead to greater student-body diversity. This was a laudable goal for a university, he said, for it would allow it to achieve "a robust exchange of ideas."

Sandra Day O'Connor recapitulated Powell's argument in her opinion for the Court in *Grutter v. Bollinger*, upholding the University of Michigan Law School's policy of intentionally favoring applicants from certain racial groups over others with similar qualifications. O'Connor justified the decision largely by appealing to its supposed policy implications. She cited several amicus briefs submitted by left-wing academics, corporations, and professional organizations, all of which alleged countless studies showing that racial and ethnic diversity guaranteed greater viewpoint diversity and, in turn, increased tolerance of differing opinions.

But is this true? Has the use of racial preferences in higher education admissions achieved the "robust exchange of ideas" on which it was originally justified by the courts?

In an amicus brief supporting SFFA's challenge to race-conscious admissions policies at Harvard and the University of North Carolina, the Legal Insurrection Foundation (LIF) says "no." In the years since Grutter was decided, "the American university campus," LIF argues, "has become less ideologically diverse and more intolerant of ideas challenging campus dogmas." The group cites several nonpartisan surveys to support the claim. A 2021 survey of 37,104 students conducted jointly by the College Pulse, the Foundation for Individual Rights in Education (FIRE), and RealClearEducation found that more than 80 percent of students reported some amount of self-censorship.

Similarly, LIF notes that a Knight Foundation-Ipsos study released in January 2022 showed that 65 percent of college students felt today's "campus climate prevents people from saying what they believe for fear of offending someone." What's more, less than half of all college students "said they were comfortable offering dissenting opinions to ideas shared by other students or the instructor in the classroom." And 71 percent of students who identified as Republican "felt that the campus climate chilled speech."

The Court now seems likely to strike down the use of race-conscious admissions in higher education next June 2023. Given the originalist-bent of the Court's majority, the decision will rely most heavily on the text of both Title VI and the Equal Protection Clause, which prohibit racial discrimination. But it may also have something to say about the faulty premise underlying race-conscious admissions all these years. Contrary to what O'Connor claimed in Grutter, affirmative action has not led to greater diversity of thought on America's college campuses.

An Overt Political Litmus Test

According to the John D. Sailer and Ray M. Sanchez "An Overt Political Litmus Test" *City Journal* May 2022 report:

On May 5, 2022, the Chancellor's Office of the California Community Colleges (CCC) system amended its proposed diversity, equity, inclusion, and accessibility (DEIA) competencies. Issued in March, the original proposal sought to establish "diversity" and "anti-racism" evaluations for every employee of the 116-college system—a political litmus test. The newly issued changes are merely cosmetic, indicating that, despite notable pushback to the proposal, it will likely become policy.

While DEI requirements are quickly becoming common, CCC's proposal stands out for its thoroughness and ideological aggressiveness. It defines "cultural competency" as "the practice of acquiring and utilizing knowledge of the intersectionality of social identities and the multiple axes of oppression that people from different racial, ethnic, and other minoritized groups face." It calls for all community college districts to "include DEIA competencies and criteria as a minimum standard for evaluating the performance of all employees" and "place significant emphasis on DEIA competencies in employee evaluation and tenure review processes to support employee growth, development, and career advancement."

The Chancellor's Office also provides a list of competencies. Some of them: "Includes a DEI and race-conscious pedagogy," "Contributes to DEI and anti-racism research and scholarship," and "Engages in self-assessment of one's own commitment to DEI and internal biases, and seeks opportunities for growth to acknowledge and address the harm caused by internal biases and behavior."

Requiring faculty to embrace the politically-charged concepts of "intersectionality" and "multiple axes of oppression" clearly violates academic freedom—but the CCC system seems unperturbed by that prospect. A workgroup for the system's curriculum committee created guidelines called "DEI in Curriculum: Model Principles and Practices," which explain what "DEI and race-conscious" pedagogy looks like in practice.

One of the document's recommended "culturally responsive classroom practices" reads: "Protect the cultural integrity of an academic discipline to support equity by no longer weaponizing 'academic integrity' and 'academic freedom' that impedes equity and inflicts curricular trauma on our students, especially historically marginalized students."

Perhaps unsurprisingly, the proposal has gained significant pushback. The Foundation for Individual Rights in Education referred to the policy as "unacceptable and unconstitutional." The Pacific Legal Foundation condemned it in equally strong terms: "The proposed regulation will entrench a political orthodoxy, reduce intellectual diversity on college campuses, threaten First

Amendment freedoms, and impair the education of students who deserve exposure to a rich and robust range of viewpoints on the critical issues facing our country."

Even Brian Leiter, law professor at University of Chicago and certainly no conservative, agreed with the Pacific Legal Foundation's First Amendment argument, noting on his blog that the "letter gets it right on the constitutional infirmities."

But the criticism seems to have fallen on deaf ears, as the new amendments are trivial. Per the changes, evaluators should have a "consistent," rather than "uniform," understanding of the DEIA evaluation process. Cultural competency involves "developing cultural knowledge" rather than "learning specific bodies of cultural knowledge." The key thrust of the policy—most notably, that every employee in America's largest system of higher education will be evaluated for his or her political beliefs—remains unchanged.

The California Community Colleges system proposes a diversity, equity, and inclusion system unique for its ideological aggressiveness.

Those concerned with higher education should pay close attention. After all, DEI competencies for promotion and tenure are the next big thing. Recently, the University of Illinois at Urbana-Champaign announced that it will require diversity statements of all faculty members seeking promotion or tenure. The Diversity Strategic Plan at Northern Arizona University promises to embed diversity "as an important component of learning outcomes, professional development, performance expectations, and performance evaluations at all levels."

Even disciplines that seem apolitical, such as medicine, have followed the trend. The UNC-Chapel Hill School of Medicine's new promotion and tenure guidelines require every candidate to submit a diversity statement and include diversity contributions in their CV. (The guidelines provide a list of sample activities.)

Oregon Health and Science University's Diversity, Equity, Inclusion and Anti-Racism Strategic Action Plan establishes a similar promotion and tenure policy, promising to "include a section in promotion packages where faculty members report on the ways they are contributing to improving DEI, anti-racism and social justice. Reinforce the importance of these efforts by establishing clear consequences and influences on promotion packages."

California often functions as a testing ground for the rest of the nation. What happens in California rarely stays in California—especially if it's an "innovation" in Progressive politics. We should hope that this overt political litmus test will be unequivocally rejected. Unfortunately, that does not look likely.

The Highest Principle

As per the Christopher F. Rufo "The Highest Principle" *City Journal* February 2023 article: Left-wing DEI bureaucracy has captured Florida State University and installed radical politics as the governing value.

Florida State University has adopted a series of "diversity, equity, and inclusion" programs that divides Americans along a "matrix of oppression," castigates Christians for their "Christian privilege," and offers a racially segregated scholarship that deliberately bars white students from applying.

Officially, Florida State officials have claimed in a recent report to Governor Ron DeSantis that they support 23 separate DEI programs and initiatives. But beneath the surface, the ideology has embedded itself everywhere in the university.

I have obtained documents through public searches and Sunshine Law requests that reveal a sprawling bureaucracy, dedicated to promoting left-wing racial narratives, including a seemingly endless array of programs, departments, trainings, certificates, committees, statements, grants, groups, clubs, reports, and initiatives.

One representative program is "Social Justice Ally Training," hosted by Student Equity & Inclusion Director Sierra Turner and the Center for Leadership & Social Change. The program provides a basic recapitulation of the critical-race-theory narrative: white, patriarchal Western societies have created a "Cycle of Socialization" that has resulted in "racism, classism, religious oppression, sexism, heterosexism, gender oppression, ableism, ageism & adultism, and xenophobia."

The trainers make the case that, in the United States, "whites" are the racial group responsible for the "systematic subordination of members of targeted racial groups who have relatively little power." Whites are also guilty of "cultural racism," or the creation and maintenance of social structures that "overtly and covertly attribute normality to white people and Whiteness." By definition, no other group can be racist—"institutional racism" can only "create advantages and benefits for Whites."

Christians, too, represent an oppressor class.

They have created "Christian hegemony," which "normalizes Christian values as intrinsic to an explicitly American identity," and have instituted a regime of "religious oppression" and the "systematic subordination of minority religions." Consequently, Christians must atone for their "Christian privilege," the training suggests, because of, for example, their "close-minded hatred, fear, or prejudice towards Islam and Muslims."

The training divides participants into "dominant groups" and "subordinate groups." Dominant groups—whites, men, Christians, heterosexuals—are told that they are at the apex of the "matrix of oppression," but if they submit to social-justice ideology, they can seek redemption through "identity development." They are told that they begin their journey as "selfish," unable to "see privilege," "not interested in the system," and hoping to "maintain the status quo." But the oppressor class can eventually overcome its nature and work to "consciously [use] unearned privilege against self" and "destroy the system."

Beyond training programs, DEI ideology at Florida State has also become pervasive in nearly every academic department. The business school has pledged to create an award for "DEI heroes." The classics department has released a statement in support of Black Lives Matter. The art history department has adopted a "land acknowledgement" that portrays white Europeans as illegal settlers. And the sociology department has created an entire course, "Critical Race Theory," that presents left-wing racialism as the gospel truth and assigns readings that traffic in overt racial hostility, such as "Whiteness as Pathological Narcissism," with no competing opinions anywhere to be found. "Do not let the constraints of the discipline stop you from being the radical you want to be," the syllabus reads.

At the administrative level, the DEI bureaucracy also serves as a filter to exclude anyone who does not commit to social-justice ideology. Some departments at FSU now require potential faculty to submit "diversity statements"—best understood as loyalty oaths to left-wing racialism—as part of the application process. Likewise, some academic programs also require graduate students to pledge allegiance to DEI in order to gain admission into the department.

The result of all these programs is a racial and ideological spoils system, in which groups are rewarded or punished based on their identity and political orientation, rather than their academic merit. Following this system of race-based judgment, Florida State even offers scholarships that explicitly exclude white students. The Delores Auzenne Assistantship for Minorities, for example, is designated solely for "African-American, Hispanic, Asian or Pacific Islander, and Native-American" graduate students—no European-Americans need apply.

The end goal of DEI ideology is to move everyone in the university's orbit toward partisan political activism. In the Social Justice Ally Training, the university makes its desire clear: participants are directly encouraged to engage in "structural change activism" and "lobbying for policy change," including "petition drives, picketing, performance art, teach-ins, vigils, overloading administrative systems, rent withholding, strikes, walk-outs, protests, marches, blacklisting, slowdowns, sit downs, dumping, [and] demonstrations."

Knowledge, it seems, has been displaced as the core mission of this university. At Florida State, the diversity commissars have busied themselves making radical politics—administrated by the bureaucracy and imposed downward on students, faculty, and staff—the highest principle.

DEI Cult

The University of South Florida turns left-wing racialism into a psychological conditioning program as reported in the Christopher F. Rufo "DEI Cult" *City Journal* February 2023 article:

The University of South Florida has adopted a radical "diversity, equity, and inclusion" (DEI) program that claims America is a force for "white supremacy," encourages students to attend racially segregated counseling programs to address their "privilege" and "oppression," and promotes a variety of left-wing causes, including "reparations," "defund the police," and "prison abolition."

I have obtained a trove of public documents exposing the university's DEI programming, much of which, according to the Internet Archive's Wayback Machine, the university tried to delete from its website following Florida governor Ron DeSantis's recent request for information on DEI in the state's public universities.

Taken together, these materials paint a troubling picture. USF's sprawling diversity bureaucracy has turned left-wing racialism into a new orthodoxy and implemented an administrative policy of racial preferences and discrimination. It divides individuals into categories of oppressor and oppressed, presents "anti-racism" as the solution, and proposes "racial identity development"—

which, in practice, resembles a form of cult programming—as the necessary method of atonement.

The first step in this programming is the condemnation of American society. Following the 2020 death of George Floyd, nearly every appendage of USF condemned the United States as fundamentally racist. Then-president Steven Currall published a statement denouncing the "systemic racism that continues to plague our nation." The English department attacked the United States for "centuries of normalized violence, structural oppression, and dehumanizing rhetoric that target Black, Brown, and Indigenous people."

The School of Interdisciplinary Global Studies blasted America for its "institutionalized, structural racism and white supremacy." The anthropology department assailed its own discipline for being "rooted in racism." The department of sociology pronounced on the "interlocking systems of oppression found throughout the institutions of our country." Literacy studies, women's and gender studies, engineering, medicine, nursing, pharmacy, public health, and other departments released similar statements.

Then the university's DEI administrators offered the solution: racial reeducation.

In the aftermath of the ensuing George Floyd riots, the USF Counseling Center offered racially segregated counseling sessions for "Black & African American," "People of Color," and "White" students, providing a "healing space for POC to discuss unique impacts of systemic racism" and a "connecting space for allies to share experiences and identify ways to take action against racism." The goal of these psychological conditioning sessions, according to organizers, was to address "COVID-19, xenophobia, killings of unarmed Black people, systemic racism, privilege, oppression, and institutional challenges." In this kind of programming, individuals are subordinated to racial categories; ideology serves as a substitute for psychological health.

Meantime, the university's DEI officers reinforced the narrative and offered a battery of resources for racial reconditioning. The Office of Multicultural Affairs published an official guidebook, "Anti-Racist Resources: The Unlearning of Racism and White Supremacy," that promoted psychological approaches to "white identity development." The premise of these programs is simple: whites suffer from "white privilege," "white guilt," and "white fragility." And the solution is clear: whites must atone for their oppression through the process of "racial identity development" and "becoming an active anti-racist."

According to one of these programs, called "Scaffolding Anti-Racist Resources," whites must first admit their complicity in racism, which includes "being confronted with active racism of real-world experiences that highlight their whiteness." Whites will then enter the process of "disintegration," experiencing "white guilt" and thinking, "I feel bad for being white." Next, after their racial identity is broken down, they will enter a phase of "reintegration," thinking, "it's not my fault I'm white" and beginning to engage in left-wing political activism.

Finally, as whites move through the stages of "pseudo-independence" and "immersion," they will begin to "work against systems of oppression" and "use [their] privilege to support anti-racist work." At the end of the program, their psychology should conform entirely to political ideology. As the final step, whites must answer various loyalty tests. "Does your solidarity last longer than a news cycle?" the training asks. "Does your solidarity make you lose sleep at night? Does your solidarity put you in danger? Does your solidarity cost you relationships?"

The endpoint of USF's DEI programming is left-wing political activism.

As part of the university's official "anti-racist" guidebook, diversity officials included materials promoting "reparations," "defund the police," and "prison abolition." One resource, "97 Things White People Can Do for Racial Justice," instructs whites to "join a local 'white space,'" "donate to [their] local BLM chapter," "participate in reparations," and "decolonize [their] bookshelf." Another, "For Our White Friends Desiring to Be Allies," demands that whites "stop talking about colorblindness" and stop oppressing those "who do not believe in a white, capitalist Jesus."

Taken as a whole, USF's DEI initiatives resemble practices of cult initiation. The path of "racial identity development" does not take as its endpoint individual psychological health but the submersion of the individual into political ideology. Whites are designated an oppressor class, born with racial guilt that can only be expiated through elaborate rituals and commitments to left-wing activism, to the point that they are alienated from previous relationships and feel compelled to "change the way [they] vote," "denounce [President Trump]," and "change how [they] read [their] Bible."

At a more practical level, the implementation of DEI ideology at USF has already resulted in a system of widespread racial preferences and discrimination. The university openly promotes racial quotas in hiring and requires potential faculty to submit "diversity statements"—best understood as loyalty oaths to left-wing racialism—to be considered for employment.

The university's Office of Supplier Diversity administers a system of racial and sexual preferences in contracting, instructing its "Diversity Champions" to hire vendors and suppliers based on identity, rather than on purely economic concerns. The university also promotes a range of racially segregated scholarships that explicitly exclude white students—the only racial group that receives such treatment.

These "diversity, equity, and inclusion" programs are a farce. In practice, they promote ideological conformity, racial and sexual discrimination, and the exclusion of any group that finds itself on the wrong side of the identity hierarchy. Governor DeSantis, who recently pledged to defund DEI programs in Florida's public universities, should not hesitate in demolishing these offices, terminating the employment of their commissars, and restoring colorblind equality, individual merit, and scholarly excellence as the guiding principles of the academy.

Racism in the Name of "Anti-Racism"

The University of Central Florida adopts DEI programming that segregates students by race and encourages discrimination against the "oppressor" class as reported in Christopher F. Rufo's "Racism in the Name of 'Anti-Racism'" Substack page in February 2023:

The University of Central Florida has adopted radical Diversity, Equity, and Inclusion (DEI) programming that segregates students by race, condemns the United States as "white-supremacist culture," and encourages active discrimination against the "oppressor" class, characterized as "male, White, heterosexual, able-bodied, and Christian."

Officially, UCF reports that it has 14 separate DEI programs, costing in the aggregate more than $4 million per year. But this dramatically understates the reality, which is that the ideology of "diversity, equity, and inclusion" has been entrenched everywhere. The university's administration and academic departments have created a blizzard of programs, classes, trainings, reports, committees, certifications, events, documents, policies, clubs, groups, conferences, and statements pledging UCF to left-wing racialism.

These programs, long in the making, exploded into prominence following the death of George Floyd in 2020. As the administration signaled that it was endorsing the Black Lives Matter movement, the academic departments immediately fell into line. The sociology department pledged allegiance to BLM and blasted the "anti-Blackness at the heart of US white-supremacist culture." The physics department released a statement promising to address "systemic anti-Black racism in policing" and its own "power and privilege." The anthropology department published a statement denouncing white European "hegemonic systems" and vowed to "advocate for a more inclusive society based on the principles of cultural relativism."

The ideology that underpins the university's DEI programming follows the basic mantras of critical race theory:

America is a racist nation divided between white oppressors and minority oppressed, and society, using the logic of "antiracism," must actively discriminate against the oppressors in order to achieve social justice. The great oppressor who occupies the "mythical norm," according to the university's official glossary, is "male, white, heterosexual, financially stable, young-middle adult, able-bodied, Christian." Other groups are "minoritized," or condemned by the "systemic and structural realities in place that push people and communities to the margins."

Following the George Floyd riots, the university's administrators and faculty renewed their dedication to the DEI narrative. Ann Gleig, an associate professor of religion and cultural studies, instructed whites on campus to begin "waking up to whiteness and white privilege," encouraging them to "educate [themselves] on systemic racism and white supremacy," "participate in anti-racist training programs," and "commit to having difficult conversations with white family and friends about systemic racism." She also directed students to a set of resources, including one that encouraged whites to attend racially segregated "affinity groups" to develop their white racial consciousness and "unravel their feelings and ways of understanding without hurting people of color."

At the same time, S. Kent Butler, a black professor of counselor education then serving as UCF's chief diversity officer, pushed the argument that minorities live in a state of constant fear and exhaustion. "Leaving the house is an action that may seem ordinary for some, but for individuals who deal with regular hatred and judgment . . . we live with anxiety and fear about walking into unwelcoming spaces," he said. The responsibility for reforming society, he explained in another interview, belongs to whites. "Racism comes from slavery, from when they used to have [Black] people swinging from trees," he said. "White people have to come to the forefront and stop the systemic system that's been put into play by white people."

How do DEI bureaucracies recommend solving these problems? Through active racial discrimination, or, to use their euphemism, a policy of "racial equity." The University of Central Florida has embedded such discriminatory practices in its programs, including faculty hiring, student activities, and scholarship opportunities.

Regarding faculty hiring, UCF has adopted the position that merit is a "myth" that advances racism and must be corrected through active discrimination on behalf of "minoritized groups." In its official guidebook, "Inclusive Faculty Hiring," the university recommends tilting the hiring process toward minorities by minimizing objective measures—dismissed as "problematic heuristics"—and peppering job announcements with left-wing buzzwords such as "racial equity," "social justice," "anti-racist," and "mention of specific group identities," with the exception of those of whites.

Equity and Inclusion Statements

To reinforce this ideology, administrators also recommend that departments require potential faculty to submit an "Equity and Inclusion Statement," which serves as a loyalty oath to left-wing ideology. At the end of the process, the university endorses explicit racial quotas. "University policy indicates that a successful search will result in a diverse pool of candidates for the final interview round that [includes at least one woman and one member of a minoritized group]," the guidebook reads [brackets in the original]. "If at the time final candidates are identified and the specified parameters are not met, the search should either be restarted or the existing candidate pool should be revisited with more equitable strategies in mind."

Students, too, must navigate a racial filter. The university has held minority-only graduation ceremonies, and its counseling center offers racially segregated "affinity groups" and psychological programs, such as "Exploring Vulnerability in POC Spaces," restricted to "Black-identified, Afro-Latinx and students from African-descent," as well as other racial-conditioning groups delineated for "Asian-identified students" and "Hispanic/Latinx students."

UCF also advertises racially discriminatory and racially segregated scholarships that intentionally exclude European-Americans and sometimes Asian-Americans. The Professional Doctoral Diversity Fellowship, Harris Diversity Initiative Scholarship, and NSF/Florida Georgia Louis Stokes Alliance for Minority Participation in Engineering & Science and National Action Council for Minorities in Engineering scholarships, for example, promise to discriminate on behalf of "underrepresented populations," a euphemism for "African American, Hispanic, or Native American" students. Others, such as the Minority Teachers Scholarship, are explicitly segregated by race. Candidates "must be a member of one of the following racial groups: African American/Black, American Indian/Alaskan Native, Asian American/Pacific Islander, or Hispanic/Latino." In other words, anyone but whites.

All these racially discriminatory scholarship programs violate Title VI of the Civil Rights Act. But university administrators have been silently embedding "racial equity" principles into every academic process. They operate with impunity because, until recently, no one has attempted to stop them.

This could change. Along with my Manhattan Institute colleague Ilya Shapiro, I have proposed a model policy that would outlaw these practices and abolish the DEI bureaucracy. Florida governor Ron DeSantis has promised to address the problem in the coming legislative session. It seems that Florida lawmakers have seen the DEI scam for what it is: an attempt to push left-wing racialist ideology in the guise of academic justice. As they prepare for action, state legislators should consider a maximalist position: demolishing the DEI bureaucracy down to its foundations and restoring the principle of colorblind equality to the Sunshine State's public institutions.

6 – George Soros: The Funding Godfather of Progressive and Democrat Causes

Credit: New York Post.

George Soros is one of the United States' top political and advocacy donors, spending billions on campaigns, think tanks, start-ups, and nonprofits that promote his agenda. His principal philanthropic network centers on the Open Society Foundations (OSF) and Foundation to Promote Open Society (FPOS), two multi-billion-dollar left-of-center advocacy grantmaking foundations.

Through OSF and FPOS Soros has funded the vast majority of the most prominent left-Progressive advocacy groups in the United States. He also created the Institute for New Economic Thinking to promote his unorthodox left-Progressive economic policy viewpoints.

Financial ties between the Black Lives Matter movement and Soros have been reported, as well as financial ties to Occupy Wall Street through intermediaries like the Tides Center. The network of Soros funded organizations indirectly touches 30 media organizations.

The day after the 2017 presidential inauguration, the "Women's March" took to the streets of Washington, D.C. Between 2000 and 2014, Soros donated to 40 of the groups affiliated with the march, his donations totaling at least $89.9 million.

Soros writes in 2022 op-ed, "If people trust the justice system, it will work." He has it exactly backward. If the justice system works, people will trust it. Trust has to be earned. Soros claims that the agenda of the prosecutors he supports is "based on both common sense and evidence." Often, it is supported by neither. For example, on his first day in office, Los Angeles District Attorney George Gascón barred the use of sentence enhancements for felons who have inflicted great bodily injury, used a gun or have prior violent felonies. He claimed that "studies show" that longer sentences increase the likelihood that a criminal will commit more crimes after release, outweighing the crime-prevention benefit of keeping him in prison. Yet Gascón cited only one unpublished manuscript for this remarkable claim.

A review by the *Wall Street Journal* of the published research found that it didn't at all support the claim. The studies on sentence length and recidivism have mixed results, and the reported effects are weak. Gascón simply cherry-picked the one study that supported his agenda and ignored the rest. Far from the "more thoughtful discussion" that Soros claims to want, his agenda is as often based on a distortion of science.

Open Society Foundations (OSF) Are Sabotaging America's Laws & Criminal Justice

As documented in *Crime Rate Madness,* which the first part of this chapter draws upon, George Soros spent over $18 million on political campaigns affiliated with the Democratic Party in 2016, $24 million on left-of-center Super PACs over the last few years—including $7 million on Hillary Clinton's primary PAC, Priorities USA—and partnered with other donors in a $15 million campaign to mobilize specific demographics.

In 2013, Soros had agreed to become co-chair for the Clinton-aligned Ready For Hillary Super PAC, as well as investing over $2 million in a left-of-center data analytics company, Catalist. After Hillary Clinton's defeat in the 2016 Presidential election, Soros met for three days with elite donors and Democrats to come up with new plans. Soros also spent $2 million in 2016 to help defeat then-Maricopa County Sheriff Joe Arpaio (R) as part of a nationwide push for criminal justice reform.

In the 2012 election, Soros announced that he would contribute $1 million each to the voter mobilization group America Votes and the Democratic super PAC American Bridge 21st Century. According to the Center for Responsive Politics, Soros gave American Bridge 21st Century $2 million in the 2015-2016 election cycle.

In the first three months of 2020, George Soros had put $28.3 million into various efforts to support the Democratic side in the 2020 election. Soros is using his Democracy PAC to distribute these payments, a new super PAC he launched in 2019 for the purpose of handing a victory to the Democrats in the upcoming presidential election.

Of the $28.3 million, $10 million went to Win Justice for its programs against voter disenfranchisement, namely, to mobilize "people of color and other infrequent voters" that might be affected by states choosing to suspend in-person voting come November due to the coronavirus pandemic. The voters that Win Justice talk to are "are among those who will most deeply and disproportionately affected by the upheaval the Covid-19 pandemic appears likely to cause in November," said a Soros spokesperson.

Soros also gave $5 million to left-of-center PAC Priorities USA and $7 million to the Democratic Senate Majority PAC. Soros' early 2020 giving also targeted several feminist groups, including EMILY's List and Supermajority.

In 2020, Soros funded political organizations that supported the campaigns of left-wing Illinois State Attorney Kimberly Foxx, Philadelphia District Attorney Larry Krasner, and Dallas County District Attorney John Creuzot. His contributions have supported these attorneys who seek to reduce theft-related prosecution. In 2017, State Attorney Kimberly Foxx was elected to office after receiving financial support from the Illinois Justice & Public Safety PAC that received $400,000 from Soros.

Foxx, whose jurisdiction includes Chicago, announced that her office sought to quit prosecuting shoplifters unless they possessed a record of over 10 previous felony convictions or had stolen more than $1,000 worth of goods. Similarly, Dallas County District Attorney John Creuzot announced in 2019 that his campaign received national funding through Soros and said that his office would no longer prosecute individuals for the theft of items valued under $750.

The office of Philadelphia District Attorney Larry Krasner states that refusing to prosecute certain crimes such as public camping, offering, or soliciting sex, and public urination is working to "decriminalize poverty and homelessness." Soros contributed $1.45 million to a super PAC that supported District Attorney Larry Krasner in the Democratic primary in May 2017.

Open Society Foundations (OSF)

Per *Crime Rate Madness,* the Open Society Foundations (OSF; formally Open Society Institute) is a private grantmaking foundation created and funded by billionaire financier and liberal philanthropist George Soros. OSF was founded in 1993 as the Open Society Institute (OSI), which remains the foundation's formal name; OSF has since become the main hub of a Soros-funded network of more than 20 national and regional foundations, making it one of the largest political philanthropies in the world.

Built on Soros' anti-capitalist, redistributionist political philosophy, the organization gives away nearly a billion dollars per year to left-wing organizations around the world to advance his vision of an "open society." Among those groups is the Foundation to Promote Open Society (FPOS), another foundation created after OSF which has since become the primary grant maker in the Soros network.

In 2018, OSF reported revenues of $376 million, expenditures of $215 million (including grants of $20.3 million), and assets of $3.7 billion.

In the United States, OSF's U.S. Programs have given hundreds of millions to left-wing political organizations, including multi-million dollar gifts to the American Civil Liberties Union (ACLU), Planned Parenthood, the Robin Hood Foundation, the Tides Foundation, the Brennan Center for Justice, and Alliance for Citizenship, among numerous others.

Confidential documents indicate that the OSF's U.S. Programs agenda prioritizes a number of liberal issue prerogatives and funds left-wing organizations to carry out these policies. Some of these prerogatives include enacting liberal comprehensive immigration reform (including a pathway to citizenship for illegal immigrants), cutting the number of prison inmates by 50 percent, increasing welfare handouts, and raising taxes to redistribute wealth. OSF has also been criticized for "compromising" American foreign policy.

Soros Bankrolls a Broad Range of Political and Cultural Causes

Per Stefan Kanfer's Winter 2017 *City Journal* article "Connoisseur of Chaos: The dystopian vision of George Soros, billionaire funder of the Left" he observed the following:

In the United States, Soros bankrolls a broad range of political and cultural causes. One is to destabilize the Roman Catholic Church in the United States. In 2015, he dedicated $650,000 for the purpose of shaping Pope Francis's U.S. visit, using left-leaning Catholic groups to promote gay marriage, abortion, and physician-assisted suicide. Leading the effort was Hillary Clinton's campaign manager John Podesta, a self-professed Catholic.

Bill Donohue, outspoken president of the Catholic League, vainly called for Podesta's dismissal. "He is fomenting revolution in the Catholic Church, creating mutiny and is totally unethical," Donohue said. "He is the front man for George Soros to create a host of phony anti-Catholic groups. These are not just bad comments, as some have suggested. These words are orchestrated, calculated and designed to create fissures in the Catholic Church."

Another Soros favorite is Black Lives Matter, the radical protest group dedicated to the proposition that police are inherently racist. Working the streets with incendiary rhetoric, at odds with the truth about black-on-black crime, BLM has helped foster "depolicing," as Heather Mac Donald describes it, in high-crime urban areas.

In 2015, after days of rioting in Baltimore in response to the death of Freddie Gray in police custody, an Open Society Foundations memo excitedly commented that "recent events offer a unique opportunity to accelerate the dismantling of structural inequality generated and maintained by local law enforcement and to engage residents who have historically been disenfranchised in Baltimore City in shaping and monitoring reform."

Three straight acquittals of police officers involved in the matter left the prosecution's case in shreds but made no difference to the Open Society Foundations. It has donated at least $650,000 to Black Lives Matter and pledged more assistance to antipolice factions across the country. These activities prompted the father of one of the Dallas police officers killed during a Black Lives Matter protest to sue Soros (along with other individuals and groups) for inspiring a "war on police."

Soros's Open-Borders Obsessions

From the SAPIENT Being's *Crime Rate Madness,* Soros's open-borders obsessions can be seen in the $2 million he gave to opponents of Maricopa County, Arizona, sheriff Joe Arpaio, an outspoken critic of illegal immigration. The sheriff's "influence on the national conversation about immigration has been poisonous," said a Soros spokesman. Arpaio fired back, calling the billionaire a "far-left globalist" who was trying to "buy a local race." The sheriff failed to ride in on Trump's November wagon, though, and Soros enjoyed one of his few election-night victories. Soros also spent millions backing liberal-minded district attorneys—they all opposed jail time for nonviolent drug offenders—in Louisiana, Mississippi, Florida, Illinois, New Mexico, and Texas. Some of these candidates won; most lost.

The emphasis on leniency for drug offenders is no accident. Two decades ago, Soros began an ardent campaign to decriminalize marijuana and other illegal drugs, which he promoted as an issue of fairness. Since then, Alaska, California, Colorado, Maine, Massachusetts, Nevada, Oregon, and Washington have all legalized marijuana, and Heads, a pro-drug magazine, enthusiastically dubbed Soros "Daddy Weedbucks." But data on the opioid epidemic confirms what skeptics had argued all along: that legalization serves as a forerunner to more drug use rather than less, more emergency-room visits rather than fewer, increased danger to the health of the young, and a consequent weakening of the social fabric.

As the 2016 post presidential fever abates, Soros's work carries on. In a New York City luxury hotel, Soros recently huddled with other devastated operatives in the so-called Democratic Alliance, including former House Democratic leader Nancy Pelosi, Massachusetts senator Elizabeth Warren, and Congressional Progressive Caucus cochairman Keith Ellison.

According to Politico, they discussed strategies to combat then President-elect Trump's "terrifying assault on President's Obama's achievements." Not all Democrats were pleased with the occasion. "The DA itself should be called into question," said one attendee. "You can make a very good case it's nothing more than a social club for a handful of wealthy white donors and labor union officials to drink wine and read memos, as the Democratic Party burns down around them."

Soros Indoctrinates Students Around the World

From the "Special Report: George Soros: Godfather of the Left" by the Media Research Center (MRC), left-wing donor George Soros spent more than $400 million world-wide to indoctrinate students and teach them to promote liberal, and in some cases extremist, causes. He has even founded his own university that promotes his own unique philosophy of open society. His reach and influence far surpasses that of the Koch brothers, who have been vilified by the left and the media for their grants to universities.

While the left shrivels at the thought of the Koch brother's donations to universities, their beloved Soros gave more than 50 times as much. Central European University and Bard College received the most from Soros. One professor at CEU praised the Occupy movement combining environmentalism, feminism, the labor movement, and social justice. Grants to Bard College for "community service and social action" included a Palestinian youth group and an initiative to educate prisoners across the country. To top it off, all of the Ivy League universities, along with a variety of state schools, private institutions, and even religiously-affiliated institutions, were also funded by Soros.

Soros funded programs and classes at universities around the world promote his radical ideology. Soros's Open Society Foundations granted $407,790,344 in gifts and commitments to higher education since the year 2000. The Koch brothers were vilified by the American political left for donating almost $7 million to universities while their beloved Soros gave more than 50 times that amount to the same type of groups. Alternet, funded by Soros complained about a "shady deal" that helped the Kochs fund Florida State University. Colorlines, also funded by Soros, said of the same donation: "FSU Trades Academic Freedom for Billionaire Charles Koch's Money."

David and Charles Koch are the libertarian businessmen in charge of Koch Industries. They have donated to libertarian and conservative groups along with medical research, the arts, and various other causes. Even with billions of dollars in funding from Soros, the left feels the need to criticize many of the Kochs much smaller endeavors.

Soros's Center for American Progress, which received $7.3 million from his foundations, posted a report on their Think Progress blog titled "Koch Fueling Far Right Academic Centers at Universities across the Country." In the article, the Koch-hating leftist Lee Fang lists universities that received money from the Kochs to include George Mason University, Utah State, and Brown. Totaling nearly $7 million, grants as small as $100,000 were criticized. A donation of $1.5 million to Florida State University supposedly gave the Kochs "a free hand in selecting professors and approving publications."

While Charles Koch is referred to as "a dominant player when it comes to meddling with academic integrity," Soros's name appears nowhere in the article. Giving 50 times the amount cited by the Center for American Progress is ignored by liberal bloggers that are funded by Soros.

Money from Soros goes to everything from general operating funds to specific pet projects that influence the local community and the world. Whether it's a top ranked university or a religiously-affiliated one, Soros has managed to find a left-wing cause to back with the help of his foundations.

There's no product the Soros family likes better than Obama. The Democratic president has received more money from Soros and his kin than any other political candidate in the last 11 years–$16,000 and counting. They gave an additional $250,000 to the inauguration fund, with five members of the family each giving the maximum contribution of $50,000.

Given limits on donations, that's an impressive amount of support. Obama leads a list of the most doctrinaire liberals running for office–all funded by Soros and his family. Those include former comic-turned Sen. Al Franken, lefty Calif. Sen. Barbara Boxer and new "Progressive" darling and Massachusetts Senate candidate Elizabeth Warren.

Soros Outspent Koch Brothers in Individual Political Donations 8 to 1

To put that in perspective, he vastly outspent the libertarian Koch Brothers in individual political donations 8 to 1. Promoting left-wing ideology to include everything from electing judges to immigration reform, Soros has exerted his power over the nation's liberal political elite.

While Soros has been known worldwide for his investment skills, he hasn't always managed to stay clear of the authorities. He was found guilty in France of an insider trading case about 20 years ago and has repeatedly failed having it pulled from his record. According to The *New York Times*, in September 2011, a French panel upheld his conviction because "he had bought and sold shares of Société Générale in 1988 with the knowledge that the bank might be a takeover target." He was fined $3 million.

His fund ran into problems in Hungary, where Soros was born and lived till his late teen years. At issue was how he handled an investment into the "the country's largest bank," OTP. "His fund was fined $2 million by Hungarian regulators for having manipulated OTP's stock price," wrote the *New York Times* in 2009.

Soros has spread billions around the world–even to helpful projects. Some of that is true, even in the United States. Soros funds after-school programs, hospitals, and the arts. While some organizations have a liberal spin, they aren't necessarily left-wing. However, his liberal and leftist views and aggressive undermining of criminal justice makes everything he does suspect.

But much of it flows to hardcore left-wing organizations. Eighty different liberal groups have received $1 million or more of Soros's charity in that time. Human Rights Watch, The Drug Policy Alliance, Tides Center and Foundation, National Public Radio (NPR), social justice initiatives and more all join the lefty millionaires club—thanks entirely to Soros.

The Drug Policy Alliance alone has received more than $31 million in those 10 years to oppose the "taboo associated with drug use." That commitment has earned Soros the title "sugar daddy of the legalization movement" from conservative columnist Charles Krauthammer. Prominent supporters of drug legalization - Sting, Soros himself, and former talk show host Montel Williams—are featured in a Drug Policy Alliance video that calls the drug war a "war on people."

Some of Soros's other donations go to fund his extensive network of liberal media outlets, which have received more than $52 million. Those operations include a wide range of liberal news operations as well as the infrastructure of news - journalism schools, investigative journalism and even industry organizations.

All of that is designed to create what Soros has been pushing for decades to achieve—what he calls an "open society." But what exactly is an open society? In "Open Society: Reforming Global Capitalism," he wrote that the concept is "an ideal to which our global society should aspire." But his influences are more complicated and more twisted.

Soros says he based the concept on works by philosopher Karl Popper, who Soros considers his mentor. "Popper proposed a form of social organization that starts with the recognition that no claim to the ultimate truth can be validated and therefore no group should be allowed to impose its views on all of the rest," Soros wrote in "The Age of Fallibility: Consequences of the War on Terror." "Open Society denotes freedom and the absence of repression," he summed up.

Where Does Other Soros Money Go?

Judicial Watch provides a detailed list below of groups receiving funds from OSF and they are universally "Progressive" in their philosophy. Some recipients cover the full range of radical and Progressive causes, including:

- The American Civil Liberties Union (ACLU).

- The Brookings Institution.

- The Center for American Progress.

- Common Cause.

- Planned Parenthood.

Other groups receiving financial support from the Soros network address specific issues. They include:

- Anti-Israel (Al-Haq, Amnesty International, Arab American Institute Foundation, New Israel Fund).

- Anti-conservative judicial appointments (Alliance for Justice).

- Anti-educational choice (American Federation of Teachers).

- Pro-abortion rights (Catholics for Choice, Center for Reproductive Rights, National Women's Law Center).

- Radical and LGBT agenda (Human Rights Campaign)

Soros' support also goes to groups involved in two issues that are extremely important to Judicial Watch: illegal immigration and honest elections. Here is a partial list of open-border and pro-amnesty groups that have received money from the OSF:

- America's Voice (pro-"comprehensive immigration reform").

- American Bar Association Commission on Immigration Policy ("opposes laws that require em-ployers and person providing education, health care or other social services to verify citizenship or immigration status").

- American Immigration Council (pro-amnesty).

- American Immigration Law Foundation (legal actions in support of amnesty).

- Brennan Center for Justice (legal actions, pro bono support to activists, media campaigns).

- Casa de Maryland (radical state lobbying organization for amnesty and expanded rights for illegal aliens living in Maryland).

- Center for Constitutional Rights (pro-open-borders).

- National Immigration Forum (pro-amnesty for illegal aliens and more visas for individuals wishing—to immigrate legally to the U.S.).

- National Immigration Law Center (pro-full access to government social welfare programs for illegal aliens).

- Unidos US (formerly National Council of La Raza) (pro-amnesty and expanded rights for illegal aliens).

Judicial Watch research has also identified Casa de Maryland, National Immigration Law Center and Unidos US as recipients of U.S. taxpayer dollars (through U.S. government grants).

The following groups have received Soros funding and are reportedly active in promoting, organizing, and supporting the "migrant caravans" from Central America which helped ignite the current unprecedented numbers of illegal aliens attempting to cross our border with Mexico.

- Amnesty International.

- The Catholic Legal Immigration Network (CLINIC) (the "largest network of nonprofit immigration legal services programs" in the country.

- The American Constitution Society (highly critical of Trump immigration policies).

- Center for Legal Action in Human Rights (active in OSF programs in Guatemala).

- Church World Service (compared Trump administration response to the migrant caravans to turning away Jewish refugees from Europe aboard the MS St. Louis in 1930).

- Human Rights First (actively opposes Trump administration immigration efforts).

- The Lawyers Committee for Civil Rights (sued Trump administration over his immigration executive order and the inclusion of a citizenship question on the 2020 Census form).

- The National Immigration Project of the National Lawyers Guild (provided legal assistance to caravan migrants);   "

Judicial Watch research has also identified the Catholic Legal Immigration Network as a recipient of U.S. taxpayer dollars through grants from three U.S. government agencies.

Following is a partial list of Soros-funded groups determined to weaken ballot integrity, undermine election integrity laws, and make it easier for illegal aliens to vote in American elections.

- The Advancement Project (which advertises itself as "the next generation, multi-racial civil rights organization).

- Bend the Arc Jewish Action (condemns voter ID laws as barriers that make it harder for minorities to vote).

- Demos (whose board is now chaired by the daughter of radical U.S. Senator and Democratic presidential candidate Elizabeth Warren).

- Project Vote (the voter-mobilization arm of the discredited ACORN organization, which also received Soros support).

- Southern Coalition for Social Justice (involved in several challenges to voter ID and redistricting legal challenges in the South).

The Soros network clearly dwarfs both national political parties in its financial resources. Its impact on American public policies (both foreign and domestic) is only now beginning to be understood...thanks in large part of Judicial Watch's research, investigations and litigation, and other sapient organizations.

There is much more to be learned about the influence of the Soros network, and especially when U.S. taxpayer dollars are awarded to groups within the Soros network, therefore using public taxpayer funds to advance George Soros' radical left agenda.

Soros Caps Off Midterm Spending With $50M Super PAC Contribution

As reported in the Elena Schneider "Soros caps off midterm spending with $50M super PAC contribution" Politico December 2022 article: Billionaire George Soros, the biggest disclosed Democratic donor in the 2022 election cycle, gave another $50 million to a super PAC in the fall, building on an already large investment in Democratic groups and candidates for the 2024 election cycle and beyond.

Democracy PAC, which has served as one of Soros' major political spending vehicles since 2019, received another eight-figure infusion of cash from Soros earlier, according to a person directly familiar with the group's new Federal Elections Commission filing, which will be publicly released. It's the latest sign that Soros will continue to play an enormous role in the Democratic campaign finance ecosystem, particularly ahead of the next presidential election.

All of Soros' 2022 campaign spending—including direct contributions to candidates and committees, as well as donations to a pair of super PACs—totaled about $50 million, likely placing atop the list of the biggest Democratic donors during the midterms, according to OpenSecrets. Soros has long been one of the Democratic Party's most generous donors, spending millions on everything from presidential and congressional races to state offices, ballot measures and even local prosecutor races.

Either directly or through his affiliated super PACs, Soros in the 2022 cycle, gave $14 million to Senate Majority PAC, the flagship Senate Democratic super PAC. That includes $1 million for the Georgia runoff, which Sen. Raphael Warnock won on Tuesday night, giving Democrats a 51-seat majority in the Senate. Soros sent another $5 million to House Majority PAC, the main House Democratic super PAC, according to the person directly familiar with the Democracy PAC filing.

Other major recipients of Soros' contributions this election cycle included: Stacey Abrams, who received $4 million but lost her bid for Georgia governor; the Democratic Party of Wisconsin, which received $1.5 million; and Planned Parenthood, the Working Families Party and J Street, each of which got $1 million.

Last January, Soros seeded Democracy PAC with $125 million, a "long-term investment" in his political priorities. The group was formed to support pro-democracy "causes and candidates, regardless of party" and to invest in "strengthening the infrastructure of American democracy: voting rights and civic participation, civil rights and liberties, and the rule of law," Soros said in a statement at the time.

Soros' son, Alexander, has served as the PAC's president.

What George Soros Gets Wrong

George Soros took to the Wall Street Journal to defend his financial support for "reform prosecutors." He began by asserting that "Americans desperately need a more thoughtful discussion about our response to crime." I couldn't agree more.

Sadly, Progressive approaches to law enforcement carry a steep price for the victims of violent crime, and the Soros's piece failed to deliver that thoughtful discussion. Instead, the philanthropist offered a shallow, essentially data-free collection of platitudes—"If people trust the justice system, it will work"—and incomplete observations.

As shown in the Rafael A. Mangual "What George Soros Gets Wrong" *City Journal* August 2022 article: Soros highlights the statistic that "black people in the U.S. are five times as likely to be sent to jail as white people." This is, he says without explanation, "an injustice that undermines our democracy."

Such a contention is meant to persuade the reader that these incarcerations are mostly (if not overwhelmingly) illegitimate—the product of racial animus more than anything else. What else could it be? Well, how about disparate rates of criminal offending? A Bureau of Justice Statistics study of homicides between 1980 and 2008 found that blacks commit homicide offenses at a rate "almost eight times higher than the rate for whites."

Presenting a disparity without any mention of what its causes might be is not a responsible way of arguing that "injustice" is afoot. That's a serious charge, and, as we've seen over the last few years, many who believe it will push (often successfully) for serious policy changes couched in breezy phrases like "reimagining public safety."

When relevant factors are taken into account, the disparities that Soros point to as obvious evidence of injustice shrink substantially, undercutting his claim.

As a 2014 report on incarceration from the National Academies of Sciences shows: "Racial bias and discrimination are not the primary causes of disparities in sentencing decisions or rates of imprisonment. . . . Overall, when statistical controls are used to take account of offense characteristics, prior criminal records, and personal characteristics, black defendants are on average sentenced somewhat but not substantially more severely than whites."

I wish Soros were as interested in even starker, more persistent disparities: namely, those regarding violent victimization. We often speak of crime in national, state, or citywide terms. While crime does affect society writ large, some communities feel its sting more than others. In 2020—a year in which homicides rose nearly 30 percent across the U.S.—the share of white homicide victims actually declined by 2.4 percentage points relative to 2019, while the share of black and Hispanic victims increased by 2.2 percentage points.

The black homicide victimization rate was almost ten times the white rate that year. In my home city of New York, at least 95 percent of shooting victims every year, going back at least to 2008, are either black or Hispanic. Blacks and Hispanics don't constitute anywhere near 95 percent of the city's residents. A University of Chicago Crime Lab analysis found that, in that city, just under 80 percent of homicide victims were black. It also found that almost 20 percent of gun-violence suspects in 2015 and 2016 had at least 20 prior arrests.

Soros and his beneficiaries have built a movement around the proposition that criminal offenders in cities like New York and Chicago are treated too harshly and are systematically denied "second chances." In addition to the data on the degree to which serious violence is committed by repeat offenders, this claim is also undercut by the fact that that those released from state prisons and tracked by the Bureau of Justice Statistics had, on average, around ten prior arrests and five prior convictions before their most recent stints.

Soros offers nothing in the way of support for the victims of violent crimes committed by those who have received many "second chances." Perhaps that's because, in his mind, there is "no connection between the election of reform-minded prosecutors and local crime rates." In support of that claim, he cites a single analysis, whose authors are, as they say in the very paper he references, unable to "rule out large increases or decreases in any particular type of crime."

Rather than engage the substance of his critics' arguments, Soros implies that they're hypocrites by highlighting the overlap between them and opponents of Progressive gun control measures—ignoring, of course, the substantial overlap between supporters of such measures and those who want to divert gun offenders and would-be shooters away from incarceration. It does not seem to have dawned on Soros that sending shooters with lengthy criminal histories back onto the street actually worsens gun violence.

Here's hoping that voters will begin to see the truth to which George Soros and his supporters seem blind—that, while our system is imperfect, true justice requires that dangerous offenders be stopped from harming innocent people.

A Litany of Failure

For the last decade, radical prosecutors and Progressive politicians have been proposing and enacting illogical criminal-justice policies, often with little consideration for the real-world effects of these ideas. Per the Thomas Hogan "A Litany of Failure" *City Journal* August 2022 report: Enough time has passed for an evidence-based assessment of how these policies have played out in the real world.

Gun Buybacks: Politicians in big cities believe that gun-buyback programs will reduce the violent crime that is spiking in America's urban centers. But comprehensive research shows no evidence that such programs work. Philadelphia just completed a three-year gun-buyback program that yielded over 1,000 firearms. Not a single recovered firearm was linked to violent crime and, during the course of the program, Philadelphia set new all-time records for homicides. "It's not reaching the area of the community that's possessing illegal guns and using them," says criminologist Joseph Giacalone. "It's political theater."

"Violence Interrupters": Progressive prosecutors tout violence interrupters—former gang members and convicts who mediate disputes on the streets—as a serious weapon against crime. Cities led by "reform" prosecutors, such as Baltimore, Indianapolis, and Philadelphia have staked a lot on this idea. The results have not been encouraging. Multiple violence interrupters have been murdered in Baltimore. In Indianapolis, the former convict in charge of training violence interrupters was arrested for threatening a woman and had to be fired. In Philadelphia, a violence interrupter shot three people in a bar while he was working his anti-violence job. And a recent research paper states that violence interrupters, despite their tough histories, are suffering from severe trauma, mainly because they are being exposed to the type of violence that police officers face every day (imagine that). The real question for violence-interruption programs is whether they might be adding fuel to the fire of violent crime.

Decarceration: Liberal policy groups like the Prison Policy Initiative, with the support of legal academics, have railed against "mass incarceration" in the United States for decades, asserting that the United States could free thousands of prisoners, even violent criminals, without affecting public safety. For their argument to make any sense, they have to push for the release of violent criminals because—as even leading decarceration advocate John Pfaff concedes—the vast majority of criminals are incarcerated for violent crimes. The decarceration advocates largely have seen their wishes granted.

According to the Pew Research Center, by 2019, incarceration rates in America had fallen to the same level as 1995, then were reduced even further during the Covid-19 pandemic. How is that working out? The United States saw its biggest single-year rise in homicide in 2020, and the murder rates continued to rise in 2021. Homicides in many cities reached levels unseen since the 1990s, when incarceration rates were as low as they are now. The incarceration-versus-violent-crime relationship is statistically complex, but the wholesale release of violent criminals serves as one more contributor to increasing murders in American cities.

No Cash Bail: Fair and Just Prosecution, a think tank for radical prosecutors, has long championed a "no cash bail" policy, claiming that detaining people pretrial is simply a way of locking up the poor. In 2020, New York passed legislation substantially reducing the state's ability to keep even violent criminals detained after they were arrested. The resulting spike in violent crimes by defendants released back to the streets led even Democratic New York governor Kathy Hochul to roll back this misguided reform in 2022, much to the relief of police and citizens. It turns out that detaining violent criminals between arrest and trial is vital for public safety. Who knew?

De-Prosecution: From Alvin Bragg in Manhattan to George Gascón in Los Angeles to Larry Krasner in Philadelphia, the Progressive-prosecutor playbook relies on a policy of de-prosecution, the decision not to prosecute crimes even when the facts and evidence are sufficient to convict defendants. Prosecutors' decision effectively to nullify criminal laws passed by state legislatures has had a disastrous effect on violent crime in big cities.

A recent study using a synthetic control algorithm attributes an extra 74 homicides per year to the de-prosecution policy in Philadelphia, where prosecutions have dropped by a staggering 70 percent for both felonies and misdemeanors. The same methodology estimated an additional 70 homicides per year in Baltimore and 169 more homicides per year in Chicago, two other cities with de-prosecuting prosecutors. Electing prosecutors not to enforce the law was as crazy as it sounded.

Defund the Police: From the members of "The Squad" in Congress to city councils across the United States, a powerful political movement has emerged to defund police, based on the belief that law enforcement does more harm than good. Seattle tested this theory in 2020, when it declared a section of the city a "police-free zone" after protests related to the death of George Floyd.

A sophisticated analysis by professors Eric Piza and Nathan Connealy determined that the lack of police led not only to an increase in violent crime in the police-free zone—an unsurprising result—but also to a spillover effect of crime in surrounding areas of Seattle. On a broader level, highly respected researchers Aaron Chalfin and Justin McCrary did a quantitative analysis demonstrating that, if anything, American cities are under-policed, and that adding more police would result in both net savings and reduced violent crime, especially murder.

In raw statistical terms, adding ten police officers to a department prevents one homicide per year in that jurisdiction. A strong case can be made, in fact, that we are under-policed: the U.S. ranks in the bottom half of developed nations for the number of police officers per capita. Fortunately, the defund movement appears to be in retreat, as city residents see the dreadful results and politicians scramble to adjust.

A curious but notable trend is developing in the study of crime. Law school professors long have been the leading advocates for many of these Progressive policies, but these legal academics have little practical experience and are not bound by any actual data, acting instead as an elite class of professional philosophers. However, a cohort of quantitative researchers is starting to look at the actual crime data and publish the results, which often reveal that these policies not only don't work but also actively harm communities, particularly those with the poorest residents.

As each of these policies meets its predictable demise, some might ask: What does work, then? The answers to that question have been demonstrated clearly and exhaustively: re-empower the police to protect law-abiding citizens. Arrest violent offenders, prosecute them vigorously, and incapacitate them with stiff sentences. And elect prosecutors who uphold and enforce the law, and who prioritize protecting law-abiding citizens, not violent criminals.

Legendary Green Bay Packers coach Vince Lombardi used to start training camp every year by stressing the importance of fundamentals. He'd hold up a pigskin and say, "Gentlemen, this is a football." It's time for the criminal-justice system to get back to the basics of blocking and tackling.

7 – Criminal Chaos Rising in Progressive Sanctuary States, Cities & Mexican Border

George Soros must be feeling the heat of rising crime rates. The leftist billionaire recently penned an opinion column in *The Wall Street Journal* explaining why he financially supports Progressive prosecutors. Cloaked in platitudinous language devoid of substance, Soros asserts that "reform-minded prosecutors" have an agenda that promotes safety and justice and are "popular and effective."

That's absurd, as we have been writing about for years, explains the Charles "Cully" Stimson and Zack Smith "Soros' Claim About Leftist Prosecutors Is Big Lie" report from The Heritage Foundation in August 2022:

His attempt to defend his scheme of replacing real prosecutors with rogue prosecutors is belied by the facts. His bought-and-paid-for prosecutors encourage lawlessness, harm law-abiding residents (especially minorities), drive businesses out of cities, and demoralize the police by treating them as the criminals.

His prosecutors claim otherwise, of course. They insist that not prosecuting entire categories of crime; not asking for bail; refusing to add sentencing enhancements; releasing hardened, convicted felons from prison; and declining to prosecute violent juvenile offenders in adult court; as well as ignoring shoplifting, drug possession, and prostitution (among other crimes) are sound policies that do not contribute to spikes in crime.

The facts, data, and truth of these matters, indicate otherwise, and covered extensively in the SAPIENT Being's second sapient conservative textbook *Crime Rate Madness: A SAPIENT Being's Guide to the Color of Crime, Antifa, BLM, SPLC & OSF Impacts on Criminal Justice.*

Soros' Claim About Leftist Prosecutors Is Big Lie

Crime rates, including violent crime rates, overall have been dropping for the past 30 years, yet incarceration rates peaked in 2008—long before Soros or his "reform" prosecutors came along.

Why? Because genuinely Progressive prosecutors, working with other stakeholders, created domestic violence courts, drug courts, veterans courts, family justice centers, and countless other alternatives to incarceration that are compassionate, create accountability, and provide opportunities with the right incentives for defendants to recover their lives by changing their thinking and behaviors.

If someone wouldn't complete these programs, though, the prosecutors could still seek incarceration.

Violent crime is geographically and demographically concentrated in inner cities, many of which are presided over by rogue prosecutors, where minority members of those communities are disproportionately victimized, including constituting a majority of homicide victims.

As Rafael Mangual of the Manhattan Institute noted in his recent book, "Criminal (In)Justice: What the Push for Decarceration and Depolicing Gets Wrong and Who It Hurts Most," while blacks constitute 13.4 percent of the population, "they made up more than 53 percent of the nation's homicide victims in 2020."

In other words, the policies of these prosecutors are harming the very individuals they are supposed to be helping.

To truly help those individuals—and their communities as a whole—these prosecutors should seek appropriate bail and prison sentences for dangerous defendants.

The idea that appropriately long prison sentences won't help protect communities is nonsense. Studies show that the longer the prison sentence, the lower the recidivism rate.

In fact, the U.S. Sentencing Commission in June released a report on a study that found that "the odds of recidivism were lower for federal offenders sentenced to more than 60 months' incarceration compared to a matched group of offenders receiving shorter sentences. ... The odds of recidivism were approximately 29 percent lower for federal offenders sentenced to more than 120 months' incarceration ... ."

The authors also found that "[t]he odds of recidivism were approximately 18 percent lower for offenders sentenced to more than 60 months up to 120 months of incarceration ... ."

Not requiring bail for violent criminals also causes increases in crime. That's common sense.

Moreover, in the primary academic paper on the subject, two law professors analyzed a Cook County, Illinois, bail reform study, which supposedly showed that lax bail laws do not impact the crime rate, and found, contrary to the study's findings, that the "bail reform" changes in Cook County "appear to have led to a substantial increase in crimes committed by pretrial releasees in Cook County."

Their analysis also found that the "number of released defendants charged with committing new crimes increased by 45%." Worse yet, the number of pretrial releasees charged with committing new violent crimes increased by an estimated 33%.

No wonder the public is souring on these rogue prosecutors' radical policies and the havoc they wreak. Voters in liberal San Francisco recently removed rogue District Attorney Chesa Boudin from office. His successor has pledged to hold criminals accountable while still offering diversionary treatment programs such as drug court for appropriate individuals—something prosecutors have been doing for many, many years.

Ironically, after voters recalled Boudin, one of George Soros' representatives objected to the *Washington Free Beacon* calling Boudin a "George Soros darling," trying to put distance between Soros and the failed DA.

A similar issue occurred when we wrote about Baltimore's now-defeated (and federally indicted) rogue prosecutor Marilyn Mosby. A Soros representative reached out and objected to our characterization of her as a Soros-backed prosecutor since he never directly contributed to her campaign, even though she took numerous trips paid for by groups either funded or inspired by Soros. Her disastrous Progressive leadership as a rogue prosecutor is covered in the next section.

The rogue prosecutor movement operates under two related principles; namely, that the entire criminal justice system is racist and that the only way to address that supposed racism is to reverse-engineer and dismantle the current system by electing pro-criminal, anti-victim zealots to office.

Flush with cash or support from Soros and his like-minded wealthy friends, candidates like George Gascon (Los Angeles), Larry Krasner (Philadelphia), Kim Foxx (Chicago), Kim Gardner (St. Louis), and others have been elevated to office and have imposed their pro-criminal agendas on an unsuspecting electorate.

The consequences have been predictable and deadly.

Prosecutors are the gatekeepers to the criminal justice system. Our nation's approximately 2,300 elected district attorneys have a solemn duty to enforce the law and to do so fairly, compassionately, and without favor.

That shouldn't be a left or right, blue or red, Democrat or Republican issue. You either support law and order and equality under the law, or you back a radical social experiment that so far has led to chaos and misery.

Meet Marilyn Mosby, the Rogue Prosecutor Wreaking Havoc in Baltimore

Do the residents of Baltimore ever look back on the TV series "The Wire"—which aired from 2002 to 2008—with its focus on guns, drugs, and gangland violence as the "good old days," when violent crime was low and life was good?

Shockingly, they could as reported by The Heritage Foundation's "Meet Marilyn Mosby, the Rogue Prosecutor Wreaking Havoc in Baltimore" by Charles "Cully" Stimson and Zack Smith in October 2020:

And Baltimore City State's Attorney Marilyn Mosby deserves a large part of the blame—as do her liberal billionaire backers. Since she was first sworn into office in January 2015, homicides, rapes, aggravated assaults, burglaries, and robberies in the gritty city have exploded.

As one FBI chart shows, once Mosby took command, homicides skyrocketed in Maryland, because the vast majority of Maryland killings take place in Baltimore city. (We focus here on the city of Baltimore, as distinct from Baltimore County, which has its own elected state's attorney.)

But that's not all. As the Johns Hopkins University shows, once Mosby took over, all manner of violent crime in Baltimore city shot up, too. That increase is even more shocking when you consider that violent crime across America—including homicides—has been falling for more than 20 years.

Yet, in cities that have elected rogue prosecutors, such as Baltimore, violent crimes have shot up dramatically. So, how did Baltimore get here, with an elected prosecutor who doesn't want to prosecute broad swaths of the criminal code?

Liberal billionaire George Soros realized early on that prosecutors are the gatekeepers to the criminal justice system, and he decided to hand select attorneys who would do his bidding by refusing to prosecute entire categories of crimes, fundamentally "reimagining prosecution" and reverse-engineering the criminal justice system into something unrecognizable in the process.

There are four fundamental problems with this rogue prosecutor movement.

- First, rogue prosecutors usurp the constitutional role of the legislature by refusing to prosecute entire categories of crimes.

- Second, they abuse the role of the county prosecutor by refusing to faithfully enforce the law.

- Third, they contribute to increases in violent crime in their cities through their reckless policies.

- Fourth, they ignore victims, in addition to public safety suffering overall.

But replacing independent, Progressive traditional prosecutors with rogue district attorneys became the game plan, and Baltimore became the guinea pig.

So, when Soros decided back in 2014 to spend millions to fund the election efforts of rogue prosecutors, one of the first people he backed was Marilyn Mosby in Baltimore city.

The crime statistics, reported each year by jurisdictions to the FBI, tell the story.

In the eight years before Mosby was elected, there were fewer than 300 homicides per year in Baltimore city, averaging 229 per year. Every year since Mosby has been in office, there have been more than 300.

Murders Numbers Up

Between 2015 and 2019, there was an average of 331 homicides each year, a whopping increase of 102 killings per year. The vast majority of those killed are African-Americans, the very people Mosby claims to care about the most.

From 2009 to 2014, the homicide rate in Baltimore city fell from fewer than 8 per 100,000 to 6 per 100,000, but the rate shot up in 2015 and has remained well above 8 per 100,000 ever since.

Put another way, from 2015 to 2019, there were 1,659 homicides in Baltimore city, meaning that about one out of every 350 residents was slain during that time frame.

For 2020, under Mosby's leadership, Baltimore is on pace to have the most homicides since she was elected. As of Oct. 26, there have been 271 homicides.

Rape Numbers Up

Rapes have gone up as well. The average number of rapes per year in the five-year period before Mosby was elected was 292 annually. Since Mosby was elected, the average has been 330 per year. In other words, there were 190 more people raped in the first five years of Mosby's tenure, compared with the five years before she assumed office.

Aggravated Assault Numbers Up

Aggravated assaults, which can include the use of a gun, have predictably soared under Mosby's tenure as well.

In the five years before Mosby was elected, there were 23,707 aggravated assaults. In the five years since she was elected, there have been 26,519 aggravated assaults, representing an additional 2,812 such assaults in total, or 562 additional aggravated assaults per year.

Burglary Numbers Down

Burglaries have gone down on Mosby's watch. In the five years from 2010 through 2014, there were 38,275 burglaries in the city, averaging 7,655 per year. After Mosby showed up, between 2015 through 2019, there have been 34,635 burglaries, averaging 6,927 per year.

Robbery Numbers Up

Under Mosby's hands-off approach to enforcing the law, Baltimore city has become the most dangerous city in the country for robberies.

In the five years from 2010 through 2014, there were 17,809 robberies in the city, averaging 3,562 per year. After Mosby arrived, between 2015 and 2019, there have been a staggering 25,350 robberies in the city, averaging 5,070 robberies per year.

Put another way, 7,541 additional people were robbed, many at gunpoint, while Mosby acted as Baltimore's gatekeeper to the criminal justice system.

It's so bad that even the deputy police commissioner and his wife were robbed at gunpoint in 2019. In fact, in 2019, Baltimore city was the No. 1 city in America for robberies, topping out at 95 robberies for every 100,000 residents.

Rogue Prosecutors' Achilles' Heel

The Achilles' heel for the rogue prosecutor movement is the fact that crime rates, especially violent crime, rise in cities where they are in charge.

When you listen to them talk, they use the same pet phrases: mass incarceration; structural racism; prosecutorial discretion; school-to-prison pipeline; restorative justice; reimagining policing or prosecution; over-policing; institutional change; and correctional-free lunch. The latter would require prosecutors to take into consideration the cost of incarcerating people.

But when you look at the actual crime rates in the cities where these prosecutors have been elected, those rates have gone up dramatically, and the rogue prosecutors from those cities don't like to hear it.

In 2020, Mosby participated in a discussion at the Hastings School of Law at the University of California in San Francisco with three other prosecutors. The topic was "Progressive Prosecution and the Carceral State."

When McGregor Scott, a fellow panelist, former elected California district attorney, and sitting U.S. attorney, made the point that violent crime was rising in Baltimore under her non-prosecution policy, Mosby said defensively, "You're not from Baltimore" and claimed that Scott's crime statistics were just "rhetoric."

But Mosby never rebutted those statistics because they were correct.

The Regression of America's Big Progressive Cities

If there's anything productive to come from his past Twitter storm in 2019, President Trump's recent crude attacks on Baltimore Congressman Elijah Cummings have succeeded in bring necessary attention to the increasingly tragic state of our cities. Baltimore's continued woes, per the Joel Kotkin "The Regression of America's Big Progressive Cities" report in August 2019: After numerous attempts to position itself as a "comeback city," illustrates all too poignantly the deep-seated decay in many of our great urban areas.

Baltimore represents an extreme case, but sadly it is not alone. Our three largest urban centers—New York, Los Angeles and Chicago—lost people while millennial migration accelerated both to the suburbs and smaller, generally less dense cities. These demographic trends, as well as growing blight, poor schools, decaying infrastructure and, worst of all, expanding homelessness are not merely the result of "racism" or Donald Trump, but have all been exacerbated by policy agendas that are turning many great cities into loony towns.

Politics run amok

Take tech rich San Francisco, where decades of tolerance for even extreme deviant behavior has helped create a city with more drug addicts than high school students, and so much feces on the street that one website has created a "poop map." In Southern California's far more proletarian city of Los Angeles, we have a downtown filled with overbuilt, overpriced apartments and is, like Baltimore, being overrun with rats. A UN official compared conditions on the city's Skid Row to those of Syrian refugee camps.

One would think such nasty problems would spark something of a political rebellion, as seen in previous decades with the rise of successful, pragmatic mayors—Bob Lanier and Bill White in Houston, Rudy Giuliani and Michael Bloomberg in New York, and Richard Riordan in Los Angeles. But so far, at least, many of today's big city mayors seem more interested in bolstering their "resistance" bona fides than governing effectively.

Los Angeles' Eric Garcetti, for example, speaks enthusiastically about his own "green new deal" and turning the city into a transit Valhalla even as blight and homelessness expand inexorably. The mayor is less rhapsodic about practical things that people actually need, such as decent roads, reliable water supply or electricity.

Economic growth generally is not much of a priority for the woke urban political class. In New York, Rep. Alexandria Ocasio Cortez's allies succeeded in driving Amazon's new headquarters out of her district. Meanwhile her socialist comrades in Seattle have helped persuade the on-line giant to relocate more of its employees to a massive new building in the suburb of Bellevue while the Emerald City hosts a rising homeless population.

The demographics of ultra-Progressivism

Ironically, this far-left trend can partially be traced to the post-2000 urban resurgence, sparked by the now unappreciated pragmatic mayors who made cities safer and more business friendly. Safe streets and thriving businesses lured large numbers of young people, many well-educated and mostly liberal, to the urban core in numbers not seen for generations.

Yet since the 1970s the middle class in cities has been in a precipitous decline while poverty has remained stubbornly high. Philadelphia's central core, for example, rebounded between 2000 and 2014, but for every one district that gained in income, two suffered income declines. In 1970, half of Chicago was middle class; today, according to a new University of Illinois study, that number is down to 16 percent. Meanwhile, the percentage of poor people has risen from 42 to 62 percent.

The most attractive blue cities—led by New York, San Francisco, San Jose, Los Angeles and Boston—now suffer, according to Pew research, the largest gaps between the bottom and top quintiles of all U.S. cities.

The post-2000 urban success increased housing prices but failed to create a new stable urban middle class. Most young urbanites don't stay long enough to build long-term communities; once they hit the family formation period in their thirties, they still largely depart for the suburbs. As the Atlantic recently noted the number of babies born in Manhattan this decade dropped nearly 15 percent; already home to a majority of single households, the nation's premier urban center could see its infant population cut in half in 30 years.

Remaking urban politics

The new demographics have hollowed out the political middle in most cities.

The old urban middle class leaned Democratic, but they were largely interested in practical outcomes—like paved roads, fixed lights, and access to jobs. Their departure, and replacement by temporary hipster populations, has helped insulate city governments from constituents who would be most adamant about reforming usually failed school districts or demanding improvements in public infrastructure or maintaining public order.

Electoral engagement has faded in most cities, with turnout for mayor averaging 15 percent for mayoral races in our most populous cities. In Los Angeles, the 2013 turnout that elected Progressive Eric Garcetti was roughly one-third of that in the city's 1970 mayoral election. Garcetti's 2017 re-election boasted a similarly low turnout.

The prime beneficiaries of these changes have been the well-organized. Rep. Alexandria Ocasio Cortez's primary victory rested on 16,000 votes out of a total Democratic registration of almost 215,000. She won not by sweeping the proletarian or minority masses, but marshalling the votes of white young educated hipsters. These voters are driving the rise of far-left socialists in other cities, including Denver, who seek to replace not Republicans but more traditional liberal Democrats.

Can this be turned around?

The new urban politics threatens the future of family neighborhoods, local entrepreneurial ventures as well as an apolitical, exuberant diversity. Immigrants and aspiring minorities want good schools, safe streets and less onerous regulation. Resolutions on sanctuary cities, condemnations of Trump tweets, social justice demands and boasts about combating climate change do little to improve tangibly reality that cities like Baltimore or even superstars like San Francisco, Washington, and New York.

Only when grassroots people and concerned businesses decide to challenge the urban status quo and the virtue-signaling political class can decay and the relentless bifurcation of our cities be reversed. After all, large and powerful companies, like Amazon, can always pack up and migrate to less insane political environments. But those with a strong stake in the local economy and neighborhoods have fewer options. It will be up to them to restore our cities' historic role as places for both families and middle-class economic aspiration.

Anarchy in Seattle

As per the Christopher F. Rufo "Anarchy in Seattle" *City Journal* June 2020 article: Seattle's hard-Left secessionist movement has claimed its first territory: six blocks in the Capitol Hill neighborhood. Antifa-affiliated activists seize control of a city neighborhood and declare an "autonomous zone."

For the past week, Black Lives Matter and Antifa-affiliated activists have engaged in a pitched battle with Seattle police officers and National Guard soldiers in the neighborhood, with the heaviest conflict occurring at the intersection of 11th and Pike, where law enforcement had constructed a barricade to defend the Seattle Police East Precinct building.

 Hoping to break through the barricade, protesters attacked officers with bricks, bottles, rocks, and improvised explosive devices, sending some officers to the hospital. At the same time, activists circulated videos of the conflict and accused the police of brutality, demanding that the city cease using teargas and other anti-riot techniques.

Then, in a stunning turn of events, the City of Seattle made the decision to abandon the East Precinct and surrender the neighborhood to the protesters. "This is an exercise in trust and de-escalation," explained Chief Carmen Best. Officers and National Guardsmen emptied out the facility, boarded it up, and retreated. Immediately afterward, Black Lives Matter protesters, Antifa black shirts, and armed members of the hard-Left John Brown Gun Club seized control of the neighborhood, moved the barricades into a defensive position, and declared it the Capitol Hill Autonomous Zone—even putting up a cardboard sign at the barricades declaring "you are now leaving the USA."

On the new rebel state's first night, the atmosphere was festive and triumphant. Hooded men spray-painted the police station with slogans and anarchist symbols, renaming it the "Seattle People's Department East Precinct." Raz Simone, a local rapper with an AK-47 slung from his shoulder and a pistol attached to his hip, screamed, "This is war!" into a white-and-red megaphone and instructed armed paramilitaries to guard the barricades in shifts.

Later in the night, Simone was filmed allegedly assaulting multiple protestors who disobeyed his orders, informing them that he was the "police" now, sparking fears that he was becoming the de facto warlord of the autonomous zone. A homeless man with a baseball bat wandered along the borderline and two unofficial medics in medieval-style chain mail stood ready for action.

Nikkita Oliver, a radical activist and former mayoral candidate, emerged as a critical voice of the protest movement and assumed a leadership role in the newly declared autonomous zone. After night fell and a light rain began falling, she spoke to the crowd and outlined the ideological commitments behind the occupation. "[We need to] align ourselves with the global struggle that acknowledges [that] the United States plays a role in racialized capitalism," she told protestors.

"Racialized capitalism is built upon patriarchy, white supremacy, and classism."

The following day, a coalition of black activists associated with the autonomous zone released a more specific list of demands, including the total abolition of the Seattle Police Department, the retrial of all racial minorities serving prison time for violent crimes, and the replacement of the police with autonomous "restorative/transformative accountability programs." Activists pledged to maintain control of the Capitol Hill Autonomous Zone until their demands are met—setting the stage for a long-term occupation and the establishment of a parallel political authority.

The city government has not developed a strategic response to the takeover of Capitol Hill. According to one Seattle police officer with knowledge of internal deliberations, the city's "leadership is in chaos" and "the mayor has made the decision to let a mob of 1,000 people dictate public safety policy for a city of 750,000." The officer said that Chief Best had dispatched high-ranking police officials to the autonomous zone to establish a line of communication, but the officials were immediately sent away by armed paramilitaries at the barricades. "The tide of public opinion is on the side of the activists and they're pushing the envelope as far as they can," said the officer. "It's not hyperbolic to say the endgame is anarchy."

Politically, the Seattle City Council has already begun to champion the protesters' demands. Socialist Alternative councilwoman Kshama Sawant declared the takeover a "victory" against "the militarized police force of the political establishment and the capitalist state." Three councilmembers have signaled support for a 50 percent reduction in the police budget, with additional councilmembers likely to support a similar policy in the coming weeks. Sawant also opened Seattle's City Hall—which had been closed by the mayor—to protesters, who immediately occupied the building.

The Capitol Hill Autonomous Zone has set a dangerous precedent: armed left-wing activists have asserted their dominance of the streets and established an alternative political authority over a large section of a neighborhood. They have claimed de facto police power over thousands of residents and dozens of businesses—completely outside of the democratic process. In a matter of days, Antifa-affiliated paramilitaries have created a hardened border, established a rudimentary form of government based on principles of intersectional representation, and forcibly removed unfriendly media from the territory.

The Capitol Hill Autonomous Zone is an occupation and taking of hostages: none of the neighborhood's residents voted for Antifa as their representative government. Rather than enforce the law, Seattle's Progressive political class capitulated to the mob and will likely make massive concessions over the next few months. This will embolden the Antifa coalition—and further undermine the rule of law in American cities.

From Woke to Broke in Chicago

'The fact is there is no more money. Period," says former Chicago mayor Lori Lightfoot regarding the political contradictions of Progressivism as noted in the Matthew Continetti "From Woke to Broke" *National Review* October 2019 article:

She's talking about the teachers' strike that has paralyzed her city's public schools—enrollment 360,000—for the past week. The public employee union is demanding more: more money for salaries (only eight states pay teachers more than Illinois), more support staff (Illinois ranks first in spending on administrators), more teachers per student. Their cause has attracted national attention. Elizabeth Warren joined the picket line.

Which is ironic. Lightfoot is not some stingy Republican. Nor is she a centrist Democrat like her predecessor Rahm Emanuel. She's as Progressive as you can get. But she now finds herself in the same position as many of her political brethren: facing criticism for failing to reconcile the contradictions in the left's agenda.

Lightfoot has discovered that there is no limit to the appetite of the constituencies generated by government spending. She has learned that the special interests bargaining for higher benefits also desire policies that make such benefits unattainable. I hope she's taking notes.

Chicago Public Schools has run a deficit for the past seven years. Why? Pensions granted to earlier generations of teachers are expensive. And the cost is growing. A quarter of the school budget is devoted to benefits—money that can't be spent on classrooms, facilities, and instruction. Expect that number to rise as America goes gray and the bill comes due for the promises we made to ourselves.

The federal government can put Social Security and Medicare on the credit card for as long as demand for U.S. Treasuries is high. States and municipalities don't have that luxury. There is an upper bound to what even the most Progressive mayors and governors can grant the lobbies that mobilize voters for their campaigns. But it's a glass ceiling. Public sector unions are eager to break it.

Nor does being woke protect you. It's impossible to appease fully the groups fighting to claim resources and honor. They often won't take yes for an answer. GM might tout to investors the fact that it is "leading in gender equality." That didn't stop the UAW from striking.

Public policy inspired by the ethic of social justice inflames the tension between Progressive leaders and the voting public. Andrew Cuomo might sympathize with Mayor Lightfoot. His fealty to environmental groups has backed him into a corner. Banning fracking and canceling pipelines hasn't just denied New York revenues, jobs, and lower energy bills. It also led energy supplier National Grid to cancel gas hookups in Long Island. Cuomo had to retaliate before the company restored service. Want to be a Progressive? Claim credit for resolving a crisis of your own making after threatening to unleash state power on private actors responding to price signals. Cuomo makes it look easy.

Gavin Newsom also has been struggling to reduce the conflict between the imperatives of the new Progressivism and the quality of life of everyday people. He has his hands full. Rising numbers of homeless have led to a breakdown of public order in areas of Los Angeles and San Francisco. Land-use regulations have restricted the supply of housing, leading to high prices and shortages, and Newsom's answer is statewide rent control that will make things worse. California's budget depends so heavily on revenues from the wealthy that it might not recover from another out-migration like the one the state experienced after a 2012 tax hike.

Pacific Gas & Electric is a case study in the Progressive self-own.

The state-regulated utility spent years deferring maintenance while it invested in renewable energy and promoted the ideology of diversity, equity, and inclusion. Among the consequences of its neglect were terrible wildfires that devastated communities. The ensuing legal bills drove PG&E into bankruptcy. It says it's been forced to engage in "de-energization": purposeful mass blackouts to prevent further damage and legal action. In early October more than two million people were left in the dark. No house, no power, no prospects—welcome to the California Republic.

The contradictions of Progressivism generate crises of affordability and governance. But the political class suffers few consequences. Chicago, New York, and California remain Democratic strongholds. What scattered opposition exists is internal to the political machine. On rare occasions parts of the coalition splinter from the whole and are able to defeat radical measures. Think of Bill de Blasio's stalled plans to cancel entrance exams for New York City's magnet schools. For the most part, though, the Democrats' hold on power continues. It's one monopoly Progressives don't seem to mind.

Are the voters in these communities merely complacent? Are they so content with the patchwork of benefits and status the jerry-rigged welfare state provides that they tolerate dysfunction? Or is the partisan alternative so appalling they won't even consider it?

Questions worth pondering as Progressives prepare to scale up their model nationwide.

San Francisco's Heart of Darkness

Seen in the Soledad Ursúa "San Francisco's Heart of Darkness" *City Journal* February 2022 article: Overrun by drug addiction and squalor, the City by the Bay wants to bring its disastrous experiment in harm-reduction to the rest of California.

Over the past two years, San Francisco has seen more than 1,360 drug overdose fatalities—more than double the number of Covid-19 deaths over roughly the same period. Open drug use and escalating violence in the city's Tenderloin neighborhood forced Mayor London Breed to make an "emergency declaration" last December, resulting in the opening of a "Linkage Center" intended to connect the mentally ill or addicted homeless to basic services.

The city selected Urban Alchemy—the 800-pound gorilla in the world of private, nonprofit social-services contractors—as the site's operator. Mere days after opening, news emerged that the Linkage Center was also operating as a drug-consumption site, in apparent violation of the federal Controlled Substances Act.

Supervised and "safe" consumption sites are part of a long list of troubling ideas to come out of Progressive-run cities. In my neighborhood of Venice—a three-and-a-half-mile-long seaside community in Los Angeles with more than 2,000 homeless people living on its streets—residents have grown concerned by rumors that the city has approved a consumption site. Over the past few weeks, Urban Alchemy has moved into our Senior Center, adjacent to an elementary school—though the city recently put on hold plans to open a "decompression center" at the site for people suffering drug-related or mental-health crises.

So I decided to visit San Francisco's Tenderloin to witness firsthand what those Progressive ideas had created. My guide was Jenny Chan, a Chinese immigrant who grew up in the Tenderloin.

We visited the main branch of the San Francisco Public Library, which, in 2018, made Curbed's list of America's 20 most beautiful libraries for its dramatic skylight and grand staircase that rises four stories. On our visit, we witnessed a man being held down and strapped into a stretcher bed by San Francisco sheriffs and paramedics. As we waited for safe passage, we overheard that the man was homeless and suffering from schizophrenia. Schizophrenia-sufferers require lifelong treatment, since their disordered thinking and behavior impair daily functioning; here in California they are left to sleep on our streets.

The library's parking lot has become notorious as the largest of the city's "safe sleeping villages." Seventy tents are spaced out in painted squares, providing access to steady meals, electricity for charging phones, toilets, fresh water, hand-washing stations, and showers for homeless individuals. The city government pays Urban Alchemy $60,000 per tent, per year to manage this site. Locals have criticized the steep price tag—around twice as expensive as the median cost of a one-bedroom apartment—but city officials tout its success and praise it as a model.

Observing the sleeping village from inside the library, I found the name ironic, as there was little sleeping going on. A group of men were dismantling bikes and motorcycles in what appeared to be a chop-shop operation. Unleashed dogs ran around. Small plumes of white smoke billowed out from the tents. I didn't see much difference between these well-funded municipal encampments and L.A.'s street encampments.

As we walked to the Linkage Center, I noted how drug dealers had lined up neatly in a row outside, with several backpacks on hand to supply their customers. I asked why the police didn't just arrest the dealers. Jenny explained that many are here from Central America, and their illegal status provides them with an unusual form of protection: she showed me a video of San Francisco district attorney Chesa Boudin saying that "perhaps as many as half" of the city's drug dealers come from Honduras and were forced into drug-running by the cartels, so arresting them is not an option, since they are victims themselves.

Between the Linkage Center and the dealers was an area occupied by "indentured customers," who shuttled back and forth between the two—an image I won't soon forget. I observed individuals standing on two feet but hunched over, with their limbs in unusual formations, a posture described as the "fentanyl fold." The sight of a needle puncturing flesh makes me faint, so I had to look away frequently. It was easier to observe individuals smoking, snorting, or huffing from a multitude of contraptions. Disheveled people with visible track marks and bruises walked nervously in circles, scratching at their skin and open sores. Bodies lined the plaza, some naked from the waist down, some missing an arm or a leg, and most missing teeth.

A representative of the Tenderloin merchants and property owners association showed us around the commercial area and explained the hardships of local business owners. I asked him how many of the homeless in the area were from out of town. He estimated about 95 percent, mostly from the Midwest, where meth addiction is rampant. They made their way to San Francisco, where they are free to use without fear of incarceration.

It became apparent to me that San Francisco had all but replaced its police response and presence with "ambassadors"—privately contracted, unarmed social workers. We toured the neighborhood with one such ambassador, who effectively functioned as our security detail. We passed a small children's park surrounded by a wrought-iron fence and secured by ambassadors on all sides.

Now lawmakers want to bring San Francisco's growing squalor to the rest of the state. California Senate Bill 57, sponsored by Scott Wiener, a Democrat representing San Francisco, would remove the state prohibition on safe-consumption sites for pilot programs in San Francisco, Oakland, and Los Angeles Counties. I was eager to return home and warn my own neighborhood of its future if we continue down this path.

The Progressive Call for Compassion at the Border Is a Political Prop

As a storm of a crisis continues to roil on our southern border, with hundreds of thousands of migrants pouring into the U.S., Progressives are once again demanding "basic humanity" from the immigration system. 24 House Democrats signed a letter demanding the Biden administration end contracts between Immigration and Customs Enforcement and the local jails and detention centers where they are housing migrants.

As revealed in the Pedro L. Gonzalez "The Progressive Call for Compassion at the Border Is a Political Prop" Chronicles March 2021 article: More than 60 House Democrats sent a letter urging Secretary of Homeland Security Alejandro Mayorkas to repeal Title 42, a Trump administration public health order that allowed for the rapid removal of certain border crossers during the pandemic.

But though Progressives drape their appeals for unrestricted migration in the cloak of compassion, the reality of what they are enabling is far more hideous than they care to admit. In encouraging migrants to come to the U.S. illegally, they are effectively incentivizing behavior that leads to the rampant abuse of children, all disguised with cheap pieties of racial and social justice.

It defies belief that Democrats could truly be unaware of the consequences of their messaging in favor of mass migration. Between October and February, 30,000 people under the age of 18 presented themselves at the border without a parent. As many as 120,000 could arrive this year, the *Economist* reported. Some 86 percent are between the ages of 13 and 17, and 14 percent are even younger, between the ages of six and 12.

In other words, they are children. But the crew that brayed "Kids in cages!" as President Trump sought to staunch this flow seems insensate to the horrors these same children face when they are encouraged to come to the U.S. by the so-called humane approach that would let them in. One investigation found that 80 percent of women and girls crossing into the U.S. by way of Mexico are raped during their journey. And the horrors continue when the news cycle leaves them behind.

In early 2016, the Permanent Subcommittee on Investigations published a report about children released by the Office of Refugee Resettlement. In the 13 documented cases, children were handed over to human traffickers masquerading as sponsors. The report noted more than a dozen other cases possibly linked to human trafficking. Among the most prominent incidents, eight minors were trafficked and forced to work 12-hour days for little pay under substandard living and working conditions at an Ohio egg farm.

This is slavery begotten by cries for "compassionate" immigration policy.

And it's guaranteed to occur again because there is no easy way to stop it or even monitor the children once they're in the country. "According to ORR officials," a Government Accountability Office report found, "the agency is generally not required by law to track or monitor the well-being of these children once they are released to sponsors."

The horrified progressive rallying cry against "kids in cages" serves mainly as a political prop for the media and Democratic Party. Once these children are released, nobody seems to care what happens to them, an indifference and unseriousness with a terrible social cost for citizens and foreign nationals alike.

In the absence of a family—of social, cultural, and familial bonds—criminality fills the vacuum; the areas in the United States most afflicted by MS-13 gang violence correspond with locations that received the bulk of the 130,027 children from Central America that the government resettled in the U.S. between October 2014 and December 2017.

Where is the compassion? How is it humane to allow children into a country where they are likely to encounter the very gangs they fled? As researcher Heather MacDonald has pointed out, participation in gangs and drug culture is rising in the second and third generation of Latino immigrants.

The United States immigration system is essentially creating a social bomb by inviting masses of people we cannot properly care for, feed, or educate. Nearly 2 million Latino households in California alone cannot afford the cost of basic needs such as housing, food, health care, childcare, and transportation.

What have we gained by allowing children into this country if they are going to live in poverty here, too? How is this humane or compassionate? And how is it fair to the millions of Americans who are struggling in a cage of destitution, yet are instructed to care about even more desperate people?

And it's not just Democrats and Biden who are the problem. Amid a border crisis they're blaming Biden for, nine House Republicans just joined Democrats voting in favor of a massive amnesty bill that would include a path to citizenship for approximately 4 million illegal aliens. And thirty Republicans voted in favor of the Farm Workforce Modernization Act, which amounts to legalized indentured servitude.

Democrats get their political props; Republicans get their cheap labor. In other words, if there's one thing Republican and Democratic elites can agree on, it's that there's something in unlimited immigration for all of them.

Biden and the Democratic Party may have triggered the catastrophe at hand, but the bomb set by an irresponsible American ruling class has been a long time ticking. Nature abhors a vacuum, and in the absence of a responsible ruling class, nothing good will fill the void.

8 – Yes, Critical Race Theory (CRT) is Being Taught in Schools: Stop Denying It!

Credit: Education Next.

Critical race theory is fast becoming America's new institutional orthodoxy. Yet most Americans have never heard of it—and of those who have, many don't understand it. This must change. We need to know what it is so we can know how to fight it.

To explain critical race theory, it helps to begin with a brief history of Marxism. Originally, the Marxist Left built its political program on the theory of class conflict. Karl Marx believed that the primary characteristic of industrial societies was the imbalance of power between capitalists and workers. The solution to that imbalance, according to Marx, was revolution: the workers would eventually gain consciousness of their plight, seize the means of production, overthrow the capitalist class, and usher in a new socialist society.

However, during the twentieth century, a number of regimes underwent Marxist-style revolutions, and each ended in disaster. Socialist governments in the Soviet Union, China, Cambodia, Cuba, and elsewhere racked up a body count of nearly 100 million people. They are remembered for gulags, show trials, executions, and mass starvations. In practice, Marx's ideas unleashed man's darkest brutalities.

By the mid-1960s, Marxist intellectuals in the West had begun to acknowledge these failures. They recoiled at revelations of Soviet atrocities and came to realize that workers' revolutions would never occur in Western Europe or the United States, which had large middle classes and rapidly improving standards of living. Americans in particular had never developed a sense of class consciousness or class division. Most Americans believed in the American dream—the idea that they could transcend their origins through education, hard work, and good citizenship.

Per the Christopher F. Rufo "The Courage of Our Convictions" *City Journal* April 2021 report: But rather than abandon their political project, Marxist scholars in the West simply adapted their revolutionary theory to the social and racial unrest of the 1960s. Abandoning Marx's economic dialectic of capitalists and workers, they substituted race for class and sought to create a revolutionary coalition of the dispossessed based on racial and ethnic categories.

Fortunately, the early proponents of this revolutionary coalition in the U.S. lost out in the 1960s to the civil rights movement, which sought instead the fulfillment of the American promise of freedom and equality under the law. Americans preferred the idea of improving their country to that of overthrowing it. Martin Luther King Jr.'s vision, President Lyndon Johnson's pursuit of the Great Society, and the restoration of law and order promised by President Richard Nixon in his 1968 campaign defined the post-1960s American political consensus.

But the radical Left has proved resilient and enduring—which is where critical race theory comes in.

Critical race theory is an academic discipline, formulated in the 1990s and built on the intellectual framework of identity-based Marxism. Relegated for many years to universities and obscure academic journals, it has increasingly become the default ideology in our public institutions over the past decade. It has been injected into government agencies, public school systems, teacher training programs, and corporate human-resources departments, in the form of diversity-training programs, human-resources modules, public-policy frameworks, and school curricula.

Its supporters deploy a series of euphemisms to describe critical race theory, including "equity," "social justice," "diversity and inclusion," and "culturally responsive teaching." Critical race theorists, masters of language construction, realize that "neo-Marxism" would be a hard sell.

Equity, on the other hand, sounds non-threatening and is easily confused with the American principle of equality.

But the distinction is vast and important. Indeed, critical race theorists explicitly reject equality— the principle proclaimed in the Declaration of Independence, defended in the Civil War, and codified into law with the Fourteenth and Fifteenth Amendments, the Civil Rights Act of 1964, and the Voting Rights Act of 1965. To them, equality represents "mere nondiscrimination" and provides "camouflage" for white supremacy, patriarchy, and oppression.

In contrast to equality, equity as defined and promoted by critical race theorists is little more than reformulated Marxism. In the name of equity, UCLA law professor and critical race theorist Cheryl Harris has proposed suspending private property rights, seizing land and wealth, and redistributing them along racial lines. Critical race guru Ibram X. Kendi, who directs the Center for Antiracist Research at Boston University, has proposed the creation of a federal Department of Antiracism. This department would be independent of (i.e., unaccountable to) the elected branches of government, and would have the power to nullify, veto, or abolish any law at any level of government and curtail the speech of political leaders and others deemed insufficiently "antiracist."

One practical result of the creation of such a department would be the overthrow of capitalism, since, according to Kendi, "In order to truly be antiracist, you also have to truly be anti-capitalist." In other words, identity is the means; Marxism is the end.

An equity-based form of government would mean the end not only of private property but also of individual rights, equality under the law, federalism, and freedom of speech. These would be replaced by race-based redistribution of wealth, group-based rights, active discrimination, and omnipotent bureaucratic authority. Historically, the accusation of "anti-Americanism" has been overused. But in this case, it's not a matter of interpretation: critical race theory prescribes a revolutionary program that would overturn the principles of the Declaration and destroy the remaining structure of the Constitution.

What Does Critical Race Theory Look Like in Practice?

In 2021, Christopher F. Rufo authored a series of reports focused on critical race theory in the federal government. The FBI was holding workshops on intersectionality theory. The Department of Homeland Security was telling white employees that they were committing "microinequities" and had been "socialized into oppressor roles."

The Treasury Department held a training session telling staff members that "virtually all white people contribute to racism" and that they must convert "everyone in the federal government" to the ideology of "antiracism."

And the Sandia National Laboratories, which designs America's nuclear arsenal, sent white male executives to a three-day reeducation camp, where they were told that "white male culture" was analogous to the "KKK," "white supremacists," and "mass killings." The executives were then forced to renounce their "white male privilege" and to write letters of apology to fictitious women and people of color.

In 2022, Rufo produced another series of reports focused on critical race theory in education. In Cupertino, California, an elementary school forced first-graders to deconstruct their racial and sexual identities and rank themselves according to their "power and privilege." In Springfield, Missouri, a middle school forced teachers to locate themselves on an "oppression matrix," based on the idea that straight, white, English-speaking, Christian males are members of the oppressor class and must atone for their privilege and "covert white supremacy."

In Philadelphia, an elementary school forced fifth-graders to celebrate "Black communism" and simulate a Black Power rally to free 1960s radical Angela Davis from prison, where she had once been held on charges of murder. And in Seattle, the school district told white teachers that they are guilty of "spirit murder" against black children and must "bankrupt [their] privilege in acknowledgement of [their] thieved inheritance."

Per Rufo: I'm just one investigative journalist, but I've developed a database of more than 1,000 of these stories. When I say that critical race theory is becoming the operating ideology of our public institutions, I am not exaggerating—from the universities to bureaucracies to K-12 school systems, critical race theory has permeated the collective intelligence and decision-making process of American government, with no sign of slowing down.

This is a revolutionary change. When originally established, these government institutions were presented as neutral, technocratic, and oriented toward broadly held perceptions of the public good. Today, under the increasing sway of critical race theory and related ideologies, they are being turned against the American people. This isn't limited to the permanent bureaucracy in Washington, D.C., but is true as well of institutions in the states—even red states. It is spreading to county public health departments, small midwestern school districts, and more. This ideology will not stop until it has devoured all of our institutions.

So far, attempts to halt the encroachment of critical race theory have been ineffective. There are a number of reasons for this.

First, too many Americans have developed an acute fear of speaking up about social and political issues, especially those involving race. According to a recent Gallup poll, 77 percent of conservatives are afraid to share their political beliefs publicly. Worried about getting mobbed on social media, fired from their jobs, or worse, they remain quiet, largely ceding the public debate to those pushing these anti-American ideologies. Consequently, the institutions themselves become monocultures: dogmatic, suspicious, and hostile to a diversity of opinion. Conservatives in both the federal government and public school systems have told me that their "equity and inclusion" departments serve as political offices, searching for and stamping out any dissent from the official orthodoxy.

Second, critical race theorists have constructed their argument like a mousetrap. Disagreement with their program becomes irrefutable evidence of a dissenter's "white fragility," "unconscious bias," or "internalized white supremacy." I've seen this projection of false consciousness on their opponents play out dozens of times in my reporting. Diversity trainers will make an outrageous claim—such as "all whites are intrinsically oppressors" or "white teachers are guilty of spirit murdering black children"—and then, when confronted with disagreement, adopt a patronizing tone and explain that participants who feel "defensiveness" or "anger" are reacting out of guilt and shame. Dissenters are instructed to remain silent, "lean into the discomfort," and accept their "complicity in white supremacy."

Third, Americans across the political spectrum have failed to separate the premise of critical race theory from its conclusion. Its premise—that American history includes slavery and other injustices, and that we should examine and learn from that history—is undeniable. But its revolutionary conclusion—that America was founded on and defined by racism and that our founding principles, our Constitution, and our way of life should be overthrown—does not rightly, much less necessarily, follow.

Fourth and finally, the writers and activists who have had the courage to speak out against critical race theory have tended to address it on the theoretical level, pointing out the theory's logical contradictions and dishonest account of history. These criticisms are worthy and good, but they move the debate into the academic realm—friendly terrain for proponents of critical race theory. They fail to force defenders of this revolutionary ideology to defend the practical consequences of their ideas in the realm of politics.

No longer simply an academic matter, critical race theory has become a tool of political power. To borrow a phrase from the Marxist theoretician Antonio Gramsci, it is fast achieving cultural hegemony in America's public institutions. It is driving the vast machinery of the state and society. If we want to succeed in opposing it, we must address it politically at every level.

Critical race theorists must be confronted with the following questions and forced to speak to the facts.

- Do they support public schools separating first-graders into groups of "oppressors" and "oppressed"?

- Do they support mandatory curricula teaching that "all white people play a part in perpetuating systemic racism"?

- Do they support public schools instructing white parents to become "white traitors" and advocate for "white abolition"?

- Do they want those who work in government to be required to undergo this kind of reeducation?

- How about managers and workers in corporate America?

- How about the men and women in our military? How about every one of us?

There are three parts to a successful strategy to defeat the forces of critical race theory: governmental action, grassroots mobilization, and an appeal to principle.

We already see examples of governmental action.

In 2020, one of Rufo's reports led President Trump to issue an executive order banning critical race theory–based training programs in the federal government. President Biden rescinded this order on his first day in office, but it provides a model for governors and municipal leaders to follow.

In the following years, several state legislatures have introduced bills to achieve the same goal: preventing public institutions from conducting programs that stereotype, scapegoat, or demean people on the basis of race. And I have organized a coalition of attorneys to file lawsuits against schools and government agencies that impose critical race theory–based programs on grounds of the First Amendment (which protects citizens from compelled speech), the Fourteenth Amendment (which provides equal protection under the law), and the Civil Rights Act of 1964 (which prohibits public institutions from discriminating on the basis of race).

On the grassroots level, a multiracial and bipartisan coalition is emerging to fight critical race theory.

Parents are mobilizing against racially divisive curricula in public schools and employees are increasingly speaking out against Orwellian reeducation in the workplace. When they see what is happening, Americans are naturally outraged that critical race theory promotes three ideas—race essentialism, collective guilt, and neo-segregation—that violate the basic principles of equality and justice. Anecdotally, many Chinese-Americans have told me that, having survived the Cultural Revolution in their former country, they refuse to let the same thing happen here.

In terms of principles, we need to employ our own moral language rather than allow ourselves to be confined by the categories of critical race theory. For example, we often find ourselves debating "diversity." Diversity as most of us understand it, is generally good, all things being equal, but it is of secondary value. We should be talking about and aiming at excellence, a common standard that challenges people of all backgrounds to achieve their potential. On the scale of desirable ends, excellence beats diversity every time.

Similarly, in addition to pointing out the dishonesty of the historical narrative on which critical race theory is predicated, we must promote the true story of America—a story that is honest about injustices in American history, but that places them in the context of our nation's high ideals and the progress we have made toward realizing them. Genuine American history is rich with stories of achievements and sacrifices that will move the hearts of Americans, in stark contrast to the grim and pessimistic narrative pressed by critical race theorists.

Above all, we must have courage, the fundamental virtue required in our time: courage to stand and speak the truth, courage to withstand epithets, courage to face the mob, and courage to shrug off the scorn of elites. When enough of us overcome the fear that currently prevents so many from speaking out, the hold of critical race theory will begin to slip. And courage begets courage. It's easy to stop a lone dissenter; it's much harder to stop 10, 20, 100, 1,000, 1 million, or more who stand up together for the principles of America. Truth and justice are on our side. If we can muster the courage, we will win.

You can find a link to the "Critical Race Theory Briefing Book" in the Appendix:

Critical Race Theory (CRT) Counterpoints: Which Ones Are True? Or False?

In a *New York Times* op-ed, co-authors David French, Kmele Foster, Thomas Chatterton Williams, and Jason Stanley present themselves as a "cross-partisan group of thinkers" sending a warning signal about the threat of authoritarianism in states such as, Alabama, Arkansas, Florida, Georgia, Idaho, Indiana, Iowa, Kentucky, Mississippi, Missouri, Montana, Nebraska, New Hampshire, New Jersey, North Dakota, Oklahoma, South Carolina, South Dakota, Tennessee, Texas, Utah, Virginia, West Virginia, and Wyoming.

As noted in the Christopher F. Rufo "The Enablers" *City Journal* July 2021 report: All these states have passed some form of legislation prohibiting public schools from promoting the core principles of critical race theory, including race essentialism, collective guilt, and state-sanctioned discrimination. Are these new laws against the racist policies and outcomes of CRT pedagogy, sapient? Or illiberal, by prohibiting freedom of speech and expression about racism? Let's find out.

Defending phantom freedoms, certain intellectuals usher in the concrete tyrannies of critical race theory objectors.

These authors may imagine themselves to be defending liberal-democratic freedoms against the threat of illiberalism. But in practice, they enable, and would leave American families defenseless against, the worst ideologies of the Left. They advance three specious arguments:

- That critical-race-theory restrictions violate free speech.

- That state legislatures should stay out of the marketplace of ideas.

- That citizens should pursue civil rights litigation instead.

These fallacious arguments they postulate—would serve to usher in the concrete tyrannies of critical race theory, which explicitly seeks to subvert the principles of individual rights and equal protection under the law.

Despite the superficial differences among the four heterodox authors, they all serve a single function: to prevaricate, stall, and run interference for critical race theory's blitz through American institutions.

The authors' primary error is to frame the debate as one about free speech.

The First Amendment was designed to protect citizens from the government, not to protect the government from citizens.

Public schools, which have the power of compulsion, are pushing toxic racial theories onto children, teaching them that they should be judged on the basis of race and must atone for historical crimes committed by members of their racial group. Critical race theorists have the right to express their beliefs as individuals, but voters and taxpayers are obligated neither to subsidize their speech nor to include it in the public school curriculum.

After all, the public education system is not a "marketplace of ideas" but a state-run monopoly. Even under the most dogmatic libertarian philosophy, monopoly conditions justify, even require, government intervention.

The anti–critical race theory bills <u>do not</u> restrict teaching and inquiry about the history of racism.

They restrict indoctrination, abusive pedagogies, and state-sanctioned racism. In Idaho, for example, the law tells public schools that they cannot "compel students to personally affirm, adopt, or adhere to" noxious ideas, such as one race "is inherently superior or inferior" or that an individual "should be adversely treated on the basis of race."

The *Times* op-ed authors argue that the public must not interfere directly in public institutions, even those that promote state-sanctioned racism. They argue that anti–critical race theory legislation constitutes a "speech code" and that any such limitations on the public school curriculum "threaten" democracy itself.

But some restrictions on speech are inevitable, even obligatory, in public schools.

Do state educators have the absolute right to propound any ideology they desire—say, eugenics or gay conversion therapy—immune from legislative restriction?

During a recent conversation on the Bari Weiss podcast, I asked David French, one of the coauthors of the *Times* article, a simple question to test the implications of his theory: if a public school adopted a Klan-sponsored curriculum that promoted white supremacy, would he support or oppose state legislation to ban it? He ducked the question, as did his co-authors on social media.

But the question remains, and opponents of bills restricting critical-race-theory instruction seem to have two possible answers—and one evasion. They could support a ban on white supremacist instruction, in which case their opposition to banning critical race theory would constitute an unprincipled endorsement of such instruction. Or they could oppose a ban, which would be internally consistent but morally backward.

But French and his colleagues evade the question, claiming that many of the practices of critical race theory are already illegal under federal civil rights law and, therefore, that new legislation is unnecessary.

This might be theoretically true, but in reality, thousands of public schools are already engaging in these abusive practices.

Most parents do not have the resources to file a federal civil rights lawsuit at every infraction; and the Biden administration has dropped all enforcement against critical race theory in public education, eliminating another avenue of protection. The status quo burdens individual families while shielding public schools from democratic oversight.

This position, presented as a principled third way, is an illusion: it might make for a compelling law-review article, but in practice, it will move the country further down the path of racial abuse in the classroom, affording parents no recourse except for the abstract satisfaction that, in the mind of some intellectuals, these practices are already illegal.

The difference between action and inaction is significant.

With state prohibitions on critical race theory indoctrination, schools have clear guidance about their curricula and families have immediate recourse. If teachers are pushing divisive racial theories in the classroom, parents can point to a clear, specific legal statute and force the school into compliance; if that fails, they can appeal to state attorneys general or state superintendents, who can immediately enforce the law.

With the French-Foster-Williams-Stanley approach of maintaining the status quo, schools can continue to promote race essentialism, collective guilt, and racial-superiority theory, and parents would be obligated to file an expensive, multiyear federal lawsuit to challenge these programs in the courts one by one, with no guarantee of success. In the end, state legislation tilts the playing field in favor of parents; the status quo tilts the playing field in favor of bureaucrats, lawyers, and diversity officers.

Is it possible that these writers simply aren't aware of the illiberal nature of critical race theory?

No. French, in particular, denounced critical race theory in 2012 as a dangerous cult that enforced its orthodoxy with "vicious" harassment on the Harvard University campus; in 2017, he described it as "racial poison" that "leads to sheer cruelty and malice."

In our recent podcast conversation, after I suggested that critical race theory was nearing hegemony within our institutions, he pushed back, arguing that if the critical theorists had truly achieved hegemony, our conversation would not have been possible—it would have been outlawed, censored, banned.

This is telling: French understands that critical race theory is a totalitarian ideology that, if it were to achieve absolute power, would immediately dismantle liberalism, beginning with the right to free speech. But he and his coauthors neglect the obvious question. If critical race theory is "racial poison," why allow it to seize control of our schools? If critical race theorists are "magnetic, preacher-like personalities" who seek totalitarian power, why defend their pursuit of this power in the name of liberalism?

This argument turns tolerance into a farce.

It purports to defend Enlightenment rationalism, equality under the law, and individual rights themselves while ceding substantive power to those who explicitly oppose these things. Those making such arguments wind up enabling the most intolerant voices in our society, who would end up perverting the very values they claim to cherish.

Public school teachers forcing first-graders to denounce themselves as racists would become "free speech;" university diversity officers forcing students through race reeducation programs would become "academic freedom." For these "heterodox" thinkers, the ratchet only goes one way: states such as California, Oregon, Washington, and Illinois can mandate critical race theory in their state curricula and teacher training programs; but if states such as Texas, Oklahoma, Idaho, and New Hampshire prohibit it, that is an "un-American" threat to "the expression of ideas."

Luckily, the American public has more sense.

The revolt against critical race theory has inspired millions of parents to engage in the political process, protest at school board meetings, run for office, file lawsuits, and lobby state legislators to stop the madness through the rightful exercise of democratic power.

According to a recent YouGov/Economist poll, 64 percent of Americans have heard about critical race theory and 55 percent "have a good idea what it is." Of that second group, 58 percent view it unfavorably, including 72 percent of independents who believe including it in school curricula is "bad for America."

These citizens understand implicitly that public schools are being devoured by a hostile ideology that seeks to divide the country by race and undermine the core principle of democratic control. They understand a simple truth: in a democracy, voters get to decide how to shape, guide, and restrict public institutions, especially those that have power over children.

As one can learn at any Alcoholics Anonymous meeting, the solution to enablers is to cut them out of the process. Political leaders should prioritize protecting American families and ignore the nitpicking and prevarications of the intelligentsia. The war against critical race theory is a war worth fighting and winning. The alternative is a path to demoralization, empty gestures—and defeat.

Yes, Critical Race Theory Is Being Taught in Schools: Stop Denying It!

To what extent, if at all, are critical race theory (CRT) and gender ideology being taught or promoted in America's schools? With little data available, and no agreement about what constitutes the teaching of critical social justice (CSJ) ideas, the answer up to now has remained open to political interpretation.

However, a new survey of young Americans vindicates the fears of CRT's critics per the Manhattan Institute "Yes, Critical Race Theory Is Being Taught in Schools" *City Journal* October 2022 report:

Motivated by the work of Manhattan Institute senior fellow and *City Journal* contributing editor Christopher F. Rufo, many on the right allege that CRT-related concepts—such as systemic racism and white privilege—are infiltrating the curricula of public schools around the country.

Educators following these curricula are said to be teaching students that racial disparities in socioeconomic outcomes are fundamentally the result of racism, and that white people are the privileged beneficiaries of a social system that oppresses blacks and other "people of color." On gender, they are being taught that gender identity is a choice, regardless of biological sex. But are the cases Rufo and others point to representative of American public schools at large—or are they merely outliers amplified by right-wing media?

The response to these charges from many on the left has been to deny or downplay them.

CRT, they contend, is a legal theory taught only in university law programs. Therefore, what conservatives are up in arms about is not the teaching of CRT, but the teaching of America's uncomfortable racial history.

But strong connections exist between the cultural radicalism of CRT and the one-sided, decontextualized portrayal of American history and society that Democratic activists endorse. And these ideas have also influenced many Democratic voters. Indeed, according to a 2021 YouGov survey, large majorities of Democratic respondents support public schools' teaching many of the morally and empirically contentious ideas to which opponents of CRT object.

These include the notions that racism is systemic in America (85 percent support), that all disparities between blacks and whites are caused by discrimination (72 percent), that white people enjoy certain privileges based on their race (85 percent), and that they have a responsibility to address racial inequality (87 percent).

Whatever one thinks of these ideas, they are hardly "settled facts" on the same epistemic plane as heliocentrism, natural selection, or even climate change. To the contrary, they are a moral-ideological just-so theory of group differences, an all-encompassing worldview akin to a secular religion, whose claims can't be measured, tested, or falsified.

They treat an observed phenomenon (disparate group outcomes) as evidence of its cause (racism), while specifying causal mechanisms that are nebulous, if not magical.

Their advocates have not refuted counterarguments; they've merely asserted empirically unverified statements about the nature of group differences. Publicly funded schools that teach and pass off left-wing racial-ideological theories and concepts as if they are undisputed factual knowledge—or that impart tendentiously curated readings of history—are therefore engaging in indoctrination, not education.

The question before us, then, is not whether or to what extent public schools are assigning the works of Richard Delgado, Kimberlé Crenshaw, and other critical race theorists. It is whether schools are uncritically promoting a left-wing racial ideology.

To answer this and other related questions, we commissioned a study on a nationally representative sample of 1,505 18- to 20-year-old Americans—a demographic that has yet to graduate from, or only recently graduated from, high school. A complete Manhattan Institute report of all the findings from this study will be published in the coming months; what follows is a preview of some of them. Our analysis here focuses mainly on the results for the sample overall rather than for various subgroups.

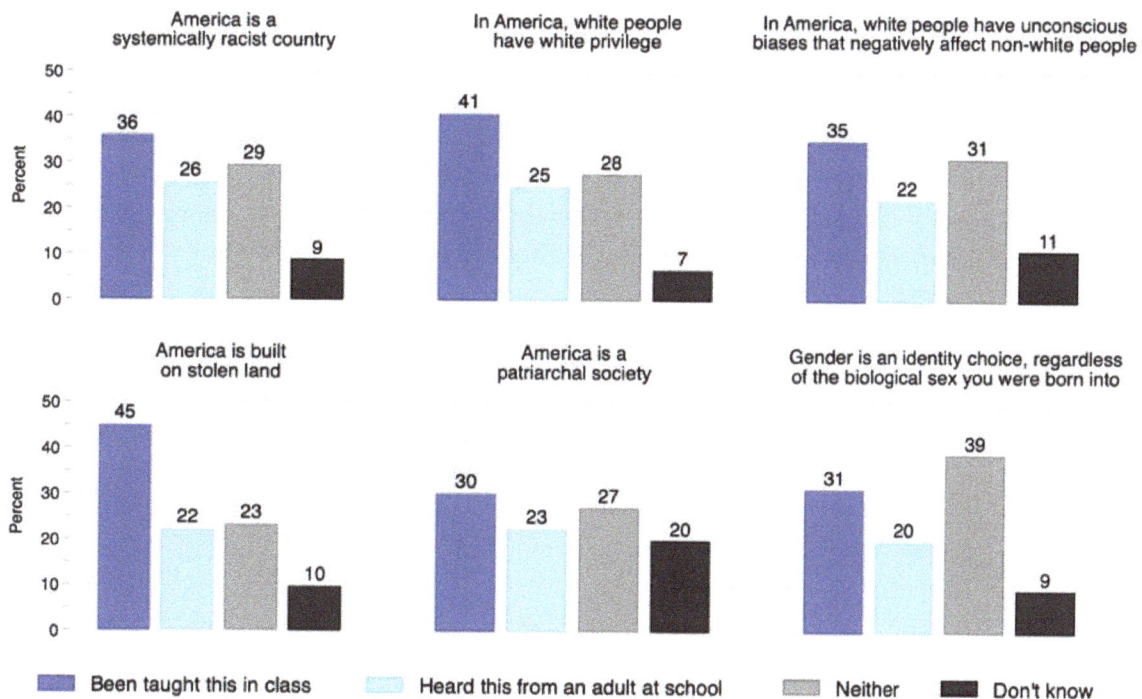

Credit: City Journal-Yes, Critical Race Theory is Being Taught in Schools. Chart # 1.

We began by asking our 18- to 20-year-old respondents (82.4 percent of whom reported attending public schools) whether they had ever been taught in class or heard about from an adult at school each of six concepts—four of which are central to critical race theory. The chart below, which displays the distribution of responses for each concept, shows that "been taught" is the modal response for all but one of the six concepts.

For the CRT-related concepts, 62 percent reported either being taught in class or hearing from an adult in school that "America is a systemically racist country," 69 percent reported being taught or hearing that "white people have white privilege," 57 percent reported being taught or hearing that "white people have unconscious biases that negatively affect non-white people," and 67 percent reported being taught or hearing that "America is built on stolen land."

The shares giving either response with respect to gender-related concepts are slightly lower, but still a majority. Fifty-three percent report they were either taught in class or heard from an adult at school that "America is a patriarchal society," and 51 percent report being taught or hearing that "gender is an identity choice" regardless of biological sex.

Perhaps it's wrong to assume that the teaching of these CSJ concepts necessarily amounts to ideological indoctrination.

After all, such concepts are salient on social and other media, and have also been uttered or invoked by prominent politicians. Perhaps, then, most teachers are merely using them as fodder for healthy classroom debate or presenting them as perspectives among other competing ideas.

Yet our data suggest that this is hardly the majority experience. Specifically, we asked those who reported being taught at least one of the listed concepts in a high school class what, if anything, they were taught about arguments opposing them. Unsapiently, 68 percent responded that they either were not taught about opposing arguments or were taught that there are no "respectable" opposing arguments. Importantly, this rate does not meaningfully vary by race, political orientation, or high school type.

Whites (30 percent) and nonwhites (34 percent), Democrats (29 percent) and Republicans (31 percent), liberals (29 percent) and conservatives (31 percent), and public (32 percent) and private or parochial (28 percent) schoolers were equally likely to report being told about respectable counterarguments. No evidence, then, suggests that this response reflects respondents' political biases.

Instead, the data suggest that large majorities in all groups have been given the impression that the concepts they were taught are beyond reproach. And these data hardly tell the full story: in our forthcoming report, we additionally show that the number of concepts respondents report being taught is positively related to the probability of being told there that opposing arguments are not "respectable."

If this isn't indoctrination—unwitting or otherwise—then what is?

The prevalence of students' classroom exposure to left-wing ideological concepts raises the question of its attitudinal effect. Are students who report receiving such instruction more "woke" than those who do not? Given the many other sources of attitudinal influence with which any effect of exposure must compete, there is ample reason for skepticism. At the same time, our respondents are in a phase of life in which, by some accounts, social and political attitudes are malleable.

The potential for exposure to shape related attitudes is plausible. In fact, in a dissertation chapter, one of us found that having white respondents read a short "racially woke" op-ed article led to eight- to 12-point increases (mostly via increases in collective shame and guilt) in support for race-based affirmative action, government assistance, and reparations to African-Americans. If attitudinal shifts of this magnitude can be produced over a span of just minutes, what might be the effects of more protracted exposure?

It's also fair to say that many educators incorporating such concepts into their instruction expect, or at least hope, that doing so makes a difference in the minds of students. Indeed, the notion that concepts like "white privilege" and "systemic racism" are solely taught for knowledge's sake strains credulity, especially when such instruction usually entails the omission or delegitimization of competing arguments. The hope instead seems to be that students will come to see white people as ultimately responsible for the creation and persistence of racial inequality; and that this realization will inspire support for race-conscious, "equity"-oriented policies.

Perhaps this hope is ill-founded, but our data indicate otherwise.

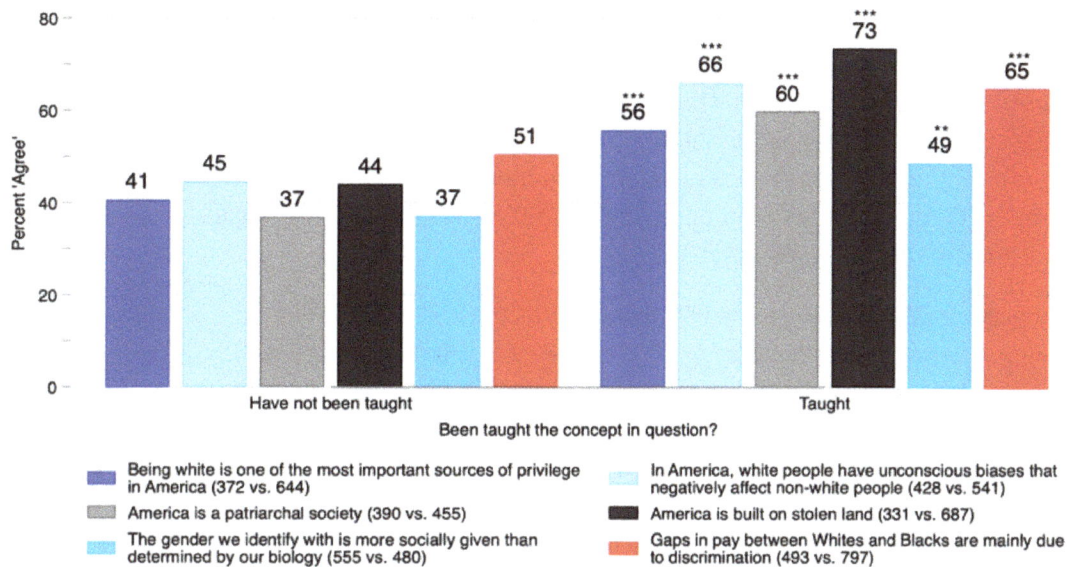

Credit: City Journal-Yes, Critical Race Theory is Being Taught in Schools. Chart # 4.

As an initial test, we examined whether those who report being taught a given concept are more likely to endorse it. For instance, relative to those who reported they were not taught the related concept, those who indicated they were taught it were 14 points more likely to agree that the black-white pay gap is mainly due to discrimination, 15 points more likely to agree that "being white is one of the most important sources of privilege in America," 23 points more likely to agree that "white people have unconscious biases that negatively affect non-white people," and 29 points more likely to agree that "America is built on stolen land."

These differences, all statistically significant at the 99.9 percent level, persist after adjustments for a host of theoretically plausible alternative explanations, including race, political orientation, county rurality, county partisanship, county racial liberalism, and county school segregation.

Our next analysis thus examines whether the volume of CRT-related classroom exposure—which we define as the total number of CRT-related concepts respondents reported being taught in school (from zero to five) affects attitudes toward white Americans and pro-black policies like affirmative action and race-based government assistance.

First, we consider whether exposure to a larger share of the five concepts increases agreement with the view that white Americans "are ultimately responsible for the inferior social position of black people." Per the survey results, this indeed appears to be the case. Support is lowest (32 percent) among those who didn't recall being taught any of the five CRT-related concepts (the "no exposure" group), and agreement rises—albeit non-linearly—to a high of 75 percent among those who report being taught all five concepts. Adjusting for alternative explanations has a minimal effect on this 43-point difference in attitudes between those taught no CRT concepts and those taught all five, which remains statistically significant.

We next consider whether exposure increases agreement with the broad-brush generalization that white Americans are "racist and mean"—an item one of us has previously tested and used as an indicator of collective moral shame among whites. Similar to the previous results, agreement with this statement begins at a low of 40 percent among those in the "no exposure" group and increases (again non-linearly) to a high of 72 percent for those who report being taught all five concepts. This difference remains significant when controlling for alternative explanatory variables.

If greater CRT-related classroom exposure increases the endorsement of negative moral appraisals of white Americans, we'd also expect it to boost support for group-based policies that afford preferential treatment to African Americans—even when descriptions of such policies explicitly speak to the risk of discrimination against whites (as our measure of support for affirmative action, adopted from the General Social Survey, does).

Consistent with this prediction, our data show that support for the preferential hiring and promotion of black people falls to a low of 17 percent among those who reported hearing no CRT, while reaching a high of 44 percent among those who reported being taught all five CRT-related concepts.

Similarly, the belief that the government should help black people (versus "our government should not be giving special treatment to black people") is endorsed by 35 percent of those in the "no exposure" group, compared with 43 percent of those who reported being taught one concept, 51 percent to 54 percent of those who reported being taught two to four concepts, and 72 percent of those who reported being taught all five concepts.

Again, a 30- to 40-point difference emerges between those who were not taught CRT material and those who received the maximum dose of it.

Here we should note that the above results are similar for white and non-white respondents alike—even if not always to the same degree. One relationship that is necessarily exclusive to whites, though, is that between exposure and white guilt,. Whereas 39 percent of whites who did not report any CRT-related classroom exposure indicated feeling "guilty about the social inequalities between white and black Americans," this share rises to about 45 percent among whites who reported being taught one or two CRT-related concepts, and to between 54 percent and 58 percent among whites who reported being taught three or more concepts.

These findings indicate that those reporting being taught more CRT-related concepts are more likely to endorse negative moral appraisals of and to view white Americans as responsible for black disadvantage. Among whites, greater CRT exposure is also linked to higher levels of guilt over racial inequality. Finally, and perhaps consequently, greater CRT exposure predicts a higher likelihood of both white and minority young people supporting race-conscious policies that afford preferential treatment to African-Americans.

The same is true for gender. Among those that were taught that gender is a choice, 53 percent say "the gender we identify with is more socially given than determined by our biology" compared with 40 percent of those who were not taught this, a significant difference. Those taught about gender as an identity are more likely to view it as detached from biological sex.

While we can't be certain that exposure causes attitude change—those with progressive attitudes could have had parents more likely to select into schools where CRT is taught (or to recall being exposed to it)—we used data from a person's zip code and county (rurality, diversity, education, voting patterns) that make such competing explanations unlikely. We can also rule out the possibility that these relationships are the product of alternative explanatory factors in our dataset.

While only scratching the surface of what will feature in the full report, our findings have several important takeaways.

First, the claim that CRT and gender ideology are not being taught or promoted in America's pre-college public schools is grossly misleading. More than nine in ten of our respondents reported some form of school exposure to at least some CRT-related and critical gender concepts, with the average respondent reporting being taught in class or hearing about from an adult at school more than half of the eight concepts we measured. Eight in ten reported being taught in class at least one concept central to CRT and contemporary left-wing racial ideology, with the average respondent reporting being taught two of the five we listed. A majority were taught radical gender ideas.

Given the sheer size of these numbers, the promotion and teaching of "white privilege" and "systemic racism" in America's public schools can hardly be regarded as a rare or isolated phenomenon. It is the experience of a sizeable share of pre-college students.

Second, educators are presenting CSJ ideas to students uncritically. If such concepts were presented only as perspectives—and in conjunction with competing others—then their introduction into the classroom could very well be defensible. But our data suggest that this is not the case. Instead, most are receiving them as undisputed "facts"—or at least facts only disputed by bigots and ignoramuses.

This is indoctrination, and governments should act swiftly to put a stop to it.

More-detailed policy recommendations must await the full report. But schools and teachers that wish to teach about these concepts should be given the option of either teaching the diversity of thought surrounding them or being barred from teaching them altogether.

Third, such biased instruction is effective. Our data show that those who report being taught CRT-related concepts are not only more likely to endorse them but are also more likely to blame white people for racial inequality, to essentialize white people as "racist," and to support "equity-oriented" race-based policies. Among whites, we also observe higher levels of white guilt among those exposed to more CRT-related concepts.

Overall, then, our data would appear to confirm many of the fears of anti-CRT activists about such instruction. Anecdotes are borne out by our representative large-scale data.

Critical race and gender theory is endemic in American schools. The vast majority of children are being taught radical CSJ concepts that affect their view of white people, their country, the relationship between gender and sex, and public policy.

For those inclined toward a colorblind and reality-based ideal, these findings should serve as a wakeup call. Unless sapient voters, parents, and governments act, these illiberal and unscientific ideas will spread more widely, and will replace traditional American liberal nationalism with an identity-based cultural socialism.

9 – The Progressivism Platform is Based on Lies, Bias, Deception & False Narratives

shutterstock.com · 1036576444

Central to the idea of Progressivism is the belief that every morally significant change from the status quo is necessarily progress. If you disagree with the change, you are morally "backward-looking." The presentation of morality as a historical development is powerful because it shuts down future debate. But is the status quo by necessity morally inferior to some inevitable future condition toward which we are being driven by the mysterious force of history?

For example, the army of social justice warriors takes frequent aim at the principles of the United States' founding. For them, progress is measured by how far consciousness can be raised in society to awareness of oppressive inequalities among human beings with regard to race, class, and gender as revealed in the Clifford Humphrey "The Myth of Change as Progress in Progressivism" *Epoch Times* February 2019 article:

Attacking the historicism of Progressivism, former President Calvin Coolidge noted that "it is often asserted … that we have had new thoughts and experiences which have given us a great advance over the people of [1776], and that we may therefore very well discard their conclusions for something more modern."

Coolidge contrasted such chronological snobbery with the "exceedingly restful" finality of the Declaration. He stated, "If all men are created equal, that is final. If they are endowed with inalienable rights, that is final. … No advance, no progress can be made beyond these propositions. If anyone wishes to deny their truth or their soundness, the only direction in which he can proceed historically is not forward, but backward."

The Myth of Change as Progress in Progressivism

Opposed to the idea that some spirit in history determines what is moral is the belief that morality depends on something outside of time and is something human reason can discern.

On this idea, Leo Strauss, a notable 20th-century political philosopher, wrote: "All political action aims at either preservation or change. When desiring to preserve, we wish to prevent a change to the worse; when desiring to change, we wish to bring about something better. All political action is, then, guided by some thought of better or worse. But thought of better or worse implies thought of the good."

If both preservation and change are dependent on the good, then it is the supreme human endeavor to seek to understand what is good and the glory of a human being to make choices in accord with it. There is no escaping the often difficult task of exercising prudence to make our way through life's moral quandaries. This task cannot be outsourced to some vague notion of history.

The horrors of the 20th century easily belie the idea that history is the long story of the moral progress of mankind. Winston Churchill, through the force of his leadership, had a profound influence on limiting the spread of those horrors. He was well aware of the growing dominion that forces of technology and globalization would have over the scope of human action. Nevertheless, his reflections led him to retain hope in the vital role that statesmanship and choice played in influencing world events. He lauded "the profound significance of human choice and the sublime responsibility of men."

Citizens in a republic like ours have the sublime responsibility and profound significance of choosing our own rulers. First our choices and then theirs—not the spirit of history—will shape our future, for better or for worse.

Despite what Progressive politicians may presume, not every change is progress. Author C. S. Lewis put it well when he wrote, "We all want progress, but if you're on the wrong road, progress means doing an about-turn and walking back to the right road; in that case, the man who turns back soonest is the most Progressive."

How Progressives Are Retrogressive

Per the Philip Carl Salzman "How Progressives Are Retrogressive" *Epoch Times* January 2022 article: How often do we hear political commentators and Republican officials use the terms "liberal" and "Progressive" interchangeably when discussing Democrats? Yet the meanings of the two terms could not be more different.

Liberalism as a political philosophy emphasizes individual freedom, agency, and choice. Human nature, in the liberal view, is a mix of qualities: energy and sloth, selfishness and generosity, creativity and habit. Society exists to provide the maximum freedom to individuals, with the constraints necessary to limit the encroachment of one on another. Inequality in a liberal society reflects the differences in capabilities and motivations among individuals. Liberalism favors free elections of public officials and limited government. For liberals, economics should be based on contractual relations freely entered into by producers and consumers, entrepreneurs, and labor.

Progressivism emphasizes equality and rights. Human nature, in the Progressive view, is basically good, with vices resulting from imperfect and oppressive social arrangements. Society is perfectible, and the perfect society is one which guarantees equality and equal rights. The economy should be owned and run collectively, by the society at large. The government must be strong, able to control all aspects of society. Political parties unjustly divide the society, and are unnecessary when the government represents all of the people.

The liberal vision supports liberal democracy and capitalism, while the Progressive vision supports socialism and government economic planning. It's no accident that some members of the Progressive caucus in the House of Representatives are members of the Democratic Socialists of America. The caucus favors collectivism, as seen in government control of all major institutions and programs, such as welfare support, pre-schools, education, medicine, and the organization of labor. Progressives prefer government monopolies in all of these fields, which is why they oppose school choice, labor choice, and medical choice (except abortion, which they love).

Progressives see liberal democracies as systems of unjust inequalities resulting from inherited privilege and oppression of the weak. Liberals see Progressives as crushing individual liberty by vesting all functions in an all-powerful government, and thus favoring authoritarian rule.

Progressivism rests on the idea of progress advanced by Karl Marx: a movement driven by class conflict from capitalism to socialism and then to communism.

In classic Marxism, classes are defined by economic position, by control over the means of production. The bourgeois class are the owners of the means of production, and the propertyless proletariat are the workers who must live on the pay provided by selling their labor.

In the classic socialist society, equality is advanced for most people, although the governing elite are all powerful and rank high above the multitude. While equality increases, and in the eyes of Progressives, justice is advanced, it's an equality of poverty and misery, because the all-powerful government's central economic planning fails to build the economy and stimulate innovation, motivation, and entrepreneurship. And, notwithstanding the century-long claim that "real socialism has never been tried," all of the socialist societies—the USSR, Soviet Eastern Europe, China, Albania, Cambodia, North Korea, Cuba, Venezuela—were or are oppressive authoritarian regimes and economic failures of stagnation and poverty.

Progressives in North America, with the exception of old-line socialists such as Bernie Sanders, have innovated in ideology, jettisoning the economic class struggle and replacing it with identity classes: gender, race, sexuality, religion, nationality, ableness. Now it's (allegedly) whites (including "white adjacent" Asians and "hyperwhite" Jews), males, and Christians who are oppressors, and people of color, women, LGBTQ++, Muslims, and the disabled who are the oppressed victims.

The Progressives' identity class conflict has not only not led to "progress" in any discernible form, but also has led to social regression, resuscitating ugly forms of prejudice and discrimination while undermining public order and national sovereignty.

With the "social justice" trinity of "diversity, equity, and inclusion," Progressives have returned us to the days of deep Jim Crow, with some races seen as virtuous and others as evil, the only difference being that the colors have changed. Progressive "inclusion" means including preferred races and genders, and excluding the others, as we see in hiring, college admissions, funding, promotions, and awards. The latest example is New York State ranking people for COVID-19 medical treatment according to their race.

Equity, meaning the statistical equivalence of races and genders, in practice means more of the preferred and fewer of the despised. Objective measures, such as standardized tests, and advanced education programs, are cancelled, because they don't produce the desired "equity" results. Now institutionalized racism and discrimination are regarded as desirable by Progressives, as long as preferred categories benefit.

Typical Examples:

Because certain racial minorities are heavily overrepresented among criminals (and victims), Progressives have advocated "justice reform" to alleviate the price that minority criminals pay. Progressives thus have advocated defunding and disbanding the police, handcuffing police operations, releasing prisoners from incarceration, a halt to holding the dangerous accused prior to trial by means of no-bail release, and district attorneys who refuse to prosecute criminals, because they view criminals as "victims of society" rather than as victims of their own bad choices.

The result, a surprise to Progressives but to no one else, is a major breakdown in public order, with violent and nonviolent crime surging, particularly in Democrat-led cities, but also more broadly. For Progressives, public safety is systemic racism, so they're happy to do without it. Even though the vast number of victims of violence are racial minorities, the Progressives continue to obsess over the tiny number of police killings rather than the victims of crime. Progressives prefer criminals to victims of crime. They even encourage people to engage in illegal acts, as when they encouraged rioters in 2020 to loot, burn, and assault police, and then bailed them out until Progressive district attorneys refused to prosecute them.

Progressives particularly favor illegal aliens who have, uninvited and against our laws, entered the country. For Progressives, illegal aliens are preferred to citizens, because many are people of color, because the country is "systemically racist," and the racial balance needs to be changed in favor of people of color, and because Progressives think that they can capture illegal aliens as future voters by plying them with privileges paid for by tax-paying citizens. Progressives have coddled illegal aliens with sanctuary states, cities, and universities, thus protecting the criminals among the illegal aliens, a two-for-one benefit for Progressives.

Progressives are not fond of fair elections, which they always have a chance of losing, so they favor "electoral reform," which means a federal takeover of elections, contrary to the Constitution, and wish to remove all safeguards against illegal voting. They particularly hate the voter ID requirement, which they label "voter suppression," although IDs are heavily supported by the public and in use in most democracies around the world.

When Progressives say, "voter suppression," they mean the suppression of illegal votes, such as those cast by illegal immigrants, or multiple votes by individuals, or votes inscribed by third parties. The manipulation and undermining of voting is another manifestation of Progressives' authoritarian tendencies. Progressives don't really like democracy; they prefer the dictatorship of the proletariat, or, in today's identity politics transformation, dictatorship of the "marginalized and underserved" minorities.

To sum up: Liberals favor individual freedom, limited government, public safety, and national sovereignty. Progressives favor some races and genders over others, criminals over victims, illegal aliens over citizens, and authoritarian rule over democracy. Progressives are about illiberal as they could be. Don't call them "liberals."

Critical Race Theory's Chief Marketing Officer

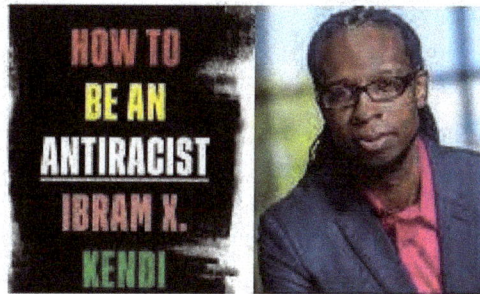

Per the Christopher F. Rufo "Critical Race Theory's Chief Marketing Officer" *City Journal* July 2021 article: Ibram X. Kendi's name is everywhere: public school curricula, corporate training programs, even the U.S. Navy's official reading list. The Boston University professor has become the latest star in the long tradition of racial activism.

But despite his laudatory reception in the press, his philosophy would jeopardize the American system of individual rights and equality under the law—and is finally getting the scrutiny it deserves. Ibram X. Kendi's brand of "antiracism" sanitizes for elite institutions the academic Left's most pernicious ideas.

Kendi's rise to prominence was swift. He published a bestselling book, *Stamped from the Beginning*, in 2016, but after the death of George Floyd in 2020, Kendi's subsequent book, *How to Be An Antiracist*, began selling an astonishing number of copies—including institutional sales to public schools, government agencies, and professional organizations, all seeking to understand the ongoing racial unrest. During the conflict, Kendi appeared constantly on television, delivered speeches to elite institutions, and positioned himself as the guru of America's racial reckoning.

But since the protests have died down, many Americans have realized that Kendi's brand of "antiracism" is nothing more than a marketing-friendly recapitulation of the academic Left's most pernicious ideas. While Kendi, born Ibram Henry Rogers, presents himself as a radical subversive, he is really an ideologist of elite opinion, subsidized heavily by America's corporations and public institutions. Kendi's work has been used and recommended by Fortune 100 companies, the federal bureaucracy, and the United States military—the very foundations of the power structure he claims to oppose.

Kendi's thesis—that if the races are equal, then racial disparities can owe only to racism and must be rectified through "antiracist discrimination"—is a simplistic reiteration of critical race theory's core concepts. As journalist Aaron Sibarium has documented, Kendi has borrowed ideas from critical race theory and translated them into a media-friendly narrative. "When I see racial disparities, I see racism," Kendi says, excluding other explanations. His logic often descends into circularity: when asked to define the word "racism," he told attendees at the Aspen Ideas Festival that it is "a collection of racist policies that lead to racial inequity that are substantiated by racist ideas."

In another nod to 1960s-style radicalism, Kendi also claims to oppose capitalism. "The life of racism cannot be separated from the life of capitalism," he says. "In order to truly be antiracist, you also have to truly be anti-capitalist." But Kendi, like fellow traveler Patrisse Cullors of Black Lives Matter, is a prolific capitalist in his personal life. He charged Fairfax County schools $20,000 an hour for a virtual presentation and has merchandised his entire line of ideas, releasing self-help products and even an "antiracist" baby book. He has accepted millions from tech and pharmaceutical companies on behalf of his Antiracism Center. Fighting against capitalism, as it turns out, is a lucrative enterprise.

Posturing aside, Kendi's actual proposals, from "defunding the police" to restricting free speech, are alarming. Kendi advocates race-based discrimination, arguing that "the only remedy to past discrimination is present discrimination." He proposes a federal Department of Antiracism that would be unaccountable to voters or legislators, permanently funded, and granted the power to suppress "racist ideas" and veto, nullify, or abolish any law at any level of government not deemed "antiracist."

As Americans begin to consider his ideas more seriously, Kendi finds himself on the defensive. In recent months, he has released a series of short-tempered articles and statements, claiming that "there is no debate about critical race theory" one moment, then distancing himself from critical race theory the next—notwithstanding that, only two weeks before, he had claimed that critical race theory was "foundational" to his work. When he's put on the spot, Kendi reverts to word games and deflection, rather than defending his position on substance.

Perhaps that is because Kendi's chief proposal—so-called "antiracist discrimination"—remains deeply unpopular. Despite the recent push to replace equality with "equity," Americans still support the system of individual freedom, equality under the law, and colorblind public policy. Even in deep-blue California and Washington State, voters have recently rejected affirmative action at the ballot box, notwithstanding heavy support for those measures from multinational corporations and the Democratic establishment.

Kendi fashions himself a revolutionary, but more and more of the public opposes his ideas. Like many activists before him, he will likely be absorbed into the fabric of elite institutions—where supposedly radical ideas are cosseted into conventional wisdom.

Critical Race Theory in Six Logical Fallacies

Logic is the friend of the wise person (a sapient being), and illogic is a snare to all (particularly Progressives). We ought to follow the logic and evidence wherever it leads as shown in the

Douglas Groothuis "Critical Race Theory in Six Logical Fallacies" National Association of Scholars Summer 2022 report:

On those issues that matter most—questions about God, humanity, meaning, morality, and society—we dispense with logic to our own peril. Illogic can damage individuals and entire societies, as Marxism has done repeatedly and worldwide. Illogic is damaging America as well through the acceptance of and application of Critical Race Theory (CRT), which has a penchant for fallacy production.

Some intellectual mistakes or fallacies are so commonly committed that they have been inducted into a canon of cognitive ignominy. Logical fallacies are divided into formal and informal fallacies. A formal fallacy is a blunder in a deductive argument, which invalidates the argument's form. We will instead concentrate on informal fallacies, which deceive in various ways, often through the use of irrelevant information, false assumptions, or incorrect or misleading uses of evidence. Let me define CRT and inspect its cognitive corruptions.

CRT is a neo-Marxist theory that grew out of Critical Theory (spearheaded by Herbert Marcuse). It was augmented by Critical Legal Studies and focuses more on racial and gender categories than on economic exploitation. Racism is everywhere and every white person is part of a system of racism that oppresses people of color (but mostly blacks). This system as a whole must be taken down and replaced by one that ensures "equity" (proportional representation for people of color) through socialism. Now to the fallacies.

1. Begging the Question

Begging the question assumes a conclusion without giving an argument. It substitutes an assertion for a logical case. "I am against capital punishment because two wrongs don't make a right," begs the question, since it assumes that capital punishment is another wrong in addition to the wrong of murder. A real argument against capital punishment requires reasoning that leads to the conclusion.

CRT lends itself to begging the question because it claims that its critics are animated by false consciousness, white supremacy, white privilege, or some other moral or cognitive impairment. The CRT advocate believes that those who disagree with CRT are not just wrong in a few ways, but are systemically deceived. Marxism originally applied this idea to economic actors, but it is now applied on a racial and gender basis by CRT. The oppressors are deceived; the oppressed are in the know (standpoint epistemology).

If someone begs the question and foreswears any counterevidence, then the idea becomes unfalsifiable. This is irrational. Every challenge to one's viewpoint can then be dismissed a priori. Proponents of CRT apply this idea to racism. White people are racists because they are part of systemic racism. No evidence to the contrary can exonerate them from this odious whiteness. When a claim is taken to be impervious to criticism, it loses rationality given its irrefutable dogmatism.

Things get worse when some CRT advocates claim that logic, critical thinking, appeals to standard logic, objective truth, objective evidence, normative grammar, and a linear approach to history and thinking in general are constitutive of the oppressor's ideology. If so, they can be denied. This denial leaves nothing to rationally argue with or to rationally argue from. But those who negate logic, truth, evidence, grammar, and linearity, quickly jettison their negations when arguing for their cases, since these elements are required for sharable discourse. They thus contradict themselves and disqualify themselves from rational discussion.

2. Argumentum Ad Hominem

This means "argument against the man." Instead of giving reasons against a position, those who hold the position are insulted as defective in some way that negates their view.

Of course, not all insults are fallacies. An insult can be justified by another's actions. Or an insult may be given that is unattached to any further claim. Saying "You are an idiot" or "You are a fascist," is true or false, but if it is unrelated to advancing another truth claim, there is no fallacy.

But, on the other hand, consider this indictment, "All who defend capitalism are racists." Of course, this statement might be true; however, a rational case needs to be made for it. One would have to demonstrate that (1) one thinks that a free-market system will disadvantage blacks, and (2) that (1) is a good thing. This case is not easily made.

If a white person advocates for merit-based admissions for higher education, this can be rejected as whitesplaining (due to false consciousness), since it supposedly favors whites over blacks. Whitesplaining means expressing a view based entirely on one's interests and privilege based on skin color. However, to advocate merit-based and race-neutral standards may have nothing to do with racism. It may simply be a color-blind endorsement of merit over race, whatever race benefits from it.

Consider sexual ethics. If you deem marriage to be a sacred and exclusive vow made between a man and a woman, this invites disparaging charges. You are homophobic since you are against gay marriage. You are also a religious bigot if your view is based on any sacred text or tradition. If you do not support some aspect of transgenderism, then you are transphobic.

The use of the term phobic is derived from psychology which uses it to refer to an irrational and pathological fear, such as agoraphobia (the fear of open places) or hydrophobia (the fear of water). Phobias are anxiety disorders. If you are homophobic, you have an irrational fear of homosexuals, which is a disorder. The question of moral judgment does not come up.

The label of phobic in these cases goes further. We pity or feel compassion for those who suffer from hydrophobia, but we resent or judge anyone who discriminates unfairly. Thus, this ad hominem vilifies people as both sick and immoral.

Admittedly, many are afflicted with phobias that impair their rationality and ability to judge fairly on diverse matters. However, to judge someone as phobic and thus untrustworthy in their judgments simply because they disagree with your views on moral matters is to commit the ad hominem fallacy.

In an essay called "Bulverism," C. S. Lewis exposed a new version of the ad hominem fallacy. Modern thinkers such as Freud and Marx have identified ways of discrediting ideas because they are "tainted at their source," either psychologically or politically. "The Freudians have discovered that we exist as bundles of complexes. The Marxians have discovered that we exist as members of some economic class." Ideas can be condemned and dismissed as stemming from psychological complexes or from one's economic class biases and prejudices. For CRT, ideas can be dismissed and condemned because those in "the dominant culture" (white) hold them.

Bulverists are right that many ideas are "tainted at their source," because of human prejudice, bias, turpitude, and other intellectual vices committed by our fallen race. However, if all ideas are tainted and thus unreliable, then CRT ideas are so affected. Thus, one could retort that, "You only say that because you are a Freudian." We could substitute "Marxist" or "CRT advocate" or anything else.

The Freudian and the Marxian are in the same boat with all the rest of us, and cannot criticize us from outside. They have sewn off the branch they were sitting on. If, on the other hand, they say that the taint need not invalidate their thinking, then neither need it invalidate ours. In which case they have saved their own branch, but also saved ours along with it.

To determine if a statement is true and reasonable, I need an argument to substantiate the claim. Everyone has biases and prejudices, but truth has neither biases nor prejudices, and finding truth through reason and evidence should be our goal. To Lewis again:

If you try to find out which [ideas] are tainted by speculating about the wishes of the thinkers, you are merely making a fool of yourself. You must first find out on purely logical grounds which of them do, in fact, break down as arguments. Afterwards, if you like, go on and discover the psychological causes of the error.

3. False Dichotomy

False dichotomy is a commonly committed fallacy. It is positively pernicious in CRT. It limits the options to two when, in fact, there are more than two options.

In some cases, there is a radical either/or. A person is dead or alive, not both. There are true dichotomies and false dichotomies, and the latter ought to be avoided. A true dichotomy is a binary such as: a woman is either pregnant or not pregnant. She cannot be both at the same time. The options are mutually exclusive and jointly exhaustive (covering all the possibilities). There is no third option. In computer coding, everything reduces to 1s and 0s. But life is more than computer coding.

Our use of the either/or may be fallacious. We may split life up by oversimplifying the case and then generating false dichotomies. In a semi-drunken stupor, a fool might say, "Look, you are either a Democrat or a Republican." This is a false dichotomy, since one might be a Libertarian or a Green Party member or something else.

The false dichotomy excludes genuine logical options, and this brings us to CRT. CRT assumes that if you do not accept CRT, then you think that racism is not a problem in America and would not want the history of slavery and Jim Crow to be taught in schools. This is a non sequitur because it is a false dichotomy. There is a third option: teach history without the ideology of CRT. One may reject CRT, and still believe racism is real, the disparities in black and white achievement need to be addressed (though perhaps not through socialism), and that America's troubled racial history should be taught, pondered, and rejected. But consider yet another fallacy.

4. Hasty Generalization

It is easy to be intellectually impatient and reach a conclusion hastily and without enough evidence. We are prone to this error, especially in the age of mediated electronic images. The image may lead one to think that a phenomenon is common and widespread when, in fact, it is the image that is common and widespread, not the phenomenon itself. A visceral image of a protestor being hit by a policeman, accompanied by persuasive commentary, supports the idea that police brutality is common and that the police ought to be "defunded" or otherwise censured. Similarly, a montage of images of unarmed blacks being shot by white police officers raises the ire of many and lends credibility to claims of systemic racism.

The adage that "a picture never lies" is false. It often lies when it is taken out of context and placed into a preset and ironclad narrative. If an innocent black man is wrongly killed or injured by the police, that is morally wrong and a fair trial should ensue. But there is more to be considered than merely a series of images, since so much can be left out, such as a violent resisting of arrest that occurred before the video images of the shooting. Getting the whole story about police violence against blacks requires hard statistics and social analysis about rates of violence and police policies. It is easier to react quickly than to reason carefully. If so, we commit the fallacy of hasty generalization.

5. The Use/Mention Fallacy

In our hypersensitive culture, one can get into deep trouble simply by speaking or writing a word or phrase deemed offensive. These terms are often epithets—words that sharply derogate others. However, one can mention an epithet without using it.

Consider a non-taboo epithet: Bill says, "John is a jerk." Here, Bill uses the epithet "jerk." That is, he is insulting John. Consider another case. Don says, "Bill said that 'John is a jerk.'" Here Don is mentioning the use of "jerk" by Bill. Don is not using the word "jerk" to describe John. He is reporting what Bill said. If someone said, "Don called John a jerk," he would be committing the use/mention fallacy in his error.

The stakes escalate quickly concerning racial epithets, such as the n-word. Neal A. Lester rightly says that the "word is inextricably linked with violence and brutality on black psyches and derogatory aspersions cast on black bodies." Thus, no one should use the n-word as an epithet.

It used to be safe to mention an epithet if it was clear that one was not using it. By mentioning it you are, as it were, putting quotation marks around the offensive term or phrase. In conversation, this can be indicated by making the scare quotes gesture. One might say with the proper gesticulation, "In the film, 'No Way Out,' several characters call the lead character a (they then say the n-word with all its original letters)." I do not advise saying or writing out the n-word, even in this context, but this person is not using the n-word in the sense I described. He is mentioning it. To say that this person used the term is to commit the use/mention fallacy.

This is simple, but some people are obtuse. Inside Higher Ed reports that "Augsburg University in Minnesota suspended a professor for using the n-word during a class discussion about a James Baldwin book in which the word appeared—and for sharing essays on the history of the word with students who complained to him about it." Professor Phillip Adamo was quoted in this piece as saying, "I see a distinction between use and mention. To use the word, to inflict pain or harm, is unacceptable. To mention the word, in a discussion of how the word is used, is necessary for honest discourse." Adamo, who is white, asked one of his students to read a quote by the black writer James Baldwin from his essay *The Fire Next Time* (1963), which used the n-word. In discussion, he mentioned the word himself.

The offended students should have taken issue with Baldwin himself, since he, a black man, used the word. Instead, they went after the Professor, who merely mentioned the word. The university suspended the Professor for two terms. Such is the power of fallacies.

6. A Newcomer: The Cancellation Fallacy

We end our sad tour of logical fallacies with a new fallacy. This fallacy is a team effort, a collection of at least five fallacies packed into one. I call it the cancellation fallacy. It is so commonly heard and so egregious that it deserves analysis.

The phrase "cancel culture" popped up in 2020 after the death of George Floyd. Angry crowds felled and defaced statues of those deemed racist. Churches were vandalized. Some schools changed their names if their namesakes were deemed racist. Donald Trump and others have been deplatformed in social media purges. An entire platform, Parler, was removed from Apple and Google apps and effectively shut down. "Cancel culture" is an epidemic.

I will put the cancellation fallacy abstractly since it helps us see its basic structure.

- Someone (especially a POC) is offended by P (any statement, person, object, process, or event).

- Therefore (i), P is wrong.

- The moral wrong committed by one who holds P is racism, homophobia, transphobia, or the like

- Therefore (ii), whoever affirms P must be cancelled.

- Unless others denounce P, (iii) they too must be cancelled, since "Silence is violence."

The cancellation fallacy is a synergistic and strenuous effort. It is a high achievement of sophistry. But it suffers from at least five errors:

- First, it equates taking offense with a proper moral judgment. Emotional reactions may be proper or improper.

- Second, it commits the ad hominem fallacy (discussed above). If you offend me, you are a bad person, and bad people cannot give good arguments, which is false.

- Third, the supposed wrongness is placed into a broad condemning category, such as racism, and thus commits the straw man fallacy. It may offend you that I don't want statues of Abraham Lincoln torn down, but that, in itself, does not make me a racist.

- Fourth, the threat of cancellation is a form of intimidation and means punishment if the threat is enacted. This commits the fallacy of argumentum ad baculum or "if you don't agree with me, I will hurt you. Therefore, agree with me." Today, this translates as: "Those critical of Critical Race Theory will be cancelled, which means losing your book contract, your employment, your social status, and more."

- Fifth, to claim that if I do not oppose P, then I must endorse P, commits the fallacy of the argument from silence. Not saying anything ("silence") cannot, in itself, be used to indict someone.

Fallacies Be Gone!

Fallacies are the bane of critical thinking. They trick us by their perennial cunning into holding false beliefs because of unsound reasoning and inadequate evidence. Anyone may be subject to deceitfulness, so we should be alert and alert others to these cognitive dangers, especially on matters as consequential as Critical Race Theory, which has a peculiar talent for racking up logical fallacies and even inventing a new one.

Statistical Disparities Among Groups Are Not Proof of Discrimination

Statistical disparities among groups are the norm in every facet of human life, including those in which discrimination cannot possibly play a role. To cling to a narrative that asserts racial discrimination as the only cause of statistical disparities turns a blind eye to reality and leads to harmful Progressivism policies.

From the Bradley Thomas "Statistical Disparities Among Groups Are Not Proof of Discrimination" Foundation for Economic Education (FEE) May 2019 report: In spite of this, however, perhaps the most prevalent pretext leftists have used for massive state coercion over the last 50 years is that disparities in outcomes between races, genders, or nationalities are de facto evidence of discrimination.

"Institutional" racism and sexism are the only possible causes of such disparities, the experts tell us. Society's prejudices and bigotry are so ingrained that only by growing the leviathan state can these negative results be corrected, they insist.

Does Disparity Entail Discrimination?

But if such disparities do arise absent discrimination perpetrated by "society," then assumptions about statistical disparities "lose their validity as evidence," Thomas Sowell notes in his book *Civil Rights: Rhetoric or Reality:*

There are many decisions wholly within the discretion of those concerned, where discrimination by others is not a factor—the choice of television programs to watch, opinions to express to poll takers, or the age at which to marry, for example. All these show pronounced patterns that differ from group to group.

The bottom line, Sowell concludes, is that "Statistical disparities extend into every aspect of human life" and that "statistical disparities are commonplace among human beings."

Income Inequality

Problems abound with how academics diagnose even seemingly straightforward measures like income inequality and discrimination.

The real issue is not with income inequality itself but with the processes put in motion in hopes of eliminating inequality.

For example, Sowell contends most income statistics are crude aggregates. The implicit assumption that the mere existence of income disparities is evidence of racial discrimination is unsubstantiated. Simply examining the average age differences among different demographics can explain away a portion of the income inequality that intellectuals proclaim exists due to discrimination. Those races and nationalities with older average ages would naturally boast higher average incomes due to being more experienced.

Adding factors like education level and personal career choices explains much of the rest.

The real issue, Sowell concludes, is not with income inequality itself but with the processes put in motion in hopes of eliminating inequality, which involve damaging government intervention and welfare programs.

Color vs. Culture

Moreover, when evaluating the "disparities are proof of discrimination" narrative, we can compare the levels of economic success among people of color. After all, a racist society just sees people of color and does not differentiate based upon different backgrounds.

As Sowell wrote, "Blacks may 'all look alike' to racists, but there are profound internal cultural differences among blacks."

As a result, comparing results for people of the same color but different culture is a valuable tool to provide an indication of other factors besides discrimination at work.

One source of data is a recent American Community Survey Report from the US Census Bureau that analyzes characteristics of selected Sub-Saharan African and Caribbean ancestry groups. Among these "ancestry groups," 60 percent or more are foreign-born.

Culture unquestionably plays a role in income and poverty disparities.

For instance, in 2012 the US poverty rate for Jamaicans was reported as 14.8 percent, Ethiopians 19.7 percent, and Nigerians 12.8 percent. All the rates were significantly lower than the rate of 28 percent for blacks as a whole.

Furthermore, the median income for Jamaican males was $41,969 and $39,155 for females; $34,018 for male Ethiopians and $30,253 for females; and $50,922 for male Nigerians and $44,874 for females.

Two of the three of these male ancestry groups noticeably out-earned the median rate of $37,526 for black males overall, while the same two groups outpaced the overall female black median income of $33,251.

Additionally, these three ancestry groups had significantly lower rates of poverty and higher median incomes than the Hispanic population.

How were these people of color, often without the benefit of growing up in America, able to clear the "barriers" of a discriminatory "system" far better than other people of color? Culture unquestionably plays a role in income and poverty disparities, even in situations comparing people of color where "discrimination" can be ruled out.

The Disparities Narrative Is a Pretext for Greater State Control

Nobody is arguing that racial or ethnic discrimination has been eliminated. But to cling to a narrative that asserts racial discrimination as the only cause of statistical disparities in measures such as income and poverty turns a blind eye to reality and leads to harmful policies.

Perhaps making matters worse is the promotion of the narrative of an all-powerful "system" that is structured unfairly and creates a sense of helplessness among those labeled "victims" of said barriers to economic prosperity.

"Why study and discipline yourself in preparation for the adult world if the deck is completely stacked against you anyway?" Sowell asked rhetorically.

Progressives like to lecture us about embracing diversity but then also deny that such diversity lends itself naturally to differences in outcomes. Instead, they choose to play identity politics based on faulty assumptions in pursuit of greater social control.

10 – BLM is America's # 1 Progressive Organization, With a Marxist Foundation

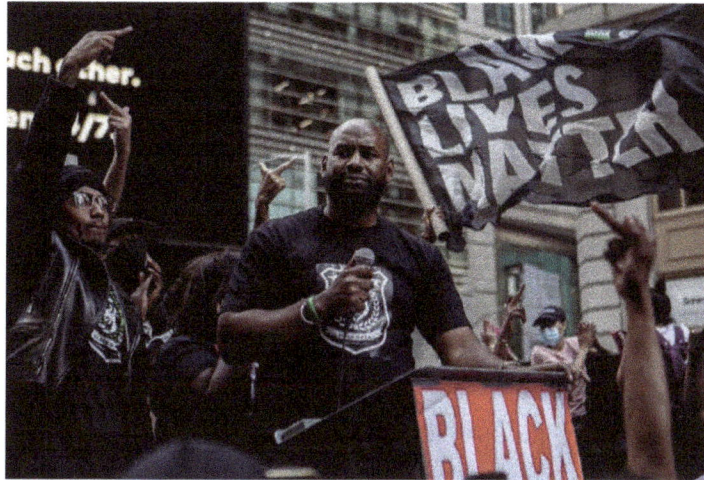

Credit: New York Post. Hawk Newsome, Greater NYC BLM chapter leader,
"If change doesn't happen, then 'we will burn down this system.'"

The George Floyd protests that have precipitated great changes throughout American society were not spontaneous events as shown in the Mike Gonzalez *BLM: The Making of a New Marxist Revolution* 2021 book:

Americans did not suddenly rise up in righteous anger, take to the streets, and demand not just that police departments be defunded, but that all the structures, institutions, and systems of the United States—all supposedly racist—be overhauled.

The 12,000 or so demonstrations and 633 related riots that followed Floyd's death took organizational muscle. The movement's grip on institutions from the classroom to the ballpark required ideological commitment. Both were provided by the various Black Lives Matter organizations.

This book examines who the BLM leaders are, delving into their backgrounds and exposing their agendas. They are shown to be avowed Marxists who say they want to dismantle our way of life. Along with their fellow activists, they make savvy use of social media to spread their message and organize marches, sit-ins, statue-tumblings, and riots. In 2020 they seized upon the video showing George Floyd's suffering as a pretext to unleash a nationwide insurgency.

Certainly, no person of good will could object to the proposition that "black lives matter" as much as any other human life. But Americans need to understand how their laudable moral concern is being exploited for purposes that many of them would not approve.

Black Lives Matter (BLM) Marxist Foundations & Anti-America Agenda

"If change doesn't happen, then 'we will burn down this system'" states the Greater New York Black Lives Matter leader Hawk Newsome.

From *Crime Rate Madness*: According to the Black Lives Matter website, their goal is to promote "Freedom, Liberation and Justice" and "to eradicate white supremacy and build local power to intervene in violence inflicted on Black communities by the state and vigilantes." The movement's ideological roots however, run deeper than bringing justice to victims of police brutality.

In a June 2020 interview with Fox News, Hawk Newsome, chairman of Black Lives Matter of Greater New York stated, "If this country doesn't give us what we want, then we will burn down this system and replace it. I could be speaking figuratively; I could be speaking literally. It's a matter of interpretation."

One of the BLM co-founders, Patrisse Khan-Cullors, explained the foundation of the movement, inspired by her and co-founders Alicia Garza and Opal Tometi, in an interview in 2015. "We actually do have an ideological frame," she told The Real News. "Myself and Alicia in particular are trained organizers. We are trained Marxists."

One click into the "What We Believe" portion of the BLM website reveals a far broader agenda for the organization. Stated goals include "disrupt the Western-prescribed nuclear family structure." Another mission statement refers to its members as "comrades" a common moniker used by communists.

In addition, the newest Black Lives Matter campaign, #WhatMatters2020, focused on highlighting certain political issues such as "racial injustice, police brutality, criminal justice reform, Black immigration, economic injustice, LGBTQIA+ and human rights, environmental injustice, access to healthcare, access to quality education, and voting rights and suppression" as well as "government corruption" and "commonsense gun laws" to emphasize and push in the 2020 election.

Using target goals, the organization hopes to increase the black voting demographic, educate, and amplify on the previously mentioned political goals, and increase voter registration for younger generations, the black demographic, and "allies." Using ActBlue, a platform dedicated to creating fundraising for "Democratic candidates and committees, Progressive organizations, and nonprofits that share our values," Black Lives Matter solicits donations to further their goals.

Vision For Black Lives: End the War on Black People

Also from *Crime Rate Madness*: The Movement for Black Lives (M4BL) launched the Vision for Black Lives, a comprehensive and visionary policy agenda for the post-Ferguson Black liberation movement, in August of 2016. The Vision, endorsed by over 50 Black-led organizations in the M4BL ecosystem and hundreds of allied organizations and individuals, has since inspired campaigns across the country to achieve its goals.

Per their website content and website link in the Appendix, after three years of consultations, writing retreats and Zoom sessions, research, and outreach, we are relaunching the Vision for

Black Lives 2020. We will be rolling out revised, updated, and expanded policy briefs for each of the six planks of the platform over the coming months, leading up to a National Black Convention in August of 2020.

We begin with the first plank of our Vision: End the War on Black People, released on Juneteenth as we converge across the country in resistance to police and state sanctioned violence.

This document does not represent the entirety of our Vision—it is only the first section of six and focuses on state violence. We will be re-releasing revised and expanded policy briefs in each of the remaining sections of the Vision—Reparations, Economic Justice, Invest/Divest, Community Control and Political Power—over the course of 2020

Per M4BL there are many wars being waged against black people. However, any sapient being knows this is not the case, nonetheless, decide for yourself and critique their policy objectives below taken from their 2020 Policy Platform on their website (the caps are theirs):

- END THE WAR ON BLACK COMMUNITIES

- END THE WAR ON BLACK YOUTH

- END THE WAR ON BLACK WOMEN

- END THE WAR ON BLACK TRANS, QUEER, GENDER NONCONFORMING AND INTERSEX PEOPLE

- END THE WAR ON BLACK HEALTH AND BLACK DISABLED PEOPLE

- END THE WAR ON BLACK MIGRANTS

- END TO ALL JAILS, PRISONS, AND IMMIGRATION DETENTION

- END THE DEATH PENALTY

- END THE WAR ON DRUGS

- END THE SURVEILLANCE ON BLACK COMMUNITIES

- END TO PRETRIAL DETENTION AND MONEY BAIL

- THE DEMILITARIZATION OF LAW ENFORCEMENT

- END THE USE OF PAST CRIMINAL HISTORY

Support for Black Lives Matter Movement Has Decreased (For Now)

Pew Research Center surveys show public support for the Black Lives Matter movement surged in June amid worldwide protests after a white Minneapolis police officer knelt on George Floyd's neck and killed him. That increase included a swell in support among white people, according to Pew. But a few months later, support returned to its pre-June levels.

Per a detailed report in The Dallas Morning News by Jared Weber in November 2020 titled "Support for Black Lives Matter movement has decreased significantly since June, local and national polls agree" the article notes: In North Texas, Tramonica Brown said, the movement against racism and police violence is at a different point than a few months ago. Worries about the coronavirus and the election mean the protests occupy a smaller place in people's minds.

As a result, she said, major events such as a Kentucky grand jury's September decision to issue no charges in the March killing of Breonna Taylor didn't draw as much outrage as they would have a few months earlier.

Still, Brown said protesters' energy remains strong—with or without the massive support they appeared to have several months ago. "Those white allies were not allies that we had to begin with," Brown said. "They were just there as an extra body. They helped fill up space."

According to Pew, 55% of respondents supported Black Lives Matter in a 2017 phone poll conducted nationally. That figure rose to 67% at the height of protests in June. More white people than ever before—including 37% of white Republicans—said they at least somewhat supported the movement then.

But both of those figures dipped in Pew's most recent survey, released in September.

Support among whites dropped to 45% and as low as 16% among white Republicans. Support among Latinos also declined by 11 percentage points, and by six points among Asian Americans. Support among Black respondents rose to 87%—adding one percentage point since June.

Where Is the BLM $60 Million?

On Jan. 5, 2022, Washington State Attorney General Robert Ferguson issued a "Closure Notice" demanding that BLM "immediately cease" all fundraising activities, because it had failed to file its annual financial disclosure report for tax year 2020, due last November.

California Attorney General Rob Bonta followed suit a few weeks later and threatened to hold individual leaders personally liable for late fees. Despite these clear directives, Black Lives Matter Global Network Foundation (BLMGNF) continued fundraising until reports exposed their flagrant violations.

As reported in the Peter Flaherty "Where Is the BLM $60 Million?" Real Clear Politics article in February 2022: According to those reports, the group's charity registration is also out of compliance in Connecticut, Maine, Maryland, New Jersey, New Mexico, North Carolina, and Virginia.

Indiana Attorney General Todd Rokita says BLM's refusal to answer basic questions about its finances and operations raises serious, even fundamental, questions about its mission, purpose, and ultimate legitimacy.

"It appears that the house of cards may be falling, and this happens eventually with nearly every scam, scheme, or illegal enterprise," the Republican attorney general told reporters. "I see patterns that scams kind of universally take: failure to provide board members, failure to provide even executive directors, failure to make your filings available. It all leads to suspicion."

BLMGNF founder Patrisse Cullors, a self-avowed Marxist who once called for the "end of Israel" during a 2015 Harvard panel discussion, resigned her post as executive director of the BLM money machine last May, with over $60 million in its coffers, ostensibly to focus on her second book and a television deal with Warner Bros.

But revelations about her personal finances, including the purchase of four homes totaling more than $3 million, were more likely the reasons for her sudden retreat from the spotlight. This news prompted criticism from local black activists, such as one black mother whose son was killed by Los Angeles police: "Black lives don't matter. Your pockets matter," she declared. "Y'all come into our lives and act like y'all got our back and y'all want to say, 'Black Lives Matter.' But after we bury our children, we don't see B, L or M, but y'all out here buying properties."

Speaking of buying properties, we do know where at least some of the $60 million went. It was transferred to BLM Canada to buy a $6 million mansion in Toronto, the former headquarters of Canada's Communist Party. Looks like BLM is returning to its roots.

There is, however, the potential for much bigger scandal. When Cullors resigned last May, she turned over the leadership to two associates. But they later issued a statement saying they never took charge since there was no agreement reached on their duties. Such a change in management requires approval by the organization's board of directors, not a unilateral decision by a resigning executive director.

Who exactly is in charge? Who is on the board? Where are the minutes of the board meetings? Where is a certified independent audit of its finances? Sixty million dollars is a lot of money, and nobody can say what's happened to it. There is more transparency and accountability in the operation of a local chapter of the Girl Scouts.

That is why the National Legal and Policy Center, an ethics watchdog group, has filed formal complaints with the attorneys general of California and Washington to do a full investigation of BLMGNF's finances and impose criminal sanctions if warranted.

Here's the Real Takeaway From Black Lives Matter's Sketchy Finances

Newly revealed IRS tax documents show the social justice nonprofit's leaders used "white guilt money" to enrich themselves. It's time to support local grassroots orgs instead as outlined in the Ernest Owens "Here's the Real Takeaway From Black Lives Matter's Sketchy Finances" Daily Beast May 2022 story:

Following the reveal of the Black Lives Matter Global Network Foundation's IRS tax documents, it's now safe to say that there's something questionable going on at the social justice nonprofit.

According to the group's Form 990, first reported by Associated Press, BLM is worth nearly $42 million in net assets—after spending more than $37 million of the $90 million it previously had on high-end real estate, familiar consultants, ambitious grants, and more.

One of the more concerning situations revealed by the financial disclosures is the fact that co-founder Patrisse Cullors was the foundation board's sole voting director, and held no board meetings, before stepping down. Under her leadership, Cullors authorized a six-figure payout to be given to her child's father for various services, paid $1.8 million to companies owned by her relatives, and ensured that her brother, Paul Cullors, was one of the highest-paid employees of BLM.

This is yet another wave of bad news for Cullors, who has constantly denied financial impropriety, as she has previously tried to quell any growing concerns around her decision-making. These tax documents not only proved that Cullors lied about misusing some of the funds (such as hosting a birthday party for her son and throwing a private Biden inauguration celebration in the multimillion dollar property intended for activists and creators), but that she did so repeatedly.

"I'm a human being that has made mistakes that want to change, want to challenge those mistakes and want to learn from those mistakes," Cullors told Trymaine Lee of MSNBC's "Into America" podcast. "And I think what's been hard is feeling like there isn't room and space for that."

While all of this news is disappointing and alarming, there's one truth that we should all take in: All politics is local, including the grassroots activism it takes to organize.

For years, much of what Cullors now describes as the "white guilt money" has been geared towards national organizations, like BLM, that say their missions are focused on addressing racial injustice. Cullors once made headlines for saying that hearing the term "990s" was "triggering" to her—but that's what nonprofit transparency looks like. If the public at large wanted to fund multimillion-dollar villas, top-flight exec travel, and cashed-out gigs for the founder's relatives, they could have easily donated to the Trump Foundation.

Local Black Lives Matter chapters across the country have for years raised concerns over how the national arm had been leaving them fiscally malnourished. And that this could happen as their co-founders garnered lucrative book deals, speaking engagements, and career opportunities.

For donors of all identities, giving to the national organization felt like an easy way to maximize impact. But I would bet that most donors are probably furious to see their money going towards anything but direct action on the ground.

It's hard not to imagine how this money could have best been spent if local chapters and other more direct on-the-ground activist groups were given a larger chunk of this money to do the actual work. To now be fully aware that a great deal of the $90 million raised for BLM during the racial uprisings of 2020 didn't actually go to fuel the continuation of similar activity on the local level—that feels like betrayal. Even worse, it's hard not to consider such fundraising as anything more than just a big grift.

Organizational Overview

Furthermore, from *Crime Rate Madness*, there is a "contentious distinction" over what Black Lives Matter is. "There are at least two versions of BLM. There's the BLM network founded by the three black female activists who created the #BlackLivesMatter hashtag. Then there's the BLM Movement, a more amorphous collection of racial justice groups."

Where the BLM Network is structured and has 34 chapters, the BLM movement is decentralized and relies "almost solely on local, rather than national, leadership." The movement "eschews hierarchy and centralized leadership." According to one of the BLM originating activists, Patrisse Cullors, the movement's "organizing is often spontaneous and not directed by one person or group of people."

The Black Lives Matter Movement's collection of groups has come to take a variety of forms and political shapes, from groups that favor protest and have no intention of supporting candidates, to others that have begun lobbying candidates and elected officials on legislative issues, to others "hoping to use money to make a difference in elections."

In October 2020, activists from St. Louis created the Black Lives Matter PAC, a political action committee designed to endorse Progressive, left-wing candidates and mobilize black voters. The Black Lives Matter movement leaders are not officially affiliated with Black Lives Matter PAC, but the Black Lives Matter Global Network Foundation does advertise the PAC to its email list.

Political Platform

In 2016, a coalition of over 50 organizations known as the Movement for Black Lives released a wide-reaching and in-depth platform detailing the coalition's policy demands. This platform was known as the "Vision 4 Black Lives" and laid out six far-left policy planks/demands pulled largely from the 1996 Black Panther Party ten-point program.

Per Weber, *The Atlantic* criticized the extremist parts of the platform as "elements unpalatable to most major politicians and people," such as extensive "reparations" that could "limit its potential to sway large audiences." The platform denounced the U.S. military, characterized Israel as an "apartheid state," demanded extensive redistribution of financial resources, and insisted upon the socialization of broad sectors of the American economy. It also demanded "special protections for trans, queer, and gender-nonconforming people ... a call for free education for black people, and a proposal to implement black economic cooperatives."

Criticisms and Controversies

Weber notes that critics blame BLM for worsening race relations in America. Even family members of Jamar Clark, who was shot by police in 2015, have urged BLM to settle the protests because "there's a fine line between protesting a cause and hurting the community." One of BLM's originating activists, Alicia Garza, has argued that black people cannot be racist, because "Racism is a system" rather than the act of merely judging people based on race.

Some commentators have argued that recent increases in crime and violence against police are the result of a so-called "Ferguson effect," named for the city that saw the first large Black Lives Matter demonstrations after the death of Michael Brown in 2014. In response to Federal Bureau of Investigation (FBI) findings that homicides of police officers have risen since then, some observers identified Black Lives Matter protests as a contributing cause to an anti-police environment.

The FBI released a report that found that 28 percent of those who used deadly force against police officers "were motivated by hatred of police and a desire to 'kill law enforcement,' in some cases fueled by social and political movements." The FBI reported that the perpetrators of attacks on police in Baton Rouge, Louisiana, and Dallas, Texas stated they were "influenced by the Black Lives Matter movement." The Dallas attack occurred at the end of a BLM protest "when a gunman who had a vendetta against white cops [killed] five and injured several other on-duty officers."

Barbara Reynolds, a veteran of the 1960s civil rights movement and an author, writes that many civil rights activists agree with BLM's goals but "fundamentally disagree with their approach." According to Reynolds, BLM uses "confrontational and divisive tactics" marked by boorish rhetoric and profanity, and rejects proven protest methods, which make it "difficult to distinguish legitimate activists from the mob actors who burn and loot." Reynolds argues that while 1960s-era civil rights activists used "loving" and "nonviolent" means to win allies and mollify enemies, the BLM Movement uses "rage and anger."

Reynolds argues that while "the civil rights movement valued all human lives, even those of people who worked against us," BLM focuses too narrowly on "black pain and suffering," shouting down "those who dare to utter 'all lives matter.'" She argued that in order to "win broader appeal [the BLM Movement] must work harder to acknowledge the humanity in the lives of others."

Black Lives Matter operations have been largely known for their extremism. Daunasia Yancey, a Black Lives Matter activist says, "We're a radical organization, with radical politics, and we have radical tactics. There's no way of softening that." BLM marches in Baltimore, Atlanta, Miami, Los Angeles, and Oakland took over interstates, forcing those cities to shut down roads. Numerous BLM demonstrators were arrested for chaining themselves to subway trains in San Francisco, to the irritation of otherwise-sympathetic locals.

The BLM Movement has also received wide coverage of its protestors interrupting and agitating 2016 Presidential candidates Hilary Clinton, Bernie Sanders, and Donald Trump. BLM originator Patrisse Cullors said the reasoning behind the protests of the Democratic Party is that the Democrats have "milked the Black vote while creating policies that completely decimate Black communities." Critics argue that Black Lives Matter "has become a movement about instilling fear—sometimes in politicians, sometimes in 'white people,' but mainly and most significantly in police."

Funding

It is estimated that groups associated with the BLM Movement have taken in $133 million since 2013. Organizations associated with liberal billionaire George Soros are said to have provided at least $33 million to various BLM movement groups since 2016, Weber reports.

In 2015, the fundraising club Democracy Alliance, led by liberal donors like George Soros and Taco Bell heir Rob McKay, recommended "its donors step up check writing to a handful of endorsed groups that have supported the Black Lives Matter movement." BLM Movement groups which received support from the Democracy Alliance were the Black Youth Project 100, the Center for Popular Democracy, the Black Civic Engagement Fund, Color of Change, and the Advancement Project.

Additionally, the Ford Foundation and the Borealis Philanthropy created the Black-led Movement Fund, a funding vehicle for the Movement for Black Lives, the coalition of groups responsible for the extremist "Vision 4 Black Lives." The fund has received "pledges of more than 100 million dollars from liberal foundations and others eager to contribute." So What is Black Lives Matter Really About?

The Hypocrisy of the BLM Movement

As reported in Diane Dimond's column in *The Winchester Star* in July 2020 that is syndicated by Creators with the heading of "The hypocrisy of the Black Lives Matter Movement," she notes that in New York, BLM organizers concentrate on painting their name on streets yet do nothing to help stop the ever-increasing civilian slaughter of mostly Black citizens.

Shootings during the first six months of 2021 are up 46%, and homicides increased more than 20%. Yet BLM's cries for defunding the police continue, and the mayor's response was to cut $1 billion from the NYPD budget. The department's anti-crime unit—focused on disarming criminals and curbing violent crime in mostly minority neighborhoods—was disbanded.

Dimond adds, "In what world does that make sense?"

In Chicago, where more than 100 mostly Black people were shot by civilians over a recent weekend, one local reverend said it's an "open season" killing field. Nearly 2,000 Chicagoans have been shot so far in 2021, hundreds fatally, and, yes, the majority of victims and known assailants are Black.

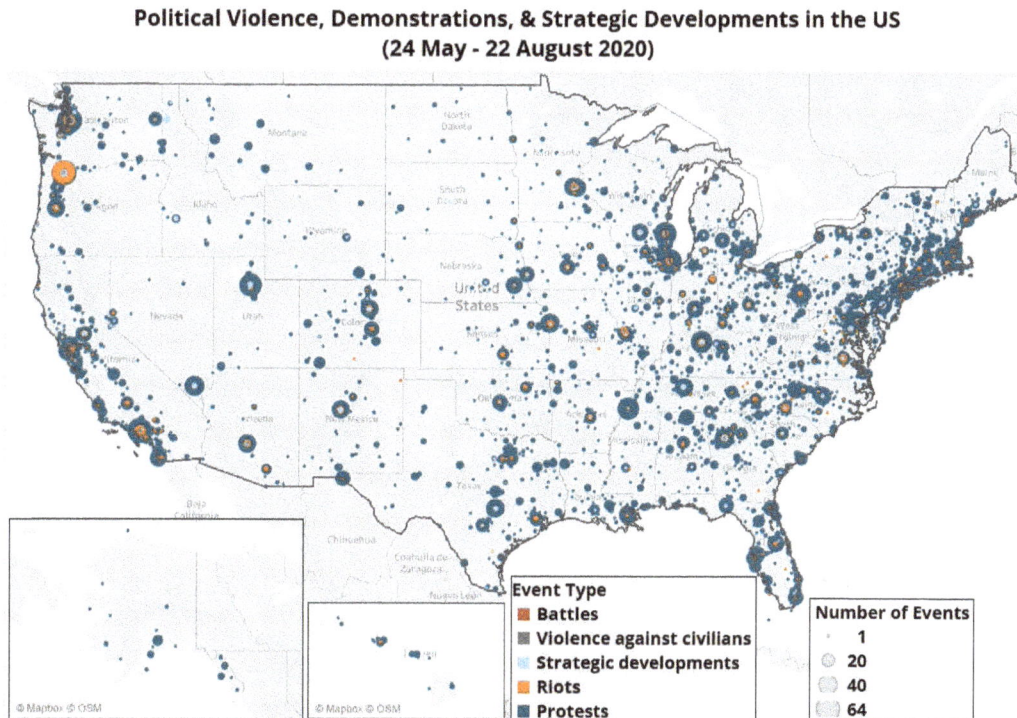

Political Violence, Demonstrations, & Strategic Developments in the US (24 May - 22 August 2020)

Credit: ACLED, US Crisis Monitor.

So, where is the Black Lives Matter movement in Chicago to try to curb this trend? Has BLM piled into the Windy City to marshal local ministers, community leaders and concerned citizens to try to combat the carnage against Black Americans? No.

In Atlanta, at the burned-out Wendy's restaurant where BLM gathered after police killed a Black man who shot at them with a Taser, another tragedy took place. An 8-year-old Black child was fatally shot as she rode by in a car. It was yet another mindless black-on-black shooting. Her father later told the criminals: "You killed a child. She didn't do nothing to nobody. Black Lives Matter? You killing your own."

The mantra of Black Lives Matter is now part of the American lexicon. All clear-thinking citizens embrace it and the idea that violent police tactics need to be abolished. Embracing those ideals and the BLM organization are two very different things.

Top 10 Reasons Why Sapient Beings Do Not Support the BLM Movement

Ryan Bomberger has a rather unique perspective revealed in his Townhall post in June 2020 with the title of "Top 10 Reasons I Won't Support the #BlackLivesMatter Movement." Adopted into a large multi-racial family of 15 (Bomberger like Obama is bi-racial), he grew up in a Christian home that exuded compassion. Today he's an adoptee and adoptive father. As an Emmy Award-winning creative professional he is passionate about igniting, in people's hearts and minds, an awareness and a love of the intrinsic value we all possess.

In Bomberger's own words, here are his top ten reasons why he will never support the BLM movement:

The premise isn't true. I hate racism. And I hate when it's used as a political weapon. According to the FBI's latest homicide statistics, I'm 11 times more likely to be killed by someone of my own brown complexion than a white person. Also, a comprehensive 2019 study concluded: "White officers are not more likely to shoot minority civilians than non-White officers." Every loss of life is tragic, but *Washington Post's* database on police-involved deaths puts things into further context. In 2020, among those killed were (all males): 2 Native Americans, 9 Asians, 46 Hispanics, 76 blacks, 149 unlabeled individuals and 149 whites (whose deaths don't get reported by national mainstream media). Only nine black individuals were actually unarmed.

There is no goal of forgiveness or reconciliation. None. It's never mentioned on their sites. You can't talk about the sins of the past and expect to move forward if there is no intention of forgiveness. I'm tired of the deeply prejudiced oppressed/oppressor critical race theory paradigm. It's not Gospel-centered. This should, immediately, be a deal-breaker for Christians.

It's all about Black Power. It's plastered all over the MFBL website. BLMF founders explain their "herstory": "It became clear that we needed to continue organizing and building Black power across the country." I don't promote a colorblind society; I love all of our diverse hues of skin. But I'm so much more than my pigmentation. Martin Luther King promoted "God's power and human power." I'm with him.

They heavily promote homosexuality and transgenderism. "We foster a queer-affirming network. When we gather, we do so with the intention of freeing ourselves from the tight grip of heteronormative thinking." I'm not embracing confusion. Loving every human being is not the same as loving every human doing.

They completely ignore fatherhood. From BLMF: "We disrupt the Western-prescribed nuclear family structure requirement by supporting each other as extended families and 'villages' that collectively care for one another, especially our children, to the degree that mothers, parents, and children are comfortable." Well, every "village" that has fatherless families is a village that suffers higher crime rates, higher drug usage, higher abortion rates, higher drop-out rates, higher poverty rates, and so much more. #DadsMatter.

They demand reparations. Ok. Sooooo, I guess the white half of me will have to pay the black half of me? If Progressives want to push reparations, start with the Party of Slavery and Jim Crow—the Democrat Party! Let them ante up. But the #BlackLivesMatter movement bizarrely demands: "Reparations for…full and free access for all Black people (including undocumented and currently and formerly incarcerated people) to lifetime education…retroactive forgiveness of student loans, and support for lifetime learning programs." Uhhh, good luck with that.

They want to abolish prisons and police forces. And…cue utter chaos. MFBL asserts: "We believe that prisons, police and all other institutions that inflict violence on Black people must be abolished…" Defund and remove the police have been rallying cries. That would be anarchy in any community. I advocate some needed police reforms and better community/police relations, but this is just foolishness.

They are anti-capitalism. Oh the irony of this declaration made by a movement that is the result of capitalism: "We are anti-capitalist. We believe and understand that Black people will never achieve liberation under the current global racialized capitalist system." The videos that make us aware of police brutality are captured on phones that are a result of capitalism. The best way to elevate people out of material poverty. Capitalism. This system is why the United States is the most charitable nation.

Colin Kaepernick supports it. A "biracial" adoptee, Kaepernick is now obsessed with his "blackness." He idolizes the late murderous Fidel Castro and Che Guevara and worships Malcolm X (just see his social media feeds). Malcolm X was anti-integration, pro-violence, and a member of the virulently racist Nation of Islam (who forced him out). Kaepernick makes millions from Nike—a company whose entire Executive Leadership Team is white (isn't this white supremacy???)—that makes its shoes in the most murderous regime in the world. Kaepernick, of course, is completely silent on that. But you know, #SocialJusticeWarrior.

Apparently, not all black lives matter. Pro-abortion BLMF declared: "We deserve and thus we demand reproductive justice [aka abortion] that gives us autonomy over our bodies and our identities while ensuring that our children and families are supported, safe, and able to thrive." Aborted children don't thrive. BLM groups announced "solidarity" with "reproductive justice" groups back in February 2015. You cannot simultaneously fight violence while celebrating it.

The Commissars Will See You Now

As revealed in the Christopher F. Rufo "The Commissars Will See You Now" *City Journal* March 2023 report: At Florida International University (FIU), DEI bureaucrats have made political activism the center of academic life. To add to the problem of DEI activism on campus, DEI administrators create internal cadres by recruiting students into publicly subsidized left-wing activism.

To this end, FIU and hundreds of other college campuses offer various programs, such as the Social Justice Badge Program, which recruit, train, and deploy student activists with the goal of implementing the "redistribution of power" and achieving "equity," or equal outcomes. The badge program invites students to participate in a long series of assessments, conferences, seminars, trainings, and initiatives—a comprehensive political education driven by the bureaucracy, rather than the faculty.

The content of these programs is pure left-wing activism. The seminar materials begin with "land acknowledgements," promote the Black Lives Matter movement, and describe life in the United States as a system of "Power, Privilege, and Oppression." In FIU's social-justice narrative, white Christians are assigned the role of oppressor—the lessons describe "Judeo-Christian holidays," for example, as a form of "cultural imperialism"—and "trans," "non-binary," and "Black people" are assigned the role of the oppressed. Whites must confront their "privilege," while minorities must work to seize "power." For one group, the work represents a spiritual purging; for the other, the work consists of bringing down the oppressor, who alone "has the power."

The endpoint is political agitation.

In a training program titled "Grassroots Activism and Protest Safety," the DEI managers encourage students to engage in protests and demonstrations to "empower social change" and "advocate for diversity and inclusion." The university valorizes Black Lives Matter, the #MeToo movement, and the March for Our Lives anti-gun movement—in other words, exclusively left-wing political activism. FIU instructs students to target "elected officials, government staff, and outside interest groups" with their messages and to prepare for violence. "Bring a bandana to cover nose and mouth," the lesson reads. "Download a messaging app that has end to end encryption."

It's worth reiterating that these programs are not part of any academic department; they are run by the bureaucracy, in the interest of the bureaucracy. The Social Justice Badge Program and the dozens of similar initiatives across FIU's sprawling administration provide employment for activist employees, most not competent to serve in academic roles. The programs also create their own demand, as students get rewarded with titles, status, and trinkets for their participation in publicly subsidized political work.

And student programs are just the beginning.

The ambition of DEI is not only to promote the ideology but also to assert its authority over every process on campus. In sum, this represents an effort, without the consent of legislators, to place the university as a whole under a new form of governance: the bureaucratic management of academic life according to the dictates of racial ideology.

On faculty recruiting, for example, the university's DEI bureaucrats have established ideological filters for potential hires by means of "diversity statements," which require applicants to confess their faith in the basic premises of left-wing racialism. At FIU, all faculty serving on search committees must submit to an intensive training program, STRIDE, which designates official "diversity advocates" who work to maintain the party line. Even in scientific and engineering fields, applicants must submit "diversity statements" to be considered for faculty positions. While such programs may conceal themselves in the innocuous language of "inclusion," they are, in reality, deeply coercive practices that limit scholarship to conventional left-wing ideas.

Like many public universities, FIU has also created what amounts to a racial spoils system.

Much of this is couched in bureaucratic terms, with an array of programs designed to "increase diversity" and "increase representation" of favored groups— those deemed avatars of historical victimhood. But others are more explicit. The Underrepresented Graduate Student Fellowship, for example, is openly advertised for "minority doctoral candidates" only—whites, in other words, are barred from applying. Another scholarship promoted by FIU, the McKnight Doctoral Fellowship Program, states simply that "applicants must be African American or Hispanic." Asians, Pacific Islanders, and Native Americans, in addition to European-Americans, are out of luck.

The most disturbing reality at public universities such as FIU is that the DEI movement is still in its infancy. In a few short years, the commissars have built intensive administrative programs, required political loyalty oaths from faculty, and implemented a system of rewards and punishments based on identity and ideology rather than character and merit. If left unchecked, the DEI bureaucracies will swallow universities whole. They will gradually re-segregate higher education according to the dictates of intersectionality and turn the principle of individual rights on its head. Political activism will replace the production of knowledge—and everyone will be worse off.

11 – Corporate, Government, Military & Non-Profit Organizations Go Woke

The modern woke-industrial complex divides us as a people. By mixing morality with consumerism, America's elites prey on our innermost insecurities about who we really are. They sell us cheap social causes and skin-deep identities to satisfy our hunger for a cause and our search for meaning, at a moment when we as Americans lack both.

Christopher F. Rufo has been reporting on Disney for more than a year, and has reliable sources inside the company when he broke a story about Disney forcing employees to engage in a critical race theory training program that denounced America as fundamentally racist, had its white employees complete a "white privilege checklist," and included exercises on "decolonizing" bookshelves.

Per the in-depth Christopher F. Rufo "Laying Siege to the Institutions" *Imprimis* April/May 2022 | Volume 51, Issue 4/5 report:

Disney's first reaction was to deflect. In response to accusations of racism, the company issued a press release denying the charge. Incredibly, it offered as proof the fact that it had produced the movie Black Panther—a kind of corporate variation on "I'm not racist, some of my best friends are black." This ridiculous response suggests that Disney executives were caught totally off guard. The elites who run our institutions, after all, are not accustomed to being challenged.

Disney eventually deleted information on the controversial training program from its internal website. But all things remaining the same, the program will resurface. This wasn't, after all, a case of well-intentioned people making a mistake. Leftist ideologies are now baked into the structures of these institutions in addition to Disney as the rest of this chapter will demonstrate.

Then a much bigger controversy began when the Disney Company waded into a political fight with Florida Governor Ron DeSantis.

DeSantis had signed a bill, passed by the state legislature, that prohibited teaching about gender ideology, sexual orientation, and sexuality in kindergarten, first grade, second grade, and third grade classrooms. Despite the fact that its opponents gave this bill an intentionally misleading name—the "Don't Say Gay" bill—it is supported, depending on the questions used by pollsters, by between 60 and 80 percent of Floridians.

The Case of the Disney Company

Acting against its own apparent business interest, Disney—the most famous children's entertainment corporation in history—came out publicly in opposition to this bill banning discussions of gender identity in elementary classrooms prior to the fourth grade. In an official statement, it declared that the company's goal was "for this law to be repealed . . . or struck down in the courts."

Shortly thereafter, my sources at Disney leaked a video to me of an hour-and-40-minute company-wide meeting about the controversy. And what did the video reveal?

- In a series of unedited clips that I released on social media, an executive producer at Disney said that she had been inserting what she called a "not-so-secret gay agenda" into children's programming, targeting kids as young as two years old, and had experienced no pushback.

- A production coordinator said that he had created a tracking program to make sure that the company was including enough transgender, non-binary, and asexual characters.

- The president of Disney's general entertainment content referenced a Disney initiative declaring that "50 percent of regular and recurring characters across Disney General Entertainment will come from underrepresented groups."

- And a diversity and inclusion manager talked about the company's new policy of doing away with the terms "ladies and gentlemen" and "boys and girls" at Disney theme parks.

These discussions weren't taking place in an Ivy League faculty lounge, but among high-level executives at Walt Disney. Americans were shocked, and rightfully so. The unmistakable gist of the video was that Disney was secretly trying to change, in a fundamental way, how children think about sexuality by engineering a narrative based on gender ideology.

Disney executives had marched into this controversy beating their chests, talking trash to Governor DeSantis, and committing the company to the overthrow of the bill protecting young children. But the leaked videos quickly generated over 100 million media impressions, and with public opinion heavily on the other side—not only in Florida, but nationwide—Disney was pummeled. People started canceling their subscriptions to Disney's streaming service, canceling planned trips to Disney theme parks, canceling Disney cruises, and thinking twice about letting their children watch Disney movies.

Elected officials noticed, too. The Florida legislature and Governor DeSantis have already revoked the special governance and tax status Disney has enjoyed since the 1960s. Disney's stock value plummeted nearly $50 billion in less than two months. And now Members of Congress are asking why Disney deserves automatic copyright extensions on things like Mickey Mouse—copyrights that customarily have a 28-year limit. If Congress lets Disney's various copyrights expire next year, it will cost Disney an additional multiple billions of dollars.

In summary, Disney's record on the issue of children and sexuality casts doubt on its claim to moral authority.

Biden Nationalizes the DEI Bureaucracy

In February 2023, President Joseph Biden quietly signed an executive order that promises to create a national DEI bureaucracy and embed the principles of left-wing racialism throughout the federal government. However, the president's recent executive order threatens to subvert the principles of liberty and equality.

Per the Christopher F. Rufo Biden "Nationalizes the DEI Bureaucracy" Substack February 2023 post:

The order, titled "Further Advancing Racial Equity and Support for Underserved Communities Through the Federal Government," relies on three key strategies: creating internal cadres and power centers through the deployment of "Agency Equity Teams;" funding third-party political activism through grants to "community[-based] organizations;" and weaponizing civil rights law by requiring federal agencies to use artificial intelligence "in a manner that advances equity."

In this video, I explain how Biden's executive order manipulates language and statistics in order to nationalize the DEI movement, suppress dissent from the new racial orthodoxy, and subvert the Constitution's promise of equal treatment under the law. Check out the Appendix under President Biden Issues Executive Order Creating National DEI Bureaucracy (Video) for the YouTube video link.

Transcript (Edited)

President Joe Biden is overhauling the entire federal government along the principles of diversity, equity, and inclusion, and it seems like nobody has noticed. In February 2023, he signed another executive order promoting DEI called "Further Advancing Racial Equity and Support for Underserved Communities Through the Federal Government."

There was very little news coverage about this, but I think that it is an extremely important development. It has ramifications for almost everything that we've been talking about the last few years, and I'd like to go into this in detail to really understand how this DEI ideology works, how it embeds itself in the bureaucracy, and what it means for our country, what it means for our constitution, and what it means for our government.

If you look at this document, there are really three key strategies that it pursues.

- First, he's creating internal cadres of DEI officers. This is really important for shaping the culture, the personnel, and the budgeting process in the federal government, which controls trillions of dollars of public resources.

- Second, he's using this initiative to justify funding third party political activists under the guise of so-called underserved communities or faith and community organizations.

- And third, he's doubling down on the weaponization of civil rights law, this time with some very interesting and very modern twists. He's pushing left wing ideology, even regulating things like the use of artificial intelligence, and this entire package is justified through this really intricate but unfortunately widespread statistical and linguistic manipulation, which I'll get into at the end.

Creating Internal Cadres

So let's begin. First and foremost—this is what I think is really the heart of DEI—is creating internal cadres.

In previous times, for example, in the Soviet Union, you'd have political commissars. These were political officers that were attached to everything from army units to bureaucracies to units of the higher administration, and they would work to maintain ideological conformity. They would push the political or ideological orthodoxy within the institution, and then monitor all of their colleagues for compliance, and then if you disagreed, straight to the gulag. This, of course, is different. It's done in an American context. It's not so dramatic, but it's really the same kind of idea. If you want to have administrative power in the government, you need to have people that are loyal to your ideology that will advance it through the apparatus.

And so, in this executive order, signed on February 16, 2023, the Biden Administration is requiring all federal departments to do an annual "Equity Action Plan" and build "Agency Equity Teams" to push training, programming, reports, data, statistical evidence with the goal of "embedding equity into government-wide processes." So this sounds very nice, right? Everyone likes "equity," everyone likes "equality." But when you actually dig into what's happening—and I've done a lot of reporting on this previously during the Trump administration—this is pure left wing racialist ideology, using the linguistic frame of "equity," which is a near-homonym to the principle of "equality."

And when you actually dig into the specifics, you understand that the Agency Equity Teams, the Equity Action Plans are not anything that is sanctioned or mandated by Congress, but is an internal executive mandate to say: "We want to push this ideology through every facet of the federal government. We want to have all of our policies, and programs, and funding filtered through the ideology of DEI and enforced by DEI bureaucrats."

These Are Hidden Expenditures

If you ask the White House today, "How much money does the federal government now spend on DEI programs?," they would not have an idea, because the idea is to decentralize it, the idea is to have it embedded everywhere in a patchwork manner that can't be then accountable to the Congress, that can't be accountable to the people.

These are fake ideological and political jobs that are rewards for people who gain them, and then they have power within the company in private sector or power within the agency in the public sector to enforce ideology through training, through programming, through kind of a bombardment of daily emails, which result in a kind of ideological conditioning. You're setting the culture by bombarding employees with a constant stream of ideological materials, programming, training, et cetera.

Now you see that everywhere throughout the federal government, tens of thousands of employees in every department pushing these pseudoscientific concepts, and then you have through the form of statistical manipulation.

So they're saying, "Well, any disparate outcome, if you measure two groups, you categorize people by race, you measure the outcomes, if there's any difference between those two outcomes, it is by definition evidence of racial discrimination," which is, of course, a kind of absurd idea we'll talk about, but you have then these two things—you have ephemeral racism, and you have statistical racism, both of which, if you submit it to a rigorous kind of analytical or logical test, fail under scrutiny. But they serve as justification to promote the ideology, and then, therefore, "embedding equity into all government-wide processes."

Funding Third-Party Political Activism

The second priority that you find in Biden's new DEI executive order is a mechanism for funding third party political activism. And then what you get, at the end of the day, is you have political operators that can enforce external norms, just like the political commissars can enforce the same norms internally within the government.

And so you're routing billions of dollars to organizations that are not subject to the same kind of scrutiny, not subject to the same civil service laws, not subject to the same FOIA or information requests. And these guys can take it, and they can run with it, and they can use federal dollars—that are taxpayer dollars—not because Congress specifically mandated them, but because they are now being used within the DEI bureaucracy.

And so again it is an inside-outside game that is self-reinforcing, that creates the external and internal sense of norms, and that they can then reward their friends on the outside. In some cases, those exact same people are now brought in as outside diversity consultants to teach NASA engineers about their white fragility, or what have you.

Weaponizing Civil Rights Law

And now the third key strategy or key principle in the DEI executive order is the extension of the weaponization of civil rights law.

Civil rights law, which promised, I think, a great promise to treat everyone equally under the law, to treat everyone as an individual, to not discriminate in our policies on the basis of race or identity really has been taken, and then in the implementation stage, used to advance a left-wing vision to the point where now you have universities, for example, explicitly violating civil rights law, racially segregating scholarships, saying, "These racial groups can apply for the scholarship.

These racial groups cannot apply for the scholarship," all in the name of civil rights, when in fact, these are explicit violations of Title VI of the Civil Rights Act. But what you see is that it becomes a lever, and it becomes a justification to advance an ideological line that is actually in some cases in contradiction with civil rights law, but is not enforced because the actual bureaucracy of the civil rights apparatus is in the wholesale control of left-wing activists that share these political priorities.

The Biden administration, though, is saying, "one of the battlegrounds that we want to play on is the battleground of information warfare." And they identify information control as what they call an "emerging civil rights risk," and they task the federal government—this is actually amazing—with "protecting the public from algorithmic discrimination," and, instruct the federal agencies to, "when designing, developing, acquiring, and using artificial intelligence and automated systems in the federal government, agencies shall do so, consistent with applicable law, in a manner that advances equity."

And so this, if you want to summarize it colloquially, is saying if the federal government is going to wage into AI, it has to be woke AI. It has to be ChatGPT that never says the naughty things, that would never praise the orange dictator Donald Trump, but would praise the great DEI advocate Joe Biden.

Linguistic and Statistical Manipulation

So if you take these three strategic priorities, really our strategic imperatives, creating internal cadres, funding third party political activism, weaponizing civil rights law, you have to ask, "Well, what is their rational justification for all of this? How do they make the argument in favor of this?" And there are only two ways that they do this. As I kind of alluded to earlier, it's a linguistic manipulation, and it's a statistical manipulation.

So let's actually read the language that they use and then break it down and parse it to try to understand not what they're saying, but what they're meaning, what their actual kind of latent content of these ideas might be. The executive order says, the mission is for "advancing equity for all, including communities that have long been underserved and addressing systemic racism in our nation's policies and priorities." Furthermore, they say that agencies "shall be responsible for delivering equitable outcomes." Again, this is poll-tested, this is marketing language, this is political language filtered through the DEI bureaucracy that's then also been filtered through corporate Madison Avenue language. You can imagine it on a splashy billboard with a Nike swoosh: "Delivering equitable outcomes for all." Sounds very, very nice.

But let's break down the phrases and let's break down the argument that's underneath these ideas.

First of all, "systemic racism." Look, the United States is not a systemically racist country in 2023, when this executive order was passed. But what they're doing is that they're setting an anchor that is the presupposition. They're treating it axiomatically. They're not proving that it is. They can't say that "these policies actively discriminated on anyone on the basis of race." They're using it as a self-evident basis for all of the arguments that come. It's a weak presupposition. We can discuss that and why it's wrong at another time, but we have to understand that that is the kind of fulcrum of this. That is the grounds that they're laying.

Second, they want to advance "equity for all," while at the same time they're saying they want to advance equity to "underserved" and" underrepresented" communities. This is incompatible.

So what they're doing is they're saying, "equity for all" is a very nice slogan. It polls well. It seems consonant with our principles from the Declaration, the Fourteenth Amendment, the Civil Rights Act, that everyone has equal protection under the law as an individual, but then they say at the same time—which again is total contradiction of the terms,—"but we're going to go for underserved and underrepresented communities and deliver them equity," meaning in practice, and you see this in corporations, in universities, in government programs, that they're actually not serving everyone equally as individuals, but they're categorizing groups on the basis of race, sexual identity, et cetera, and then tilting the playing field or treating people separately to two separate or actually multiple separate standards, based on the theory of intersectionality, where they're saying, "we categorize people by groups, and we treat them differently" through policies, through hiring, through promotions, through government contracting, through grant funding, through the distribution of assets, through, for example, BIPOC-only basic income programs that some cities have deployed recently."

And then so you have what Ibram Kendi says more honestly is "anti-racist discrimination." So yes, we want to discriminate on the basis of race. That's really what it means to do this. He's at least honest about it, and we're justifying it on the basis of systemic racism. Okay, so you have the justification. You have the argument or the actual policy. And then what is the desired outcome? What is the kind of telos of this system? It's "equitable outcomes."

"Equitable outcomes" means if you want to make the language more plain, equal outcomes. The goal, the stated goal and the stated definition, even axiomatically, is that we will not be systemically racist in the United States until we have equitable or equal outcomes on the basis of racial categories. And so when everyone has the same income, when everyone has the same number of college degrees, when everyone has the same achievement along a whole series of metrics, then we will have a society that has been redeemed from systemic racism, then we will have equitable outcomes, and we will have served "underserved" communities or "underrepresented" communities to the sufficient point that our objective is met.

The DEI Bureaucracy Can Only Lead to Tyranny

But ultimately, the problem with the theory of equitable outcomes is that you can only achieve this through bureaucratic tyranny. The Founders knew this. The Founders when they talked about diversity, they said so in this beautiful phrase, the "diversity of faculties." They knew that human beings, as individuals, some were gifted in some things, some were gifted in other things, some lacked gifts in the same categories, and they said that if we tried to level or to equalize outcomes along all of those various faculties, all of those various achievements, you could only do so through crushing excellence, through having a kind of unequal process, and then by having a government that was so strong that it could enforce it only through tyranny.

This is not to say, to be clear, that it is not our moral duty to eliminate all forms of racism and racist policies from our government, from our society, from our laws. That is a noble goal. I think it's consistent with the founding vision, and I think, for the most part, we have moved our society over the last 250 years much closer to that vision. But now the question is this: do we want to fulfill that promise of the Declaration, the Fourteenth Amendment, the promise of civil rights, or do we want to diverge from that promise with this theory of kind of critical race ideology, with this theory of anti-racist discrimination, with this theory of equitable outcomes, which throughout human history has always ended in bloodshed, tyranny, and misery, and misfortune?

The political left says: "Let's give it a try once again. We're going to put a statistical dashboard. We're going to call it equity now. We're going to equalize outcomes, but because we are sophisticates of the twenty-first century, we're going to avoid all of the errors and misfortunes of the past." I'm not so sure.

But more importantly, what I am sure about is that this can only be achieved by actually abandoning the principles of our country, the principles of equality and liberty, which are really those two sides of the same coin, and the guiding light of the last 250 years. That's not to say that we always had it in practice. That's not to say that we've always lived up to it, but I think we've always moved towards it. And some might say, "Oh, Chris, you're a kind of naive Whiggish mind, who says that we're moving towards it." But look, Lincoln thought this, the great leaders of our country have thought this, so I feel like I'm in good company.

But if we go along the lines of Biden's kind of racialist bureaucracy or government not by the will of the people, but government by the will of the DEI ideologues that are embedded through the federal agencies, we're going to be subverting our Constitution, not by passing constitutional amendments, not through the process that has been handed down through us, but subverting the constitutional order with a death by a thousand cuts, by ceding, or delegating, or really abdicating, our authority to these DEI bureaucrats that go then, cut by cut, piece by piece, dismantling the principles of liberty and equality, demolishing the foundation and moral and philosophical underpinning of our Constitution, and then doing it by changing the meaning of language and misleading the public.

And so with this video, with the work that I'm doing looking at the DEI bureaucracies, right now in universities, I hope that I can give you the tools to parse the language, the tools to understand the concepts, and then hopefully the tools to start fighting back, because we can only solve this problem through the political process, through the legislative process, and through courageous political leadership. And we have to wholly reject the ideology of DEI. We have to abolish the DEI departments in every facet of our government. And we have to make the case for those great principles of liberty and equality rightly understood, and this is the fight of our time.

This is the great constitutional battle, and we are not only right on the politics, but we are right morally, we're right philosophically, and we are right by the highest meaning of our Constitution. Let's get to work.

America's Most Woke Big City Seattle is Dangerously Progressive

From the Christopher F. Rufo "Cult Programming in Seattle" *City Journal* July 2020 article:

In July 2020, the City of Seattle's Office of Civil Rights sent an email inviting "white City employees" to attend a training session on "Interrupting Internalized Racial Superiority and Whiteness," a program designed to help white workers examine their "complicity in the system of white supremacy" and "interrupt racism in ways that are accountable to Black, Indigenous and People of Color." Hoping to learn more, I submitted a public records request for all documentation related to the training. The results are disturbing.

At the beginning of the session, the trainers explain that white people have internalized a sense of racial superiority, which has made them unable to access their "humanity" and caused "harm and violence" to people of color. The trainers claim that "individualism," "perfectionism," "intellectualization," and "objectivity" are all vestiges of this internalized racial oppression and must be abandoned in favor of social-justice principles. In conceptual terms, the city frames the discussion around the idea that black Americans are reducible to the essential quality of "blackness" and white Americans are reducible to the essential quality of "whiteness"—that is, the new metaphysics of good and evil.

Once the diversity trainers have established this basic conceptual framework, they encourage white employees to "practice self-talk that affirms [their] complicity in racism" and work on "undoing [their] own whiteness." As part of this process, white employees must abandon their "white normative behavior" and learn to let go of their "comfort," "physical safety," "social status," and "relationships with some other white people." As writer James Lindsay has pointed out, this is not the language of human resources; it is the language of cult programming—persuading members they are defective in some predefined manner, exploiting their emotional vulnerabilities, and isolating them from previous relationships.

It's important to point out that this "interrupting whiteness" training is not an anomaly.

In recent years, nearly every department of Seattle city government has been recruited into the ideological fight against "white supremacy." As I have documented, the city's homelessness agency hosted a conference on how to "decolonize [their] collective work;" the school system released a curriculum explaining that "math is a tool for oppression;" and the city-owned power company hired a team of bureaucrats to fight "structural racism" within their organization.

Dozens of private companies now offer diversity training to public agencies. The idea that all whites have unconscious, "implicit bias" that they must vigilantly program themselves to overcome has become an article of faith across corporate boardrooms, academia, and law-enforcement agencies, even though the premise is unscientific and impossible to verify.

The endgame is to make Seattle's municipal government the arbiter of the new orthodoxy, and then work outward. At the end of the session on "internalized racial superiority," the diversity trainers outline strategies for converting outsiders and recommend specific "practices for interrupting others' whiteness." In effect, the activists have organized an ideological pyramid scheme—using public dollars to establish their authority within the government, then using that authority to recruit others into the program. As Lindsay writes, "the goal is no longer to indoctrinate on what is 'rightthink' and 'wrongthink.' It is to make the [subject's] thinking be completely in line with the view of the world described by the cult doctrine."

How far can this racial-justice shakedown extend itself? The new racial orthodoxy has seen exponential growth in the past few years and has proved extremely difficult for local governments and elite institutions to resist. The movement's key rhetorical premise is designed as a trap: if you are not an "antiracist," then you are a "racist"—and must be held to account.

Skeptics might dismiss Seattle's "interrupting whiteness" training as a West Coast oddity, but it is part of a nationwide movement to make this kind of identity politics the foundation of our public discourse. It may be coming soon to a city or town near you.

In the name of social justice, Seattle government agencies conduct employee training sessions separated by race.

Nonetheless, state-sponsored racial segregation in the United States ended with the Civil Rights Act of 1964 but in Seattle, it has recently returned, and in an unlikely place: government agencies as shown in the Christopher F. Rufo "The New Segregation" *City Journal* October 2020 article:

According to new whistleblower documents, at least three public agencies in the Seattle region have implemented race-segregated diversity trainings that teach employees, in the words of one training manual, to "accept responsibility for their own racism" and "question the white power structure."

At the King County Library System, a private consulting firm called Racial Equity Consultants recently held racially segregated "listening sessions." The consultants "begin with an anti-oppression framework," internal documents show, and they use segregated sessions to root out "institutional privileges and systemic inequities." Widespread "institutional racism" is said to exist in the libraries, and employees who reject that premise are accused of "internalized racism." When reached by e-mail, Racial Equity Consultants said that it was not authorized to comment.

At the Puget Sound facility of the federal Veterans Administration, local leadership has launched racially segregated "caucuses" for "individuals who identify as white" and those who identify as "African-American or black" or as "people of color." According to whistleblower e-mails, the organizer, physician Jesse Markman, initially "felt uncomfortable suggesting, as a white person, what [he] perceived, at the time, to be segregation." After consulting with outside diversity trainers, however, Markman decided to move forward with the racially segregated sessions, calling them "an environment for sharing and discussion, which is not afforded by mixed groups." When contacted by e-mail, Markman referred the inquiry to the VA's Public Affairs Office, which did not provide comment.

Finally, at the King County Prosecutor's Office, chief prosecutor Dan Satterberg and senior staff have recently required employees to sign an "equity and social justice" pledge and assigned "continued training for white employees," who must "do the work" to "learn the true history of racism in our country." As part of the new initiative, whites are encouraged to participate in racially segregated "anti-racist action groups" and agency-wide "cultural-competency" training that teaches them how to adopt "a new non-oppressive and non-exploitive attitude." According to a leaked memo, Satterberg recently wrote a letter to staff suggesting that the "privileged white male cohort" in his office should "shut up and listen." The prosecutor's office confirmed the authenticity of the equity pledge and staff-wide memo, but Satterberg did not offer comment.

In the name of social justice, Seattle's white elites are instituting a policy of racial identification and segregated training.

In all three of these institutions, white executives have explicitly implemented such policies, arguing, in one case, that holding segregated training sessions mitigates "any potential harming of staff of color that might arise from a cross-racial conversation." As the VA's Markman explained to colleagues: "It can be challenging for people of color to feel a burden to educate others on how to be better, when at the same time being told or expected to be entirely open and unfiltered."

The policies' underlying assumption—that white leaders must shield minority employees from open dialogue—is patronizing and could lead to genuine racial division in the workplace. According to multiple sources within King County government, segregated training sessions have created suspicion and distrust. "I was truly disgusted," one library employee told me. The trainers told white staffers that "we stole the land from indigenous people, [and] we are responsible for committing genocide," the employee reports. Another staffer at the prosecutor's office described a recent diversity session as a "firing squad" and fears that any dissent would lead to immediate retaliation.

These sessions are likely illegal. As U.S. Civil Rights Commissioner Peter Kirsanow has argued, racially segregated training sessions violate the 1964 act, which prohibits employers from segregating employees based on "race, color, religion, sex or national origin." The Department of Justice is already investigating Seattle's segregated diversity trainings. It should expand its investigation to include the King County Library System, the King County Prosecutor's Office, and the VA's Puget Sound Health Care System. Segregation in the name of social justice is still segregation—and it has no place in our public institutions.

Home to leading critical race theorists like Robin DiAngelo and Richard Delgado, Seattle has long been on the vanguard of race-based Progressivism. But now, these academia-derived concepts have escaped the campuses and are finding their way into public bureaucracies. Federal officials should put a stop to it.

Senator Cotton's Stand Against Military Wokeness

In March 2021, Arkansas Senator Tom Cotton introduced legislation to ban critical race theory trainings in the United States military. The bill is concise, and desperately needed to protect the military from critical race theory indoctrination as noted in the Christopher F. Rufo "Senator Cotton's Stand" *City Journal* March 2021 article:

As I have warned, critical race theory and related ideologies have begun to make their way into the armed services, with some branches promoting "white fragility" book clubs and the West Point military academy teaching CRT as part of a leadership program.

The premise of Senator Cotton's legislation is that the military should encourage its members to "love the United States," defend the "founding principles of the United States," and maintain policies that treat people as "human beings with equal dignity and protection under the law." Critical race theory, according to the findings in the bill, undermines these three goals by presenting the United States as a racist, oppressive nation and by encouraging racial division under the guise of "social justice."

Cotton's legislation would put an end to this. (Disclosure: I reviewed and provided feedback on an initial draft of this legislation.) The bill would prohibit the armed forces from directly promoting the core tenets of critical race theory: that "the United States of America is a fundamentally racist Nation;" that "an individual, by virtue of his or her race, is inherently racist or oppressive;" and that "an individual, because of his or her race, bears responsibility for the actions committed by other members of his or her race." The bill also includes a provision against segregating members of the armed forces by race, which has become common practice in many CRT training programs.

This should be uncontroversial. America's public institutions, especially the military, should not promote the principles of race essentialism, collective guilt, and racial segregation, which are anathema to American ideals. That this legislation is even necessary is a sign of how pervasive these ideas have become, even in ostensibly apolitical environments like the military.

With Democrats in control of the Senate, Cotton's bill will likely suffer a premature death.

But it will raise a series of provocative questions. Do intellectual and political leaders on the Left believe that the United States is a fundamentally racist country? Do they believe that individuals should be judged according to their race, rather than their individual actions? Do they believe that soldiers should be segregated by race?

These are not idle questions. Reports in recent months suggest that the military is rapidly becoming politicized. Top generals have declared their allegiance to groups and concepts steeped in the ideology of critical race theory. The Pentagon and high-ranking officers launched a coordinated attack against Tucker Carlson, a cable talk show host who had dared to criticize them. And the National Guard expressed its displeasure with a sitting member of Congress by sending a detachment of soldiers in full uniform to her office on Capitol Hill.

Though the text of Cotton's bill raises direct questions about critical race theory, its subtext asks a series of deeper questions: what is the purpose of the armed forces—to promote fashionable academic trends, or to defend the nation? If we are unwilling to prevent the armed forces from promoting the idea that America is a racist oppressor-state, then what are we defending in the first place? Senator Cotton should pose these questions to his colleagues as often as possible until he gets an answer.

Wokeness in the military is being imposed by elected and appointed leaders in the White House, Congress, and the Pentagon who have little understanding of the purpose, character, traditions, and requirements of the institution they are trying to change. The push for it didn't begin in the last two years under the Biden administration—nor will it automatically end if a non-woke administration is elected in 2024. Wokeness in the military has become ingrained. And unless the policies that flow from it are illegal or directly jeopardize readiness, senior military leaders have little alternative but to comply.

Companies Are Going Woke, But Consumers Aren't

As noted in the Tom Joyce "Companies are going woke, but consumers aren't" *Washington Examiner* January 2023 story: Should businesses take public stances on political and social issues? The public is split: 48% think businesses should, while 52% think they should not, according to a Gallup poll released in January 2023.

The poll shows a divide, but the true divide here is between Democrats and everyone else. The poll found that 75% of Democrats think businesses should take public stances on political and social issues. Meanwhile, just 40% of independents and 18% of Republicans felt the same way. When businesses that do speak out on social issues tend to lean left, it's no wonder why.

No matter what the polling says, though, businesses should not wade into these issues. They should stick to providing good products and services to the public, not offering half-baked political takes. But the polling should tell companies all they need to know about this topic; taking political and social positions in public divides the people.

The primary goal of a business is to turn a profit. So what is the purpose of alienating potential customers by amplifying political stances? It will not change the minds of the people angered by the ads. They may instead choose to get a similar product or service elsewhere.

This hasn't stopped businesses from getting political, though. In recent years, major companies have supported abortion , transgenderism , the Black Lives Matter movement , and more. These are controversial topics that may have supporters in liberal boardrooms, but they also have opponents in all 50 states.

Many corporations have also fallen prey to the latest woke fad: environmental, social, and corporate governance. ESG madness results in corporations supporting left-wing social policy as a form of virtue signaling. It can also serve as a cover to distract the public from the ills a company is committing. Notably, FTX got high marks from the World Economic Forum on this topic before its recent implosion.

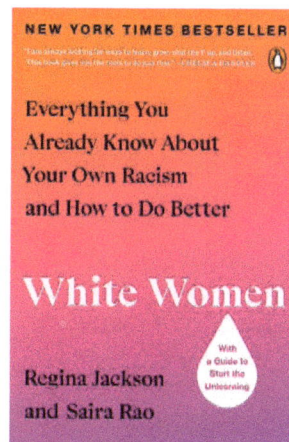

Credit: Penguin Random House-White Women
Reader's Guide by Regina Jackson and Saira Rao..

This trend is hurting consumers. It causes companies not to hire the best people or to put the best materials in their products. If a company prioritizes diversity over hiring the best people available to do the job, that will hurt the quality of its product. It may even encourage an American company to purchase Russian oil instead of American oil because of some wokeness ratings .

Leaders at companies have no obligation to surrender to this woke nonsense. Instead, they should ensure that their companies are profitable and have the brightest personnel available to offer the best to consumers.

Top 13 List of Woke American Companies

Disney – Takes the prize for the "wokest place on earth" when they mounted an internal campaign against "white privilege" and organized racially segregated "affinity groups" as part of their unintentional "go woke, go broke" campaign. Their opposition to Florida's parental-rights law demonstrates the limits of corporate virtue signaling, that in turn led to the Florida state legislature, with the support of Governor Ron DeSantis, in voting to repeal the "special independent district" enjoyed by Disney for half a century.

Walmart -- The company's new training program tells white hourly employees that they are guilty of "internalized racial superiority."

Google – Their new employee program claims that America is a "system of white supremacy" and that all Americans are "raised to be racist."

Verizon – Teaches employees that America is fundamentally racist and promotes a variety of left-wing causes.

American Express – The firm teaches employees that capitalism is fundamentally racist, then asks them to deconstruct their racial and sexual identities.

AT&T – The company's new racial reeducation program promotes the idea that "racism is a uniquely white trait."

Bank of America – The financial giant teaches that the United States is a system of "white supremacy" and encourages employees to become "woke at work."

Lockheed – The nation's largest defense contractor, sends key executives on a mission to deconstruct their "white male privilege."

Raytheon – Adopts critical race theory and tells employees to acknowledge their "privilege."

Progressive Insurance – CEO Tricia Griffith indicates that a person's viewpoint is determined by race and sex.

State Farm – Launches program to distribute LGBTQ books to kindergartners nationwide.

CVS – Launches a program that forces hourly employees to discuss their "privilege."

Major League Baseball – Moved the 2020 All Star Game from Atlanta claiming Georgia's tighter voter ID laws would disenfranchise African American voters. As it turned out, the Jim Crow 2.0 fallacy was an embarrassment for MLB, Tracey Abrams, and the Biden administrations when

Georgia's 2022 elections broke all voter turnout records for every ethnic group, including blacks. Strike three—you're out!

Woke Foundations Use Dollars Acquired Through Capitalism to Undermine Free Market Principles

Recently, the Ford Foundation announced plans to provide $1 billion in funding toward social justice programs, an extension of the $1 billion it handed out in 2015. The resulting press coverage, including a profile of its president on "60 Minutes," was effusive as reported in the Richard Graber "Woke Foundations Use Dollars Acquired Through Capitalism to Undermine Free Market Principles" The Daily Signal May 2021 update:

As we learned in Chapter 3, Ford is not alone in its philanthropic wokeism. Many other large foundations have followed suit. The Mellon Foundation, one of the largest funders of the arts and humanities, is now prioritizing social justice in all its grant-making. The Rockefeller Foundation too is committing $1 billion over the next three years to "catalyze a more inclusive, green recovery from COVID."

While well-intentioned, there has been almost no scrutiny of grant-making that supports social justice activism. "Have the billions of dollars spent on it resulted in greater equity and quality of life for those it purports to help?" asks Richard W. Graber, chairman of The Philanthropy Roundtable and president and CEO of The Lynde and Harry Bradley Foundation.

To be clear, a diverse range of philanthropies are supporting tremendous organizations with noble causes. America's ideals allow everyone from the average citizen to the wealthiest foundation to fund what they choose. And certainly, charity should continue to help the most vulnerable in society.

Grant-making through a lens that judges people by their gender and ethnicity.

The concern, though, is philanthropy that singularly looks at grant-making through a lens that judges people by their gender and ethnicity both sets America back and undermines the principles of free enterprise that have improved far more lives than any government or social justice program.

Further, such efforts are antithetical to the free market beliefs of these foundations' namesakes, who are the reason they exist in the first place. Henry Ford, John D. Rockefeller, and Andrew Mellon all embraced the free market principles that made it possible to invent, produce, fuel, and finance the transportation industry. That, in turn, enabled millions of Americans to be more upwardly mobile and generated limitless possibilities in innovation.

"The foundation is a creature of capitalism—a statement that, I'm sure, would be shocking to many professional staff in the field of philanthropy," stated Henry Ford's grandson in his letter resigning from the Ford Foundation board in 1977. He went on to say, "that the system that makes the foundation possible is very probably worth preserving."

In the decades since Ford wrote that letter, about 2 billion people worldwide have been lifted out of starvation and poverty. That feat is nothing short of a miracle, attributable to the global rise in ideas related to freedom and free markets. Research substantiates this, showing that the more economically free a country is, the greater its standard of living.

Former President Barack Obama himself has agreed, stating, "We don't dispute that the free market is the greatest producer of wealth in history—it has lifted billions of people out of poverty."

It is curious then that major foundations are committing staggering levels of funding to efforts that sound good, but in reality make it harder to start or maintain a business, value identity over initiative, and perpetuate the false, defeatist narrative that America is a land of racism, not opportunity. Such ideology detracts from how far we've come as a country and how much farther we can go if we unite behind principles that truly create parity and prosperity.

12 – Public Schools Anti-Whiteness Pedagogy, Transgressions & Indoctrination

Credit: How Can I Cure My White Guilt?-The New York Times.

Many college professors and administrators are eager to turn their students into ideological clones of themselves in hopes of ensuring that the U.S. will have the kind of governmentally controlled, collectivistic society they desire as noted in the George Leef "A Racially 'Woke' Agenda Is Now Hardwired in Public Schools" Minding the Campus November 2019 article:

Sometimes their "success" in that becomes spectacularly evident, such as the furious, vitriolic attack by the Oberlin College community against a small bakery in town over its alleged racism—for trying to prevent an underage black kid from stealing wine. That supreme exercise in "wokeness" led to a lawsuit and $33 million jury verdict against the college. (I recommend "O Oberlin, My Oberlin" by retired professor Abraham Socher for a comprehensive study in the way zealous leftists have come to dominate the school.)

Public schools are doing more and more to condition students to accept a wide array of leftist notions—notions that make them highly receptive to further leftist teaching and calls for them to act against perceived enemies of the social justice agenda.

The alliance between the public education establishment and the march of "Progressivism" is as natural as anything could be. Public education depends on the power of government: to tax, to build schools and hire teachers and administrators, to compel student attendance, to minimize or even prohibit competition. As the poor quality of many public schools has become increasingly evident over the last several decades, the education establishment has become an utterly slavish ally of the political left. It depends on the coercive fist of government.

At the same time, the political left has become ever more reliant on the education system (K-12 through college and beyond) to inculcate statist ideas in people. If voters were inclined and able to think through the harmful consequences of "Progressive" policies such as minimum wage laws, welfare payments, the Green New Deal, government-run health care, wealth taxes, and so on, they would toss the leftists out of office. It's far better for those politicians if as many voters as possible are conditioned to support candidates who mouth clichés about the evils of capitalism, the need for compassionate government, the imperative of transforming America, so it will be a just society, and many others.

Therefore, it's no surprise that public schools are ratcheting up their efforts at turning students into adults who will automatically vote to keep their political allies in power. And that calls for constant adjustments to the curriculum.

Subversive Education

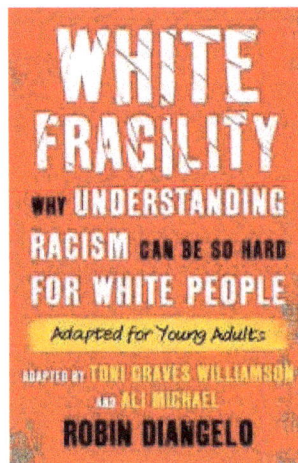

Credit: www.alimichael.org

Per the Christopher F. Rufo "Subversive Education" *City Journal* March 2021 story: In 2020, the Wake County Public School System, which serves the greater Raleigh, North Carolina area, held an equity-themed teachers' conference with sessions on "whiteness," "microaggressions," "racial mapping," and "disrupting texts," encouraging educators to form "equity teams" in schools and push the new party line: "antiracism."

The February 2020 conference, attended by more than 200 North Carolina public school teachers, began with a "land acknowledgement," a ritual recognition suggesting that white North Carolinians are colonizers on stolen Native American land. Next, the superintendent of Wake County Public Schools, Cathy Moore, introduced the day's program and shuffled teachers to breakout sessions across eight rooms. Freelance reporter A.P. Dillon obtained the documents from the sessions through a public records request and provided them to *City Journal*.

At the first session, "Whiteness in Ed Spaces," school administrators provided two handouts on the "norms of whiteness." These documents claimed that "(white) cultural values" include "denial," "fear," "blame," "control," "punishment," "scarcity," and "one-dimensional thinking." According to notes from the session, the teachers argued that "whiteness perpetuates the system" of injustice and that the district's "whitewashed curriculum" was "doing real harm to our students and educators." The group encouraged white teachers to "challenge the dominant ideology" of whiteness and "disrupt" white culture in the classroom through a series of "transformational interventions."

Parents, according to the teachers, should be considered an impediment to social justice. When one teacher asked, "How do you deal with parent pushback?" the answer was clear: ignore parental concerns and push the ideology of antiracism directly to students. "You can't let parents deter you from the work," the teachers said. "White parents' children are benefiting from the system" of whiteness and are "not learning at home about diversity (LGBTQ, race, etc.)." Therefore, teachers have an obligation to subvert parental wishes and beliefs. Any "pushback," the teachers explained, is merely because white parents fear "that they are going to lose something" and find it "hard to let go of power [and] privilege."

The Equity in Action plan encourages teachers to override parents in the pursuit of antiracism

This isn't an aberration. In fact, the district's official Equity in Action plan encourages teachers to override parents in the pursuit of antiracism. "Equity leaders [should] have the confidence to take risks and make difficult decisions that are rooted in their values," the document reads. "Even in the face of opposition, equity leaders can draw on a heartfelt conviction for what is best for students and families." In other words, the school should displace the family as the ultimate arbiter of political morality.

The equity plan outlines this new ideology in chart format, announcing the district's commitment to a series of fashionable pedagogies, including "color consciousness," "white identity development," "critical race theory," "intersections of power and privilege," and "antiracist identity and action."

The equity program in the Wake County Public School System is a massive enterprise. Founded in 2013, the district's Office of Equity Affairs has now amassed a $1 million annual budget and hosts an ongoing sequence of school trainings, curriculum-development sessions, and teacher events. In 2019, for example, the office hosted a series of "courageous conversations" about race and a five-night discussion program about the podcast Seeing White, which asks listeners to consider how "whiteness" contributes to "police shootings of unarmed African Americans," "acts of domestic terrorism," and "unending racial inequity in schools, housing, criminal justice, and hiring."

According to Wake County Public Schools, the purpose of these programs is to achieve "equity," which it defines as "eliminating the predictability of success and failure that correlates with any social or cultural factor." This is naïve, at best. Cultural traits such as family environment, transmitted values, and study habits have an enormous influence on academic outcomes. The radical-left educators believe that this is an injustice. They see their job as leveling cultural differences, grouping students into the categories of inborn identity, and equalizing outcomes.

The administrators have the logic backwards. Rather than seek to level cultural factors, they should seek to uncover and then cultivate the cultural traits that lead to academic success across all racial groups. Despite all the recent focus on racial issues in education, the greater disparity in student outcomes today is, in fact, related to social class. As Stanford's Sean Reardon has shown, the class gap in academic achievement is now twice as large as the race gap—precisely the opposite of what it was 50 years ago.

This news should suggest an opportunity to school administrators. They could pursue pedagogical strategies that help struggling students of all racial backgrounds. Sadly, rather than seizing this opportunity, teachers in Wake County are busy planning conference presentations on "toxic masculinity," "microaggressions," "trauma-informed yoga," "peace circles," and "applied critical race theory." North Carolina might be a red state, but in its largest county, the school system has fully bought in to the latest Progressive dogmas.

Parents across the U.S. should not assume that their local district is immune to these trends. The new political education is spreading everywhere.

Teaching Hate

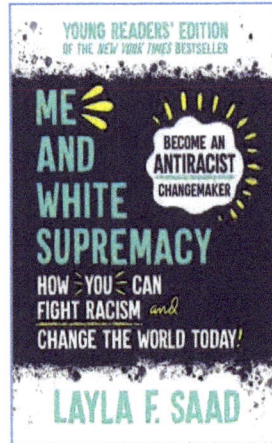

Credit: Carnegie Library Catalog-eiNetwork
at https://librarycatalog.einetwork.net.

Further documented in the Christopher F. Rufo "Teaching Hate" *City Journal* December 2020 article:

Seattle Public Schools recently held a training session for teachers in which American schools were deemed guilty of "spirit murder" against black students. The United States is a "race-based white-supremist society," the training instructed, and white teachers must "bankrupt [their] privilege in acknowledgement of [their] thieved inheritance."

According to whistleblower documents I've obtained from the session, the trainers begin by claiming that the teachers are colonizers of "the ancestral lands and traditional territories of the Puget Sound Coast Salish People." Then, next to an image of the Black Power fist, they claim that "the United States was built off the stolen labor of kidnapped and enslaved Black people's work, which created the profits that created our nation."

In the presentation materials, the organizers of the session identify themselves by both gender pronouns and race labels. For example, one speaker is identified as "He/Him, White," while another is identified as "She/her pronouns, Black (half Black and half White)." It has become commonplace in academia to use gender-pronoun identifiers, but the expectation for explicit race-labeling in the workplace appears to be novel.

The central message is that white teachers must recognize that they "are assigned considerable power and privilege in our society" because of their "possession of white skin." Consequently, to atone for their collective guilt, white teachers must be willing to reject their "whiteness" and become dedicated "anti-racist educator[s]."

The trainers acknowledge that this language might meet resistance from white teachers. They explain that any negative emotional reaction to being denounced for "whiteness" is an automatic response from the white teachers' "lizard-brain," which makes them "afraid that [they] will have to talk about sensitive issues such as race, racism, classism, sexism, or any kind of 'ism.'" The trainers insist that the teachers "must commit to the journey," regardless of their emotional or intellectual hesitations.

In the most disturbing portion of the session, the teachers discussed "spirit murder," which, according to Bettina Love, is the concept that American schools "murder the souls of Black children every day through systemic, institutionalized, anti-Black, state-sanctioned violence." Love, who originated the concept, declares that the education system is "invested in murdering the souls of Black children," even in the most ostensibly Progressive institutions.

The goal of these inflammatory "racial equity" programs is to transform Seattle schools into activist organizations.

At the conclusion of the training, teachers must explain how they will practice "anti-racist pedagogy," address the "current social justice movements taking place," and become "anti-racist outside the classroom." They are told to divide the world into "enemies, allies, and accomplices," and work toward the "abolition" of whiteness. They must, in other words, abandon the illusion of neutral teaching standards and get in the trenches of race-based activism.

Unfortunately, this indoctrination is not an aberration—it reflects deep ideological currents within Seattle Public Schools. In recent years, the district has expanded its Department of Racial Equity Advancement and deployed "racial equity teams" in dozens of neighborhood schools. The stated goal is to "advance educational racial equity," but in practice, these programs often serve to introduce, perpetuate, and enforce a specific ideological agenda.

This is a tragedy for students. Seattle public schools have been closed to on-campus learning since the early days of the Covid outbreak. In September 2020, the school district reported that fewer than half of students attended any of the school's remote instruction, with even worse attendance rates for minorities. Rather than address this crisis, which has doubtless expanded racial disparities, the district prioritized "white privilege" training for teachers.

Unless we see a change of course, this new orthodoxy—gradually replacing academics with activism—will cause educational disaster. School districts will subordinate traditional learning to the latest academic fads. When those inevitably fail, desperate teachers and administrators will be increasingly tempted to drop the old "three R's" in favor of the new "three R's": racism, racism, and racism.

As Seattle's public school administrators consume themselves with racial ideology, students will pay the price. Teachers can "bankrupt their privilege" in front of their colleagues, but their exhibitionism will do nothing for third-graders struggling to read or high school seniors preparing to graduate.

Seattle schools, which did not provide comment for this story, claim that they are "teaching tolerance." If only. In truth, they are teaching hate.

Next Step for the Parents' Movement: Curriculum Transparency

As shown in the James R. Copland, John Ketcham and Christopher F. Rufo "Next Step for the Parents' Movement: Curriculum Transparency" *City Journal* December 2021 report:

In 2021, public school parents vaulted to the forefront of America's fractured political landscape. Around the country, parents objected both to Covid-related school closures and to racially divisive curricula. Parental frustration helped secure sweeping GOP wins last month in Virginia, highlighted by Glenn Youngkin's victory over former governor Terry McAuliffe. Youngkin has promised to rein in public-school radicalism and "ban critical race theory" on his first day in office.

Perhaps the central moment in the Virginia gubernatorial race was McAuliffe's comment during a debate: "I don't think parents should be telling schools what they should teach." Like most Virginia voters, we couldn't disagree more. Research shows that greater academic success follows when parents actively engage in their children's education. To be sure, this doesn't mean that we should decide the finer points of curricular design by plebiscite; nor does it mean that a minority of objecting parents should dictate school pedagogy. But public schools are institutions created by "We the People" and should be responsive to the input of parents and the broader voting public at the state and local level.

At a minimum, parents should be able to know what's being taught to their children in the classroom. Transparency is a virtue for all of our public institutions, but especially for those with power over children. To that end, we have drafted a template—building on one of our earlier efforts at the Manhattan Institute and the work of Matt Beienburg at the Goldwater Institute—to inform state legislatures seeking to foster school transparency. The policy proposal is designed to provide public school parents with easy access—directly on school websites—to materials and activities used to train staff and teachers and to instruct children.

Recent years have demonstrated the need for transparency measures.

As many public schools migrated to "virtual only" learning in response to the pandemic, parents received a first-hand look at the divisive, racialist curricula being taught to their children. They learned that public schools were forcing third-graders to deconstruct their racial and sexual identities, showing kindergarteners dramatizations of dead black children and warning them about "racist police," and telling white teachers that they were guilty of "spirit murdering" minorities. These were not isolated incidents.

These revelations prompted parents to demand to know exactly what was being taught to their children. They felt that the public-school bureaucracies had been hiding controversial materials and exerting undue influence over their children, all in the service of fashionable left-wing ideologies.

Frustrated parents understandably pushed back, protested at school board meetings, and, in some cases, forced the resignations of school superintendents who refused to listen to their concerns. School officials often responded to parents' concerns with resentment. Some were so agitated by the parental pushback that they sought federal intervention—including through a well-publicized (and since retracted) letter from the National School Boards Association comparing parents to "domestic terrorists." Other school officials insisted that they, not parents and not voters, should be in charge of children's pedagogy. This is precisely backward. While government schools necessarily cannot meet every parent's demands, parents have a fundamental right, long recognized in law, to guide their children's education and moral conscience. To exercise those rights, parents need accurate information about the learning materials and activities their kids are encountering in government schools.

Our model for transparency adequately balances the needs for robust curricula and parents' rights in a pluralistic society. It does not attempt to define specific concepts, methods, or ideologies. Nor does it seek to ban, restrict, or discourage any materials, activities, or pedagogies. Its aim is simply to provide parents with information about the curricula used in the classroom across all subjects—and to let families, teachers, and schools negotiate disagreements at the local level. If they cannot resolve their differences, parents have options: petition elected leaders or run for school board seats themselves, move to a different area, or remove their children from the public school system.

Parents have a right to know what's being taught to their children.

According to the Education Liberty Alliance, 11 states already have state-law provisions for parental review of curricular material. Legislatures in Utah, Arizona, and Wisconsin have recently seen bills introduced to require online access. More states will surely follow.

It's important to strike the right balance. We are sensitive to the concern that state or local policy should not overburden teachers with compliance-related paperwork. Our blueprint for transparency in education thus requires listing only essential information about curricular materials and activities, such as title, author, organization, and a web link, if available. Moreover, most teachers already use free cloud storage systems, such as Dropbox, Google Drive, and Microsoft OneDrive, to organize their materials; to satisfy our proposed transparency requirements, teachers could simply share a link. For those who do not already use such systems, the parents' right to know what is happening in the classroom easily justifies the extra effort.

By focusing on transparency, our prescriptions sidestep arguments about "censorship" in public schools. (Realistically speaking, any school necessarily has to pick and choose what to teach among near-infinite options. For the record, we think Toni Morrison's acclaimed novel *Beloved* is an excellent addition to high school curricula; we're far more dubious about sharing Maia Kobabe's sexually graphic cartoon book *Gender Queer* with elementary school students.) Our transparency-based approach also ignores pointless debates about whether critical race theory is actually being taught in K-12 schools.

Openness will not necessarily engender trust. Parents will certainly disagree about pedagogy. There's no simple way to reconcile all competing perspectives. But the answer to these inevitable disagreements cannot be to hide from parents what's being taught to their own children. We believe that funding common schools in our democratic system requires information and engagement—and so we propose that public schools open their books and let parents see what's inside.

The Fight for Curriculum Transparency

The debate over America's public schools, which began in 2020 with Covid-19-related closures and continued in 2021 with the backlash against critical race theory, has shifted to a third phase: curriculum transparency where parents have the right to know what public schools are teaching their children as noted in the Christopher F. Rufo "The Fight for Curriculum Transparency" *City Journal* February 2022 article:

Last December 2021, my Manhattan Institute colleagues Jim Copland, John Ketcham, and I developed a model transparency policy, which, if adopted, would require public schools to make teaching materials available to parents online. Since then, legislators in 19 states have introduced bills to require curriculum transparency statewide. It has become, within a matter of weeks, one of the hottest public-policy ideas in the country—and, just as quickly, one of the most controversial.

As soon as conservative legislators began introducing these bills, left-wing activist organizations lined up in opposition. In states such as Kansas and Indiana, teachers' unions have rallied their members to state capitols to protest curriculum transparency. The unions object to any imposition on teachers, but they also fear—after the unprecedented public anger generated by school closures, mask mandates, and critical race theory—that giving parents a window into the classroom will strengthen the backlash.

They should be worried. In recent years, teachers' unions have been captured by their most radical elements. The NEA, which represents more than 3 million public school employees, explicitly endorsed critical race theory and other radical ideologies. The organization is fighting to block parents from knowing whether its members have implemented these unpopular pedagogies in the classroom.

Civil rights organizations have also moved to block greater transparency in public schools. The American Civil Liberties Union, which once vigorously supported legislation to provide government transparency, recently abandoned this principle. "Some of these so-called 'curriculum transparency bills' are thinly veiled attempts at chilling teachers and students from learning and talking about race and gender in schools," said ACLU staff attorney Emerson Sykes. "We are actively pursuing litigation to block these laws and policies."

Even more absurdly, one activist associated with the "free speech" organization PEN America told NPR that "school transparency is essentially this Big Brother-type regime" that could be used to "intimidate and punish instructors." This inversion would make Orwell blush: in *1984*, Big Brother was the government monitoring the people; now, to some left-wing activists, Big Brother is the people monitoring the government. For the ACLU and PEN America, speech is violence, transparency is censorship, and democracy is tyranny.

Conservative legislators should not be deterred. The case for curriculum transparency rests on an irrefutable moral argument: parents have the right to know what the government is teaching their children. Parents are not only taxpayers but also the primary stakeholders in the public education system. Approximately 90 percent of American families entrust their children's education to public schools.

That system's minimum responsibility is to provide accurate, timely, and comprehensive information about the curriculum—especially as it relates to sensitive and controversial topics such as race, gender, identity, and political ideology. The recent parent backlash underscores the importance of transparency. Millions of American families feel that the public schools are working against their values. Transparency legislation is the bare minimum for public schools to start rebuilding trust with these families.

Curriculum transparency has been a political winner, too. As I explained in January 2022, after the victory of anti-critical race theory legislation in 2021, the Left hoped that conservatives would overplay their hand. No such luck: by supporting curriculum transparency, conservatives have baited the Left into opposing a non-threatening, liberal value once embraced by citizens of all political stripes.

As Zaid Jilani noted in *City Journal*, organizations like the ACLU immediately abandoned their principles to protect the interests of teachers' unions and entrenched powers. "The ACLU of old would never have argued for government secrecy, especially when it comes to public schools," Jilani wrote. "America still needs the commitment to government transparency that the ACLU once exemplified. One might even say that we need it more than ever."

The race is now on to see which governor will become the first in the nation to sign curriculum transparency into law. He or she will not only honor parents' right to know what their children are being taught in the classroom but also initiate the long and necessary process of rebalancing the relationship between public schools and the public.

The ultimate goal of curriculum-transparency legislation is to restore trust in the school system and provide families with a mechanism for accountability. Good teachers will have no problem sharing their lessons and working with parents; bad or ideologically motivated teachers, on the other hand, will be exposed to parental oversight and can be held responsible by administrators. That is how good government is supposed to work.

"Antiracism" Comes to the Heartland

Per the Christopher F. Rufo "'Antiracism' Comes to the Heartland" *City Journal* January 2021 article: A middle school in Springfield, Missouri, in 2020, held a diversity training program that forced teachers to locate themselves on an "oppression matrix" and watch a video of "George Floyd's last words."

According to whistleblower documents and teachers who attended the program at Cherokee Middle School, the training began with a "land acknowledgement," claiming that "Springfield Public Schools is built on ancestral territory of the Osage, Delaware and Kickapoo Nations and Peoples." (At the time of publication, Springfield Public Schools had not responded to a request for comment.) The diversity trainers, Jeremy Sullivan and Myki Williamson, asked the teachers to "acknowledge the dark history and violence against Native and Indigenous People" before engaging in the day's program of "social justice work."

The trainers then forced the teachers to watch a nine-minute video of "George Floyd's last words." The film is silent, showing only white text on a black screen, illustrating Floyd's final utterances, including his cries for his mother. Such videos are a common technique in many diversity-training programs—and cult indoctrinations. The intention is to overload the senses of the participants and create an "emotional anchor" that serves to justify subsequent political arguments, even if they're non sequiturs.

Next, Sullivan announced the agenda: "We're going to look at three large concepts and those concepts are oppression, white supremacy, and systemic racism." He and Williamson provided the teachers a handout to locate themselves on an "oppression matrix," which defines white heterosexual males as the "privileged social group" and women, minorities, transgender, and LGBT people as "oppressed social groups." Presumably, those at the top of the oppression matrix, including many of the teachers in the room, are responsible for the "racism, sexism, transgender oppression, heterosexism, [and] classism" against disfavored groups.

The diversity trainers then narrowed the focus to race, distributing another handout that outlines the concepts of "overt white supremacy" and "covert white supremacy." The document claims that "lynching, hate crimes, KKK, neo-Nazis, [and] burning crosses" are "socially unacceptable" forms of white supremacy, while "education funding from property tax, colorblindness, calling the police on black people, BIPOC as Halloween costumes, not believing experiences of BIPOC, tone policing, [and] white silence" are "socially acceptable" forms of white supremacy.

This is a dangerous conflation.

The trainers are attempting to extend the stigma of true social evils—slavery, lynching, Nazism—to any deviation from Progressive political preferences, from property taxes to criminal justice to Halloween costumes. According to one teacher who attended the training, the handout originally listed "MAGA" as a form of "covert white supremacy," but it was removed after public outcry. The principle, however, has remained: diversity trainers use the emotional overload of historical evils to justify the imposition of current dogma.

Even more cynically, diversity trainers such as those at Springfield Public Schools have begun to insist on a standard of "affirmative consent." This means that teachers must not only accept the tenets of the training—in some cases even condemning themselves as white supremacists or oppressors—but also actively vocalize that acceptance. When one teacher said that he was "afraid to say anything," Sullivan quickly shut him down, telling the teacher that he must think what an "underrepresented or under-resourced student [might] say of our fear of speaking up." Remember: under the new ethics, disagreement is verboten; silence is transformed into an admission of guilt. "White silence" is a form of "white supremacy."

Finally, after more than an hour of training, one white teacher, who was raised by a black stepfather, began pushing back, asking: "Is the district saying that we should be Marxists?"

He continued: "While I don't think there's a person in the room who doesn't agree that this is an important topic that should be dealt with, the way that it's being framed comes from Herbert Marcuse who took and stripped all of the economic policies of Marxist theory and turned it into [cultural Marxism]. . . . I grew up the son of a black man, he raised me to believe in Dr. King's teachings. Dr. King did not teach the kind of vitriol that we see out of Marxism, [which] has a long replete history of countries being bigoted and prejudiced against others and then murdering millions as a result."

The diversity trainers, both white, were stunned. At first, Sullivan acknowledged the Marxist orientation of the diversity training program. "I know that that's the roots, I'm aware of all that information," he said. Then, perhaps realizing that teaching Frankfurt School Marxism in a Missouri public school could be controversial, he distanced himself: "The goal here is to take a stand against racism, it's not to be totalitarian. . . . There's not some big political agenda. It's certainly not Marxism. It's just let's make sure that all of our kids are truly valued and celebrated."

This is the tell. Many diversity-training programs—and the political movement known as Black Lives Matter—operate on the principle of bait and switch. Following Marcuse, they predicate their rhetoric on the "emotional anchor" of racial suffering, then use euphemisms to make their political arguments. In the Missouri training program, the school district proposes "empowerment" as the solution, which sounds anodyne, even appealing. However, in the documentation, the district defines "empowerment" as training students to "refuse to accept the dominant ideology and their subordinate status and take actions to redistribute social power more equitably." The district defines a euphemism with more euphemisms, but the deeper meaning is clear: that American society is white supremacist and must be replaced with a regime of race-based redistribution.

For years, Americans have watched as educators have pushed deeply divisive "antiracism" programs in coastal cities such as Berkeley, Portland, and Seattle. Now "antiracism" has come to the heartland.

Gone Crazy

From the Christopher F. Rufo "Gone Crazy" *City Journal* February 2021 article: New York's East Side Community School recently sent a letter encouraging white parents to become "white traitors" and advocate for "white abolition."

The message, sent by principal Mark Federman, showed a graphic outlining eight stages of white identity development—from the lowest form, "white supremacist," to the intermediate forms of "white confessional" and "white traitor," to the highest form, "white abolitionist." The goal of this process, according to the graphic's creator, Northwestern University professor Barnor

Hesse, is to challenge the "regime of whiteness" and eventually to "subvert white authority" and "not [allow] whiteness to reassert itself."

In the letter to parents, Federman went on a tirade against white conservatives, arguing that "racism and hate is often the underlying cause fueling their beliefs." He denounced former president Donald Trump as a "lying, racist, sexist, classist, hateful, science-denying bully" and described the Trump supporters who attended the president's January 6 rally as "a crowd of white supremacists." Federman's latest outburst came as no surprise, said one parent of children who no longer attend the school. The parent, who requested anonymity, said that Federman had pushed a divisive "Progressive line" to students and families.

The language in Federman's letter carries disturbing historical echoes.

The Ku Klux Klan and neo-Nazis used the term "race traitor" to describe whites who crossed the color line to work, marry, or associate with nonwhites. The letter's use of "white abolition" is also troubling. Federman and Hesse claim to want to abolish "whiteness" as a cultural and social construct, but they also use the term to describe an immutable racial essence. As University of New Mexico professor Geoffrey Miller has observed: "Applied to any other group, this would sound like a monstrous euphemism for mass extermination and cultural annihilation."

This isn't the first time that Federman has embroiled his school in controversy. In 2007, a 17-year-old student at East Side punched a school police officer in the face and was subsequently arrested. According to court records, Federman told the arresting officer to take the student out the back door to avoid embarrassment. When the officer refused, Federman blocked the officer from leaving the building through the front door and then "flailed his arms and kicked his legs to avoid being handcuffed when [he was] placed under arrest." Police charged Federman with resisting arrest and obstruction of governmental administration (the court later dismissed the case against him).

In 2014, following the death of Eric Garner in police custody, Federman sent a letter to students asking them to join him in a protest march to petition the United States Attorney to file criminal charges against one of the New York Police officers involved. The Education Department reined him in, telling Federman that the protest was "unsafe, did not have enough educational value and showed bias toward one side." Federman reluctantly withdrew official school support for the protest, but 70 of his students left class anyway and took the subway to Brooklyn to rally against the NYPD.

After I broke the news about these "white traitor" materials on social media, Federman sent another letter to parents. "I want to make it clear that I do not believe I did anything wrong," he wrote in a schoolwide email, as the story quickly spread to the *New York Post*, *Daily Mail*, and other outlets. Federman then instructed school families not to speak to the media. "Please do not reply to anyone. We do not want to encourage or engage these people. If anyone does email you, please share it with me," he said.

"I was appalled" by the most recent messages about white abolition, said the parent whose children formerly attended the East Side Community School. Many school families share this opinion, according to this parent, but are "afraid to come forward" out of worry that they might be denounced as racists. The parent's advice was simple: "We need to stop indoctrinating our youth and radicalizing them."

Given the rise of critical race theory in public schools, this is easier said than done.

Bad Education

As shown in the Christopher F. Rufo "Bad Education" *City Journal* February 2021 article: A Philadelphia elementary school in 2020 forced fifth-grade students to celebrate "black communism" and simulate a Black Power rally in honor of political radical Angela Davis.

According to whistleblower documents and a source within the school, a fifth-grade teacher at the inner-city William D. Kelley School designed a social studies curriculum to celebrate Davis, praising the "black communist" for her fight against "injustice and inequality." As part of the lesson, the teacher asked students to "describe Davis' early life," reflect on her vision of social change, and "define communist"—presumably in favorable terms.

At the conclusion of the unit, the teacher led the ten- and eleven-year-old students into the school auditorium to "simulate" a Black Power rally to "free Angela Davis" from prison, where she had once been held while awaiting trial on charges of conspiracy, kidnapping, and murder. The students marched on the stage, holding signs that read "Black Power," "Jail Trump," "Free Angela," and "Black Power Matters." They chanted about Africa and ancestral power, then shouted "Free Angela! Free Angela!" as they stood at the front of the stage.

The William D. Kelley School has long been one of the most troubled in the district. The school's student population is 94 percent black and 100 percent "economically disadvantaged." Academically, it is one of the worst-performing schools in Pennsylvania. By sixth grade, only 3 percent of students are proficient in math, and 9 percent are proficient in reading. By graduation, only 13 percent of Kelley students will have achieved basic literacy.

Despite this abysmal academic performance, teachers and administrators at William Kelley have gradually abandoned traditional pedagogy in favor of political radicalism. Even the school's newest public artworks illustrate this politicization. Administrators recently commissioned a mural of Davis and Huey P. Newton, who represent the Communist and Black Panther revolutionary movements of the 1960s; both figures stood trial for various crimes, including the murder of a police officer.

Unfortunately, the programs at William Kelley are no aberration. In recent years, the entire Philadelphia public school system has embraced the philosophy of "antiracism." Last summer, the superintendent released an Antiracism Declaration promising to "[dismantle] systems of racial inequity" and circulated a memo recommending racially segregated training programs for white and black educators. The local teachers' union produced a video denouncing the United States as a "settler colony built on white supremacy and capitalism" that has created a "system that lifts up white people over everyone else." The solution, according to the union, is to overthrow the "racist structure of capitalism," provide "reparations for Black and Indigenous people," and "uproot white supremacy and plant the seeds for a new world."

In practical terms, it is unclear how these "antiracist" programs will translate into academic outcomes. The gap between rhetoric and reality at schools such as William Kelley is almost beyond comprehension: the vast majority of the ten- and eleven-year-olds marching for the utopia of "black communism" can barely read and write. Rather than come to terms with the pedagogical failure of Philadelphia public schools, however, educators have shifted the blame to "systemic racism" and promises of "revolution."

That students at schools such as William Kelley could depart virtually bereft of basic literacy is a tragedy for them and a shame for the teachers and adults promising to "plant the seeds for a new world." They have condemned their students to join the ranks of the more than half of all adult Philadelphians who are "functionally illiterate."

One teacher at William Kelley, who requested anonymity out of fear of reprisals, expressed deep pessimism about the future of public education: "I've come to realize that no policy hurts African-Americans more than the public school system and the teachers' union." The teacher is right. In absolute terms, the numbers are demoralizing. The School District of Philadelphia has 18,000 employees and a $3.4 billion annual budget—and fails, year after year, to teach the basics of "reading, writing, and arithmetic." As it turns out, education is hard; political fantasy is a useful diversion.

The Dismantlers

As documented in the Christopher F. Rufo "The Dismantlers" *City Journal* August 2022 report: San Diego Unified is the latest school district to adopt the principles of academic queer theory and translate them into K-12 pedagogy, with the ultimate goal of dismantling "heteronormativity" and promoting a constellation of new sexual identities, such as "genderqueer," "non-binary," "pansexual," and "two-spirit."

I have obtained a range of publicly accessible documents from San Diego Unified that reveal the district's new ideology. The materials follow the basic premise of queer theory: white Europeans created a false "gender binary" and used the categories of "male" and "female" to dominate racial and sexual minorities.

A San Diego Unified training for facilitators of LGBTQ student groups argues that this system of "heteronormativity" forces students to conform to these norms: they are "assigned" a sex at birth, pressed into the identities of "man" and "woman," and expected to have heterosexual relationships culminating in "marriage (and kids)." This "gender binary," however, is arbitrary, socially constructed, and harmful. It is, in the words of the presentation, a "limited system [that] excludes and oppresses trans, nonbinary, intersex, and gender-nonconforming people."

According to the district, the gender binary has created an unjust society that distributes "heterosexual and cisgender privilege," the sexual analog to the concept of "white privilege." In the presentation, administrators explain that "a heterosexual/cisgender person automatically receives" this privilege, which "benefits members of dominant groups at the expense of members of target groups" and "results in institutional power" for straight men and women. Furthermore, the district claims, this sexual privilege is connected to a broader range of privileges and oppressions via the theory of intersectionality. "Racism, classism, heterosexism, etc. do not exist independently," the presentation reads. "Multiple forms of discrimination interrelate creating a system of oppression."

What is the solution? To dismantle "heteronormativity" and break the "gender binary." Following the principles of queer theory, San Diego Unified has created a program of gender-identity instruction with the explicit goal of undermining the traditional conception of sex and promoting a new set of boutique sexual identities, such as "transgender," "genderqueer," "non-binary," "pansexual," "asexual," and "two-spirit," that promise to disrupt the oppressive system of heteronormativity.

A series of curriculum documents encourages students to study the basic tenets of queer theory and then examine photographs of gender-nonconforming role models, including a woman with a beard, a boy in a dress, a teenage girl with a "genderqueer" identity, a boy wearing a tiara, and an infant with a "gender neutral baby name." In another document published by San Diego Unified, administrators celebrate "nonbinary identities," arguing that there must be a "linguistic revolution to move beyond gender binaries," including the adoption of the term "Latinx," which "makes room for people who are trans, queer, agender, nonbinary, gender non-conforming or gender fluid."

This ideology has already shifted the district's sexual-education program.

In a training produced jointly by San Diego Unified and Planned Parenthood, administrators walk teachers through the constellation of new identities and advise them to eliminate traditional language from their vocabulary. Men are to be called "people with a penis" and women are to be called "people with a vulva," because, according to the district, some women can have penises and some men can have vulvas.

Additionally, the district points out that teachers can assist in a child's gender transition without notifying parents and that, under California law, minors of any age can consent to pregnancy testing, birth control, and abortion. Finally, the training program includes sample questions on sexuality that teachers might address in the classroom, including: "Is it okay to masturbate?;" "How do gay people have sex?;" "What is porn?;" and "What does semen taste like?" In a related presentation, the district also advises teachers on leading discussions on "how to use a condom" and how to engage in "safer oral sex" and "safer anal sex."

For now, the continued spread of queer theory and gender ideology in districts such as San Diego Unified appears to be a foregone conclusion. It is remarkable to see the tenets of a once-obscure and controversial academic discipline translated into classroom orthodoxy for children. Parents, however, should begin pushing back.

If the case against queer theory as an academic discipline is strong, the case against queer theory as a K-12 pedagogy is even stronger. The goal of dismantling "heteronormativity" is nonsensical and destructive to the basic building blocks of society. To divide the world into man and woman and to encourage the development of families and children is not "oppression," but a basic process of human nature—one that should not be discarded under the false pretenses of academic postmodernism.

'Parents' Rights Advocates' Running For Local School Board Positions

Across the country, new right-leaning political action committees are pouring money into school board races, aiming to flip control of who governs schools in favor of self-proclaimed parents' rights advocates in a way that rivals the role that teachers unions have historically had in these contests.

Per the Erin Mansfield and Kayla Jimenez "These PACS are funding 'parents' rights advocates' running for local school board positions" *USA Today* October 2022 article: For much less than what it would cost them to influence a seat in the House or Senate, these PACs are putting thousands of dollars at a time—sometimes just hundreds—into races for local school boards and as a result, changing education on a national scale.

A super PAC called the 1776 Project PAC is leading the way, emphasizing opposition to lessons related to racial and social justice. With a war chest smaller than what some congressional candidates in competitive districts are raising, the group has supported and opposed school board candidates in a dozen states.

Political action committees, or PACs, and super PACs pool donations from many different people and entities and use that money to try to elect candidates who represent their interests. They may be registered at the federal or state level.

Ian Vandewalker, senior counsel for the democracy program at New York University's Brennan Center for Justice, a left leaning think-tank, said the involvement of these major PACs in local elections is a sign that politics at large have become nationalized and more partisan.

This sort of hyper-partisan, disinformation-based electioneering seems to be happening at all levels now. "This sort of hyper-partisan, disinformation-based electioneering seems to be happening at all levels now," Vandewalker said.

Other PACs are focusing on specific states and races. A grocery store heiress is behind a PAC spending to influence school board races across the state of Florida, and a federal PAC that typically focuses on federal policy got involved in one Florida county. In Texas, a PAC is raising big money to flip school board seats statewide.

Candidates with the most money in their campaign accounts tend to be the ones who win. At the school board level, that effect has the potential to be larger because the races are often so cheap.

13 – DeSantis Woke Busting Excels in Exposing Progressive Hypocrisy & Idiocracy

Credit: Daniel A. Varela/Miami Herald via AP - Florida Gov. Ron DeSantis signing of HB7, "individual freedom," also dubbed the "stop woke" bill on April 22, 2022.

With ex-President Donald Trump no longer the standard bearer for the fight against the ideological poison of Progressivism, Florida Governor Ron DeSantis takes a stand against its racialist ideologies in public institutions and businesses. As documented in Rufo's "Florida v. Critical Race Theory" *City Journal* article in December 2021:

The stakes could not be higher. Critical race theorists, and their adherents in the new Progressive movement, would replace the American system of individual rights, equality under the law, and meritocracy with a system of identity-based distribution of power. In one of the discipline's founding texts, *Critical Race Theory: The Cutting Edge*, author Richard Delgado explains that these ideas are "marked by a deep discontent with liberalism, a system of civil rights litigation and activist, faith in the legal system, and hope for progress." It is a profoundly nihilistic vision, which explains, in part, the character of recent street protests. The rioters and looters in Portland, Seattle, and Chicago are not fighting for any positive value; they are waging a war of simple negation.

The governor framed the rise of critical race theory as a mortal threat to the United States. "I think what you see now with the rise of this woke ideology is an attempt to really delegitimize our history and to delegitimize our institutions," he said. "And they basically want to replace it with a very militant form of leftism that would absolutely destroy this country."

This Progressivism madness has no bounds with more examples of Arizona claiming that babies are racist; Santa Clara County denouncing the United States as a "parasitic system;" Philadelphia teaching students to celebrate "Black communism;" San Diego telling teachers "you are racist;"

Bank of America teaching that the United States is a "system of white supremacy;" Verizon teaching that America is fundamentally racist; and Google teaching that all Americans are "raised to be racist."

At heart, the battle against critical race theory is a fight against entrenched bureaucracies that have used public institutions to promote their own racialist ideology. "This is an elite-driven phenomenon being driven by bureaucratic elites, elites in universities, and elites in corporate America, and they're trying to shove it down the throats of the American people," DeSantis said. "You're not doing that in the state of Florida."

Florida v. Critical Race Theory

As illustrations of critical race theory (CRT) in American institutions, DeSantis cited seven of Christopher F. Rufo's CRT reports as noted in the *City Journal* "Florida v. Critical Race Theory" article in December 2021.

Per Rufo: Over the past year, DeSantis has emerged as one of the most articulate political spokesmen for the anti–critical race theory movement. His new policy agenda builds on successful anti-CRT legislation in other states but goes two steps further. First, it provides parents with a "private right of action," which allows them to sue offending institutions for violations, gain information through legal discovery, and, if they win in the courts, collect attorney's fees. Second, it tackles critical race theory in corporate "diversity, equity, and inclusion" training programs, which, DeSantis says, sometimes promote racial stereotyping, scapegoating, and harassment, in violation of state civil rights laws.

Following his speech, DeSantis invited me to address the crowd. I explained that the reason critical race theory has upset so many Americans is that it speaks to two deep reservoirs of human sentiment: citizens' desire for self-government and parents' desire to shape the moral and educational development of their children. Elite institutions have attempted to step between parent and child.

DeSantis has deftly positioned himself as a protector of middle-American families. One of the guest speakers, Lacaysha Howell, a biracial mother from Sarasota, said that left-wing teachers tried to persuade her daughter that the white side of their family was oppressive. Another speaker, Eulalia Jimenez, a Cuban-American mother from the Miami area, said that left-wing indoctrination in schools reminded her of her father's warnings about Communism in his native Cuba. Both believed that critical race theory was poison to the American Dream.

As they begin their next session in January, Florida legislators have the opportunity to craft the gold standard for "culture war" policy. The governor's team has worked with a range of interested parties, including the Manhattan Institute, which has crafted model language for prohibiting racialist indoctrination and providing curriculum transparency to parents. The battle is ultimately about shaping public policy in accord with public values. "I think we have an ability [to] just draw a line in the sand and say, 'That's not the type of society that we want here in the state of Florida,'" said DeSantis. The stakes are high—and all eyes are on Florida to deliver.

No Cause for Controversy

When Florida governor Ron DeSantis signed the "Parental Rights in Education" bill into law, banning public school teachers from kindergarten through third grade from holding classroom instruction on sexual orientation and gender identity, most Progressives saw it as an attack on LGBT rights.

As noted in the Thom Nickels "No Cause for Controversy" *City Journal* May 2022 article: Overnight, the inflammatory and misleading moniker "Don't Say Gay" was applied to the new law, setting off alarms across the country. Hysteria over Florida's mischaracterized "Don't Say Gay" law largely involves obscuring the fact that it applies only to children under age ten.

New York City mayor Eric Adams launched a digital campaign in five Florida markets to condemn the law, while the ACLU began its own campaign: "Just Say 'No' to 'Don't Say Gay.'" The ACLU suggested that the Florida law could keep classic authors like Langston Hughes and American poet Walt Whitman out of school libraries. Former presidential candidate Pete Buttigieg said that the law would result in suicides of young LGBT people.

NPR's coverage of the story skirted objectivity when it highlighted the view that the law would hurt LGBT children, despite DeSantis's claim that the law would merely safeguard toddlers from a "woke gender ideology." Progressives are also fixating on what Florida state representative Joe Harding, the House bill's sponsor, was quoted as saying on February 17: that classroom instruction on such topics could be prohibited beyond third grade if it was determined not to be "age or developmentally appropriate."

There's much to unpack here, namely: Are first- and second-graders liable to commit suicide because their local public school will not support their emerging gender identity? On the contrary, the notion that third-graders can be aware of themselves as "trans" is a fantasy produced by the woke narrative industry.

There likely isn't a third-grader in the world who would find it necessary to jump from a tall building because his trans identity (and where would he have gotten this notion, anyway, at such a tender age?) is not taken seriously at school. What Buttigieg and others are really arguing for is preparatory training for schoolchildren on these issues, so that, if the kids eventually come out as LGB (but more likely trans), they will have already been "primed" in these matters.

The *Wall Street Journal* correctly observed that reaction to the bill in many quarters, both for and against, is overwrought. The bill's opponents aren't part of a covert operation literally to seduce young school children into sex. The "grooming" at issue here would be better termed "woke gender indoctrination." Meantime, the White House has joined the hysteria on the other side, referring to the bill as "cruel."

As White House press secretary Jen Psaki said, "It is certainly something that is not helping, you know, young people who are members of the LGBTQI+ community who are already vulnerable, already being bullied."

There appears to be universal consensus on the part of Progressives to ignore the fact that the law refers only to young children slightly past toddler age and not "youth" maturing into sexual awareness.

The Bogeyman

Per the Dave Seminara "The Bogeyman" *City Journal* May 2022 report: Days after the 2020 election, I wrote a column predicting that the search for a new conservative bogeyman would begin. The Left has settled on its preferred villain: Florida governor Ron DeSantis. My home state has long been reviled by Progressives, and many now view our governor as an example of everything wrong with the United States. In the DeSantis era, the Sunshine State represents either freedom or tyranny, depending on your politics.

Yet amid the avalanche of negative, misleading, and false stories about DeSantis, he enjoys a sizable lead in polling in a state that only recently gained a slim majority of registered Republicans, and at the conclusion of his 2022 reelection, he won by a landslide. Let's examine some of the spurious charges against him.

His approach to classroom issues endangers kids. To say that Florida's Parental Rights in Education law (often mislabeled the "Don't Say Gay" bill) has been controversial would be an understatement. U.S. transportation secretary Pete Buttigieg, among others, said that the bill would lead children to commit suicide (borrowing a dubious talking point), while the media painted a distorted picture of the legislation. Many outlets gave readers the impression that the law prohibited teachers from saying the words "gay" or "homosexual," but their coverage often left out or buried the fact that the law applies only to students in kindergarten through third grade, and several journalists suggested that the law would prohibit students from asking their teachers questions about gender identity or sexual orientation. In fact, the law covers only "classroom instruction" on such matters and doesn't prohibit casual conversations about these topics. A recent poll indicated that 67 percent of parents and 61 percent of overall respondents support the legislation.

His approach to Covid endangers the elderly. Florida's resistance to lockdowns and mandates has been vindicated over time, not that you'd know it from media coverage or the "DeathSantis" moniker coined by left-wing activists. Using raw Covid numbers, rather than age-adjusted mortality rates, made Florida's performance appear worse than it was. The state has the second-highest percentage (21 percent) of residents aged 65 and over, and that doesn't fully reflect the large, elderly snowbird and seasonal-visitor population that flocks to the state each year. Given Covid's disproportionate toll on the elderly, failing to adjust for age when comparing state death tolls is misleading. On an age-adjusted basis, Florida ranks 31 out of 50 in per capita Covid deaths. Florida also had significantly fewer nursing home deaths per capita than did New York or New Jersey, its schools reopened by August 2020, and its economy is booming.

He bullied kids into removing their masks. Democrats and many media outlets branded DeSantis a "bully" for scolding students at the University of South Florida into taking off their masks earlier in 2022. "You do not have to wear those masks, I mean please take them off. Honestly, it's not doing anything and we have to stop with this Covid theater. If you want to wear it, fine, but this is ridiculous." When he said it, several students started laughing and at least four of them immediately took their masks off. Some kept their masks on, and DeSantis didn't belabor the point.

In any case, the media's outrage and subsequent claims that the episode was proof that DeSantis is "anti-science" are ridiculous. The Daily Beast, for example, said that DeSantis had offered students "terrible, anti-science" advice. The Palm Beach Post opined that DeSantis's actions were a "blatant attempt to pander to the most anti-science elements of society." At the time, the media framed anyone who objected to mask mandates as anti-science, but a few weeks later, mask mandates of all sorts were scrapped.

He's bullying the Walt Disney Corporation. When Florida Republicans voted to dissolve Disney's self-governing status, Democratic state legislators howled in protest. Revoking Disney's special status is obviously political retribution for the company's distorting and grandstanding against the Parental Rights in Education Law. But Disney had a deal like no other employer in Florida—one that's impossible to justify even if the company wasn't taking a partisan stand. Don't Democrats profess to oppose corporatist special treatment?

He's banning books. In March 2022, DeSantis signed legislation that allows parents to object to educational materials used in schools. And the Florida Department of Education recently rejected 41 percent of the math textbooks under consideration. Many were ruled out for nonpolitical reasons; others were disqualified for inappropriately political material. Officials provided examples of offending books. In one, a word problem used data portraying conservatives as far more racist than liberals. CNN, NBC, and other news outlets provided images of the offending word problem but downplayed it in typically dishonest coverage. In any case, the notion of book-banning is a red herring. Publishers are producing an avalanche of woke children's literature, some with LGBT themes and pornographic content. Many schools are offering or assigning these titles to kids. Parents, with support from DeSantis, have pushed back. Liberals have met the removal of these books from libraries or curricula with outrage, but how would they feel if schools assigned children to read, say, conservative firebrand Matt Walsh's satire *Johnny the Walrus* or Bethany Bomberg's book *Pro-Life Kids*?

He's a racist. DeSantis recently signed the Stop Woke bill, which prevents schools and employers from pushing critical race theory. MSNBC host Joy Reid tweeted that DeSantis was "anti-Black" and guilty of child abuse for having some black boys around him for a photo when he signed the bill. A liberal Florida legislator and other Democrats weighed in, insisting that the boys must not have known what the law was about. Not so, says former NFL player Jack Brewer, who works with the kids, and has threatened to sue Reid for defamation.

He's a dictator. When NBA player Enes Freedom recently posted a photo with DeSantis on Instagram and Twitter, for example, hundreds of Progressives asked him how he could pose with a "dictator" or "authoritarian" while critiquing China and other repressive regimes. One liberal PAC recently compared DeSantis to Fidel Castro, while Democratic gubernatorial candidate Nikki Fried has compared him to Castro and Adolf Hitler. These attacks don't merit a response.

When DeSantis took office in January 2019, Florida had 257,175 more registered Democrats than Republicans. The GOP now has 89,528 more Republicans than Democrats—a remarkable swing of 346,703 voters during his tenure. And the state's population continues to grow. Apparently, Americans love his brand of tyranny.

Ron DeSantis's Big Night

From the Michael Hartney "Ron DeSantis's Big Night" *National Review* August 2022 article: If you think Democrats are scared of Florida governor Ron DeSantis now, just wait until they digest the results of school-board elections in the Sunshine State.

But first some context. For the past two years, Progressives and their allies in the legacy news media have tried to use Governor DeSantis's education agenda to paint him as a reckless extremist. For example, after DeSantis pushed Florida's schools to reopen for in-person learning during the pandemic, critics dubbed him "Governor Deathsantis." Later, when DeSantis fought to block public schools from teaching kindergartners about sexual orientation and gender identity—a policy that, whatever one thinks about it, appears to be favored by many voters—Progressives called him an authoritarian bigot.

Rather than run away from the critics, DeSantis went all in. He took the fight on education issues directly to his political opponents, including the state's formidable teachers' unions. In a wholly unprecedented move for a governor, DeSantis endorsed 30 school-board candidates—each of whom willingly pledged to support and campaign on his education agenda. What's more, 17 of the candidates that DeSantis endorsed faced opponents who had won the backing of the state's largest teachers' union.

Make no mistake, this move was as risky as it was courageous. In a year in which DeSantis has to worry about his own reelection (he will face competition from former governor Charlie Crist), the incumbent chose to invest his time, money, and political reputation in backwater local elections that teachers' unions have dominated for decades.

My own research on school-board elections shows just how bold DeSantis's move was. Historically, candidates endorsed by teachers' unions have won the overwhelming majority of board elections. In 2020, union-backed candidates in Florida won more than 70 percent of the time. What's more, union-endorsed incumbents almost never lose.

Despite these unfavorable odds, DeSantis's gamble paid off. On Tuesday's election night, his board candidates steamrolled the ones favored by the education establishment. Twenty-five of the 30 candidates he backed either won outright (19) or advanced (six) to November's runoff as the top vote-getter in their race. More impressive still, in the 17 contests where the teachers' unions' preferred candidate faced a DeSantis-crowned challenger, the union won just four seats.

The DeSantis education playbook offers several important lessons to Republicans.

First, it shows that when GOP governors take a more muscular approach to education advocacy at the local level, they can help even the playing field between unions and parents. Because school-board candidates run without party labels printed on the ballot, citizens can find it difficult to choose the candidate who shares their values. Far from undermining democracy, DeSantis's move helped inform voters about the candidates and their priorities.

Second, it validates the popularity of at least some elements of the party's education agenda. National polling data indicates that DeSantis's education agenda has real appeal beyond just Florida. In July, voters from several battleground states who took part in a teachers' union–commissioned poll by Hart Research Associates said they now trust Republicans more than Democrats on education issues.

Finally, it provides valuable insight into the type of standard-bearer the Republicans should choose in 2024.

Much has been made about the potential of an impending DeSantis–Trump primary showdown. As Republicans consider which man would be a better choice to lead their party, they would do well to recall that politics, like sports, is not so much about individual talents as about elevating an entire team. Effective party leaders should be able to expand their coalition and win as many elections for their team as possible.

When it comes to party building, Trump's record is marred by the half-hearted effort in Georgia's special Senate elections, which likely cost the Republicans a Senate majority. On Tuesday, Ron DeSantis struck the opposite chord in Florida, thwarting a once-dominant political force, along with any doubts about his political future.

Schooled by DeSantis

As noted in the Michael Hartney "Schooled by DeSantis" *City Journal* November 2022 article: Woody Allen once observed that 80 percent of success in life comes down to showing up. For decades, conservatives failed to heed this advice in education politics, letting unions monopolize the school boards that govern American K–12 education. That ended on November 8, 2022, as Florida governor Ron DeSantis helped conservatives defeat a record number of union-backed school board candidates.

Despite conservatives' faith in the virtue of local control, the Right's failure to engineer consistent conservative school board victories has long given Progressives in the education establishment a stranglehold on local school politics. Decades of research show, for example, that teachers' unions win roughly 70 percent of competitive school board races. What's more, because most school board races are nonpartisan, low-turnout affairs, conservative voters often unwittingly help elect union-friendly board majorities. With no reliable counterweight to hold them accountable, teachers' unions hold outsize power in school board decision-making.

This state of affairs quietly persisted until the pandemic, when conservative (and moderate) parents discovered the price of their apathy and disorganization. Conceding school board seats to the education establishment now had real and visible costs. Union-friendly boards that presided over unjustifiable school closures showed more concern for their politically active employees than they did for the parents and kids struggling with remote schooling. At the same time, classes on Zoom gave many parents their first-ever look at controversial curricula and instructional materials. Even though a majority of parents oppose elementary students learning about "sex education and LGBTQ issues," establishment forces persisted, with parents reporting one outlandish episode after another during the pandemic-plagued school year. One local union leader in Maine told complaining parents that they should just leave the public schools entirely.

Enter DeSantis

In his victory speech on Election Night, his line, "we fought the woke in the schools [and won]," made all the headlines. But the hard work that enabled this victory came from coordinated electioneering efforts during the quiet summer months leading up to Florida's August primary. DeSantis had put his political muscle behind 30 conservative school board candidates who pledged to support a parents-first and anti-woke agenda.

When the dust settled, DeSantis's conservative school board candidates had prevailed in over 80 percent of their races. More impressive still, in the 19 elections where one of DeSantis's candidates faced a union-backed opponent, the unions won just four races (21 percent). In previous elections in the same districts—when conservatives had no coordinated electioneering effort in place—union-favored candidates won more than 70 percent of their races.

These trends prevailed across the country where conservatives mounted a coordinated electioneering effort as in Florida, they did well. But where conservatives did not make such a push, teachers' unions continued their dominance of school board contests in both red and blue states. My own analysis of union electioneering in red Indiana and blue Michigan, for example, uncovered robust union win rates of 66 and 74 percent, respectively. In other words, without the coattails of a strong (and coordinated) conservative message in these local races, teachers' unions were able to maintain their historic edge and notch three times as many victories (in percentage terms) in the Midwest as they did in Florida.

There's no reason that the DeSantis/Florida GOP strategy can't work beyond the Sunshine State. Other Republican states had popular governors who stood up to teachers' unions on reopening schools and keeping unwanted and divisive ideology out of the classroom. But showing up matters. Even now, in this time of hotly contested educational controversies, numerous school board seats routinely go uncontested.

In low-salience contests, Progressive boards can easily endure in conservative communities that don't pay much attention. As Craig DiSesa, who oversees campaign operations for the Virginia-based The Middle Resolution, told me, even in some of the commonwealth's more conservative school districts, liberal boards have persisted because of a lack of political engagement. In 2022, DiSesa's group flipped several school board seats in Virginia Beach, installing school-choice advocates over union-backed establishment figures.

Basic efforts aimed at recruiting better candidates and coordinating small donations from popular conservative officials (DeSantis gave his endorsed candidates $1,000 each) can go a long way toward winning conservative majorities on school boards. The potential return on this investment is huge. Taxpayers and families will benefit by seeing their interests better represented on boards, and conservative lawmakers can begin building a stable of future candidates for other local and state offices.

For conservatives, there's a clear path forward, but they will need to get—and keep—their hands dirty. As the pandemic subsides and normalcy returns to our schools, conservatives cannot afford to take their eyes off these crucial down-ballot races.

Man in the Arena

The consensus is that, amid generally disappointing results for conservatives, Florida governor Ron DeSantis won the midterms. He defeated his Democratic opponent, Charlie Crist, by a 19-point margin and turned the state, which was once considered a battleground, deep red. He won everywhere, notching impressive victories with Hispanic and urban voters in formerly Democratic strongholds like Miami-Dade County.

How did DeSantis outperform the rest of the GOP? The answer, I believe, is that he has created a new model for "culture war as public policy," which combines popular media combat with competent, effective governance. From the Christopher F. Rufo "Man in the Arena" *City Journal* November 2022 article, Rufo analyses what happened:

DeSantis has built his profile by engaging in controversial cultural fights on critical race theory, gender ideology, and other "woke" issues. In his election night victory speech, DeSantis framed himself as a culture-war champion. "We fight the woke in the legislature. We fight the woke in the schools. We fight the woke in the corporations," he said. "We will never, ever surrender to the woke mob. Florida is where woke goes to die."

But DeSantis is not merely blustering. He has advanced a substantive agenda to rein in left-wing ideologies in Florida's institutions, passing significant higher education reforms, new curriculum guidance for K–12 schools, a ban on gender theory in grades K–3, and the Stop W.O.K.E. Act, which restricts critical race theory-style racial scapegoating in large institutions, including corporations. Most notably, DeSantis picked a fight with the Walt Disney Company, which had previously been untouchable in Florida politics—and won.

I've had the privilege of working with DeSantis and his team on some of these initiatives and have observed some of the deeper reasons for his success. First, he is a master at picking and choosing his fights. Though the media excoriated him for the K–3 gender theory ban, the Stop W.O.K.E. Act, and his fight with Disney, in all three cases, he knew that he would emerge with two-to-one public support on these issues.

He skillfully engaged in the media scrum and, to the surprise of his opponents, surfaced from those conflicts more popular than before. He doesn't engage in controversy for the sake of controversy; his strategy is calculated, and he has the self-discipline to proceed only when he can accomplish his goals.

Second, DeSantis has a keen mind for public policy. When I traveled with him to introduce the Stop W.O.K.E. Act, he arrived on the tarmac at 6 a.m. with a Red Bull and a stack of policy briefs. During the flight, he discussed a wide range of policy ideas for reforming K–12, higher education, and corporate governance, delving into the details and complexities of each.

One of his staffers told me that, during the Covid pandemic, he would pore over medical journals and call staffers in the middle of night, asking to connect with doctors who had conducted the research. Many conservative leaders stoke the culture war to generate media attention and fundraising dollars; DeSantis stokes it to advance important policy objectives and to protect his constituents from the excesses of woke ideologies.

Third, DeSantis backstops his culture-war agenda with capable governance. His administration has continued Florida's rise as an economic powerhouse, counted votes in the midterms within hours of the polls closing, and led recent disaster-recovery efforts with skill and efficiency. After Hurricane Ian, the government deployed thousands of linemen, quickly restored power, and rebuilt a vital bridge in three days.

DeSantis understands that maintaining essential services is the foundation of good government, and he has built a team to manage the complexities of administration. His communications team has been particularly impressive, swarming left-wing journalists on social media to correct the record and combat misleading narratives. DeSantis wisely delegates this work, which allows him to focus on what matters: governing.

In short, DeSantis has shown conservatives how to fight—and win. He has demonstrated courage and ability, two essential, if rare, qualities in modern politics. According to post-midterms polling data, Republican primary voters increasingly see his model of governance as the way forward.

DeSantis Tackles Divisive "Diversity, Equity, and Inclusion" Programs on College Campuses

Per the Lindsey M. Burke, Ph.D. "DeSantis Tackles Divisive 'Diversity, Equity, and Inclusion' Programs on College Campuses" The Heritage Foundation January 2023 report:

The average American university has more than 45 individuals with jobs devoted to promoting so-called diversity, equity, and inclusion. DEI programs push divisive identity politics as well as distorted narratives about American history. But Florida Gov. Ron DeSantis' administration is once again leading on this issue, taking a first step in clamping down on these counterproductive positions and administrative bloat.

In order to provide taxpayers and parents with transparency around what tax dollars are funding within the halls of state colleges and universities in Florida, the governor's office sent a letter to the state Department of Education requesting that the agency, along with public universities, provide information on initiatives and expenditures associated with DEI programs and critical race theory.

Each institution must provide by January 13, 2023, a brief description of the program or activity, the number of full and full-time-equivalent employees involved, the total funding to support the initiative, and the amount of state funding spent.

It's a welcome survey. Florida State University has at least 31 personnel dedicated to DEI efforts, and the University of Florida has at least 29, which is likely only the tip of the DEI iceberg on that campus. Numerous such staff members are on the payrolls of Florida's 38 other state colleges and universities.

Getting a full accounting of costs associated with the many programs and initiatives will paint a fuller picture of just how much taxpayer money is funding DEI efforts—efforts that are counterproductive to fostering welcoming environments for all students and that cement divisive, identity-focused politics on campus.

On average across the country, universities employ four times as many DEI staff as staff dedicated to helping students with disabilities, according to research by The Heritage Foundation's Jay Greene and the Educational Freedom Institute's James Paul. Their research also found that universities employ 1.4 times as many DEI staff as history professors.

The problem is that this proliferation of DEI personnel and initiatives is not improving student satisfaction with their higher education experience. Rather, it is increasing bureaucratic bloat and "may be better understood as jobs programs subsidizing political activism without improving campus climate," as Greene and Paul explain.

DeSantis' most recent move follows other important measures his administration has taken to rein in the Left's capture of academic institutions funded by Florida taxpayers, such as:

The Stop WOKE Act. This law prohibits public school districts and colleges from hiring critical race theory consultants and codifies Florida's prohibition on the application of critical race theory in K-12 schools. It also prohibits employers from requiring employees to participate in DEI training. "In Florida we are taking a stand against the state-sanctioned racism that is critical race theory … We won't allow Florida tax dollars to be spent teaching kids to hate our country or to hate each other," DeSantis stated when he announced the proposal in December 2021. While a federal judge paused aspects of the law in November, the governor is expected to appeal the decision.

The Parental Rights in Education Act. This law stipulates that "classroom instruction by school personnel or third parties on sexual orientation or gender identity may not occur in kindergarten through grade 3 or in a manner that is not age-appropriate or developmentally appropriate for students in accordance with state standards." It puts parents—rather than public schools, which should be focused on teaching young children to read and write—in the driver's seat on sensitive topics like sexual orientation and "gender identity."

Senate Bill 7044. This law requires universities to periodically change accrediting agencies in an effort to reduce the "inordinate amount of power" held by accrediting bodies, DeSantis said. Requiring periodic changes in accrediting agencies may also mean colleges aren't pressured to increase DEI initiatives in order to remain in good standing with the accreditation cartel. For example, the Southern Association of Colleges and Schools released a DEI position statement that reads in part that it "supports and encourages the leadership role of its institutions in promoting and sustaining diversity, equity and inclusion in all arenas of higher education." The law also requires professors to undergo "comprehensive post-tenure review" every five years to provide performance accountability.

Alternative Pathways Into the Classroom. In August, DeSantis announced changes to the Florida Administrative Code that provide a pathway for veterans and returning service members to obtain temporary teaching licenses. Downplaying or ending certification requirements to teach (including the requirement that teachers possess a teaching degree, with no consideration for real-world experience as a substitute qualification) would address purported teacher shortages while also weakening the power of ineffective and woke colleges of education.

From providing parents with more transparency relative to what their children are taught in schools and protecting children from the discrimination of critical race theory to weakening the accreditation cartel and shining sunlight on DEI, Florida is leading the way in weakening the Left's capture of education institutions.

It's a big reason—along with expansive school choice options for families and a good return on investment for taxpayers—the state ranked first on The Heritage Foundation's inaugural Education Freedom Report Card. As 2023 legislative sessions kick off across the country, it will be exciting to see what other states follow suit.

Ron DeSantis is Winning the Culture Wars

No governor has drawn more national attention than Ron DeSantis of Florida. And since DeSantis is a Republican and in the mold of Donald Trump, that coverage has been decidedly negative as noted in the Joe Concha "Ron DeSantis is winning the culture wars" *The Hill* March 2023 article:

The topic could be his handling of COVID-19. Or his decision to open businesses and beaches earlier than most other governors. Or vaccine distribution. Or his Parental Rights in Education bill (dubbed the "Don't Say Gay" bill by Democrats and echoed by many in the press). Or banning most abortions after 15 weeks. Or approving an immigration measure that doesn't allow state entities to do business with businesses and companies that transport migrant children who crossed the border illegally into Florida. Or signing a proclamation declaring Emma Weyant the true winner of a U.S. national college swimming title after she lost to transgender athlete Lia Thomas.

You can agree or disagree with DeSantis and the Florida legislature on any of these moves, measures and proclamations. What makes the governor popular among his supporters is that he doesn't appear to give a damn about what the Florida press or the national political media think about how he's leading his state. He has a plan and principles that appear to be unwavering.

Consider a recent exchange the governor had with WFLA's Evan Donovan after the reporter referenced "what critics call the 'Don't Say Gay' bill."

"Does it say that in the bill?" DeSantis shot back, refusing to allow his critics to frame the bill as homophobic. "Does it say that in the bill? I'm asking what's in the bill because you are pushing false narratives. It doesn't matter what critics say."

"It says 'classroom instruction on sexual identity and gender orientation,'" Donovan replied while leaving out a very key detail.

"For who?" DeSantis retorted. "For grades pre-K through three, no five-year-olds, six-year-olds, seven-year-olds. And the idea that you wouldn't be honest about that and tell people what it actually says, it's why people don't trust people like you because you peddle false narratives. And so we just disabused you of those narratives."

And that's true: The bill applies to kids in kindergarten through second grade being taught sexual instruction. Sounds like something that a parent of a kindergartener or first- or second-grader would support.

"Understand, if you are out protesting this bill, you are by definition putting yourself in favor of injecting sexual instruction to 5-, 6- and 7-year-old kids," DeSantis said during another recent press conference. "I think most people think that's wrong. I think parents especially think that's wrong."

The national press is largely against the bill, and headline after headline refers to it as the "Don't Say Gay" bill, in an apparent effort to push a false narrative.

Take this framing by NBC News: Its headline read, "Florida Gov. Ron DeSantis signals support for 'Don't Say Gay' bill," followed by a subhead—"The bill, which would bar the 'discussion of sexual orientation or gender identity' in primary schools, passed the Florida Senate Education Committee on Tuesday."

The headline itself was misleading, because that's not what the bill is called; it's what critics call it. And the story itself, which wasn't an opinion piece, never once mentioned DeSantis's main point—that the bill bars sexual instruction to 5-, 6- and 7-year-old kids.

Why omit that crucial element of the legislation? Unless, of course, a narrative is being peddled.

He'll almost certainly win in November to capture a second term as governor, which could serve as a springboard to a 2024 presidential run.

When 2024 rolls around, Donald Trump will be 78 years old; DeSantis will be 45.

A recent CPAC straw poll showed Trump winning the nomination easily, with 61 percent of the vote. DeSantis was second with 28 percent, up 7 points from 2022. No other candidate got more than 2 percent.

But if Trump doesn't run, DeSantis gets 61 percent of the vote. His next-nearest potential competitors, Donald Trump Jr. and Mike Pompeo, each get 6 percent.

Ron DeSantis is a culture warrior, just as Trump was before him. His positions may be unpopular with Democrats and the press—but if Florida is an indication of sentiment in other swing states, such as Georgia, Arizona, Nevada, Michigan, Pennsylvania and Ohio, this will serve him very well if he becomes 2024 GOP nominee.

Not a National Model—a National Warning

As per the Michael Lucci "Not a National Model—a National Warning" *City Journal* July 2022 article: Instead of a national model, Gavin Newsom's California is a national warning of what happens when the Progressive education establishment captures a state.

The political ads Newsom ran in Florida reveal perhaps an even greater disconnect between his rhetoric and California's reality. Newsom warned Floridians that freedom "is under attack in your state," and urged Florida residents to "join the fight, or join us in California where we still believe in freedom." Newsom's messaging turns gaslighting into a political strategy, and as it turned out, failed miserably if you look how Florida turned a deeper shade of red int h 2022 midterm elections.

If California believes in freedom, it has an odd way of showing it. After years of mask mandates, school closures, and pervasive lockdowns, Californians must be wondering what limits exist on state government intrusion into their lives. Nonetheless, they can't help but notice the newfound freedoms that criminals and street homeless have enjoyed in cities like San Francisco and Los Angeles, where the rule of law has eroded at the hands of activist district attorneys.

Meantime, Californians who vote with their feet are fleeing to Florida in record numbers. From 2010 to 2018, California lost an average of 1,000 people to Florida per year, according to IRS taxpayer migration data. Then, from 2018 to 2019, California lost 4,800 residents to Florida. And from 2019 to 2020—the first IRS data that cover the early pandemic months—California lost 11,500 residents to Florida.

California's outmigrants are bringing lots of income with them. The state shed an average of $270 million of annual income to Florida from 2010 to 2018. The annual loss jumped to $1.2 billion from 2018 to 2019, and then to $2 billion in 2019–2020. California's losses, and Florida's gains, have almost certainly accelerated in the intervening years. And Florida is not the only state picking up California exiles. The Golden State's losses are at or near record levels with other states, too—in particular, states like Texas that Newsom targets with criticism.

Newsom wants Americans to believe that he has it figured out in California, and that the new American model for freedom is a Progressive one. Yet his state's aggressive population pivot has coincided almost precisely with his tenure as governor, making Newsom the first California leader to preside over a shrinking state rather than a growing one.

No amount of political rhetoric can mask California's reality under Governor Newsom. Low-income students are being left behind, the rule of law is eroding, and residents are leaving in record numbers. The many former Californians watching Newsom's ads in Texas and in Florida can only marvel at the hubris of the man.

14 – California's Woke Madness vs. Miami—The Least Woke Big City in America

Credit: California Gov. Gavin Newsom - Fred Greaves/Reuters.

As shown in the Joel Kotkin "California's Woke Hypocrisy" *City Journal* July 2020 article: No state wears its multicultural veneer more ostentatiously than California. The Golden State's leaders believe that they lead a Progressive paradise, ushering in what theorists Laura Tyson and Lenny Mendonca call "a new Progressive era." Others see California as deserving of nationhood; it reflects, as a *New York Times* columnist put it, "the shared values of our increasingly tolerant and pluralistic society."

In response to the brutal killing of George Floyd in Minneapolis, then Los Angeles mayor Eric Garcetti announced plans to defund the police—a move applauded by Senator Kamala Harris, a prospective Democratic vice presidential candidate, despite the city's steep rise in homicides. San Francisco mayor London Breed wants to do the same in her increasingly crime-ridden, disordered city. This follows state attorney general Xavier Becerra's numerous immigration-related lawsuits against the Trump administration, even as his state has become a sanctuary for illegal immigrants—complete with driver's licenses for some 1 million and free health care.

Despite these Progressive intentions, Hispanics and African-Americans—some 45 percent of California's total population—fare worse in the state than almost anywhere nationwide. Based on cost-of-living estimates from the U.S. Census Bureau, 28 percent of California's African-Americans live in poverty, compared with 22 percent nationally. Fully one-third of Latinos, now the state's largest ethnic group, live in poverty, compared with 21 percent outside the state. "For Latinos," notes longtime political consultant Mike Madrid, "the California Dream is becoming an unattainable fantasy."

Since 1990, Los Angeles's black share of the population has dropped in half. In San Francisco, blacks constitute barely 5 percent of the population, down from 13 percent four decades ago. As a recent University of California at Berkeley poll indicates, 58 percent of African-Americans express interest in leaving the state—more than any ethnic group—while 45 percent of Asians and Latinos are also considering moving out. These residents may appreciate California's celebration of diversity, but they find the state increasingly inhospitable to their needs and those of their families.

California's Woke Hypocrisy

More than 30 years ago, the Population Reference Bureau predicted that California was creating a two-tier economy, with a more affluent white and Asian population and a largely poor Latino and African-American class. Rather than find ways to increase opportunity for blue-collar workers, the state imposed strict business regulations that drove an exodus of the industries—notably, manufacturing and middle-management service jobs—that historically provided gateways to the middle class for minorities. As a recent Chapman University study reveals, California is the worst state in the U.S. when it comes to creating middle-class jobs; it tops the nation in creating below-average and low-paying jobs.

Following Floyd's death, even environmental groups like the Sierra Club issued bold proclamations against racism, but they still push policies that, in the name of fighting climate change, only lead to higher energy and housing costs, which hurt the aspirational poor. Many businesses, including small firms, must convert from cheap natural gas to expensive, green-generated electricity, a policy adamantly opposed by the state's African-American, Latino, and Asian-Pacific chambers of commerce.

Meantime, California's strict Covid-19 lockdown policies, imposed by a well-compensated (and still-employed) public sector, have imperiled small firms. "There's a sense that there was major discrimination against local small businesses," said Armen Ross, who runs the 200-member Crenshaw Chamber of Commerce in South Los Angeles. "They allowed Target and Costco to stay open while they were closed. Many mom-and-pops may never come back." Many restaurants—roughly 60 percent are minority-owned—may never recover, notes the California Restaurant Association.

In the past, poor Californians, whether from the Deep South, Mexico, or the Dust Bowl, could look to the education system to help them advance. But California now ranks 49th nationally in the performance of poor, largely minority, students. San Francisco, the epicenter of California's woke culture, has the worst scores for black students of any county statewide.

Yet educators, particularly in minority districts, often seem more interested in political indoctrination than in improving scholastic results. Half of California's high school students can barely read, but the educational establishment has implemented ethnic-studies courses designed to promote a Progressive, even anticapitalist, and race-centered agenda. Unless the education system changes, California's black and Hispanic students face an uncertain future. A woke consciousness or deeper ethnic identification won't lead to successful careers. One can't operate a high-tech lathe, manage logistics, or engineer space programs with ideology.

California's failure to improve conditions for Latinos and blacks was evident even before the lockdowns and recent unrest. What the state's minorities need is not less policing, or systematic looting of upscale neighborhoods, or steps to reimpose affirmative action, or kneeling politicians; they require policies that empower working-class citizens of all races to ascend into the middle class.

Leaders offer platitudes and counterproductive policies rather than opportunities and better living standards for the state's minorities.

The state's leaders should prioritize improving middle-class jobs and opportunities, replacing indoctrination with skills acquisition, and encouraging local businesses. Considering the nature of California politics, this can happen only if minority Californians demand something different. That could happen if enough of these residents realize that the state's ruling Progressive class is interested in their votes—but apparently not in improving their lives.

Gavin Newsom's Real Constituents

The most charitable thing you could say about Gavin Newsom is that he's not intelligent enough to be the cause of California's troubles. The Golden State governor—born to a fabulously wealthy and politically well-connected family, establishing himself as a local power player with the funding of family friends, and entering Democratic Party politics as a political appointee—"inherited a state in decline," Rich Lowry noted in 2021.

According to the Nate Hochman "Gavin Newsom's Real Constituents" *National Review* March 2023 article: But "Newsom is the governor by and for all the forces that created this debacle. . . . From San Francisco mayor to lieutenant governor to governor, he's wedded his ambition to a Progressive elitism that can seem out of touch even in liberal California."

What he lacks in originality and competence, Newsom more than makes up for in his enthusiasm for his role as an avatar of gated-community Silicon Valley Progressivism. His public-relations strategy is an instructive example: Of the last 24 tweets Newsom has posted—spanning the four-week timeline from Biden's State of the Union address to now—nine were about California, while 14 were about Republicans in red states, usually zeroing in on MSNBC-style culture-war fodder such as guns, abortion, and, in today's favored formulation, the threat to democracy. (The one other tweet was about Pennsylvania Democratic governor Josh Shapiro banning the death penalty.)

This focus on red states is a consistent feature of Newsom's public persona. Another tally of his tweets last April yielded similar results: Of his 22 most recent tweets at the time, seven were about California, "five were about national events," and "ten out of the 22 were about Republicans in other states, with no discernible relationship to California." And it's not just his Twitter tweets: In 2021, Newsom's reelection campaign "posted billboard ads in seven red states" with "information about how to get an abortion in the Golden State."

That summer, he also launched an ad on Florida's Fox News affiliates, informing Sunshine State residents that "freedom is under attack by Republican leaders in states like Florida." The price tag for Newsom's "ads and billboards blasting Republican governors in other states," according to the *Sacramento Bee*, was "about $230,000."

That a California governor would campaign for reelection by advertising in Texas and Florida might seem counterintuitive. But it can tell us a lot about how California operates. From the standpoint of individual self-interest, Newsom's strategy makes a good deal of sense. The Golden State's golden boy knows where his bread is buttered—and it's not with the dwindling California middle class, many of whom have either packed up and left or are seriously considering doing so. (An astonishing 2019 poll found that "more than half of California voters have thought about moving out of the nation's most populous state, citing the high cost of housing, taxes or its political culture.")

It's with the same Progressive elites who propped him up in the first place and who have gone out of their way to protect their hand-picked governor from democratic forces: When the rabble got it into their heads to attempt to recall Newsom in 2021, his wealthy backers—labor unions, Big Tech, and Hollywood, among others—rallied around him to the tune of a $71 million anti-recall war chest.

Newsom, ever the faithful servant, is simply reflecting the priorities and worldview of his main constituents.

The fact that California has the highest illiteracy rates in the nation, that it's now the poorest state in America after factoring for cost of living, that its cities—wracked by crime, drugs, and homelessness—have come to resemble those in third-world countries, or that it's seen net out-migration every year this century has very little bearing on the sumptuous quality of life in Montecito or Marin County.

Insulated from the broader decay their policies have inflicted on the state, the Progressive power-players in California have the same priorities as Progressive elites everywhere: Abortion, the education system's inalienable right to teach third-graders the 1619 Project and the spectrum of gender identities, and guns—not, of course, the gun violence perpetrated in California's deep-blue cities, but the kind that can be used to stoke hysteria about the backwards, AR-15-toting rednecks in Alabama.

In response to the news that Tennessee governor Bill Lee signed a law restricting drag-show performances in public places where children might see them, Newsom fired off a characteristic tweet: "Tennessee has the 8th highest murder rate in the nation. It ranks 44th among states for health outcomes. And this is what the Governor is focused on." As Governor Lee pointed out in response, Tennessee has consistently ranked among the top states for incoming U-Haul rentals for the past few years, whereas California has had more outbound U-Haul trucks than any other state in America for the last three consecutive years. (So much so, in fact, that in 2021, "it broke U-Haul's ability to measure—because the company ran out of trucks to rent" to Californians, as Dan McLaughlin noted). But none of that matters much to Newsom: A few U-Hauls here, a lost congressional district there—so long as the Silicon Valley donor dollars keep flowing, it'll all come out in the wash.

Nationally, the Democratic Party has embraced a desire to "make America California." If the party succeeds, a neo-feudalist high-low political system—an alliance of an insulated ruling elite and a welfare-dependent urban underclass—will be coming soon to your state. The good news is, there will still be U-Hauls. The bad news is, there won't be any Tennessee's left to drive them to.

California's Progressive Betrayal

Per the Joel Kotkin "California's Progressive Betrayal" *City Journal* June 2019 article: The recent California Democratic Party convention in San Francisco exposed the divide between the state's Progressive and working-class voters. Progressives, in their militant certitude, support left-wing policies that often don't affect them; it's the working class that suffers the consequences of these proposals.

But the Green New Deal, widely embraced by party leaders, pushed too far, triggering a backlash at the convention. The state's private-sector labor unions, notably the building trades, organized a "Blue Collar Revolution" protest against the Democrats' climate legislation.

The Democrats are calling for the elimination of fossil fuels by 2030, which would result in California's immiseration, especially for workers in the state's energy-production sector, the nation's fourth-largest. In 2012, the oil and gas industry employed over 400,000 Californians, but these workers—unionized and well-paid—can expect pink slips with the green package. California's renewable mandates also threaten the building-trades unions, which count 400,000 members statewide—a sizable contingent, though considerably below the industry's 2007 numbers.

While new wealth drives demand for expensive housing, building restrictions that stymie expansion into suburbia limit the sector's growth. Not long ago, building-trade union members were considered part of California's aristocracy, but they can no longer afford median-priced homes in any of the state's urban counties. Residential sales have dropped statewide, and California's rate of new housing permits has fallen behind the national average, making construction workers' economic prospects even dimmer. And the manufacturing sector has stagnated—this despite a 4 percent national expansion, along with 5 percent and 14 percent growth in neighboring Arizona and Nevada.

The Golden State's left-wing policies hurt working-class and middle-class residents.

California's working- and middle class can expect this trend to continue as the state's climate-regulation policies become ever more draconian. The cost of living will rise, and Californians can anticipate more taxes on items like soda, guns, and tires. Yet Progressives ignore the burdens these put on residents in the name of equity and climate change. In an effort to hide their huge carbon footprint, it's worth noting, Silicon Valley's tech leaders have transferred servers and relocated facilities to Texas, the Midwest, and China—places with higher rates of greenhouse-gas emissions—and sending jobs out of state, too.

California elites insulate themselves against an economy that saddles workers with high energy and house prices, especially in the state's less-temperate interior. In mild coastal climates like the Bay Area or west Los Angeles, electricity prices aren't such a burden, but in inland cities like Bakersfield, summer temperatures regularly soar over 100 degrees, leading to massive cooling costs. In a state with the nation's highest poverty rate, high energy bills can be devastating.

The blue-collar revolt isn't limited to a party convention. In an unprecedented lawsuit against the state Air Resources Board—the agency leading the implementation of green mandates—some 200 civil-rights leaders claim that these expensive policies disproportionately affect minorities and the poor. But California's green-focused press generally ignores them, as do the state's large media entities. The Walt Disney Corporation, for example, is known for paying pitiful wages to its blue-collar workers. As former Anaheim mayor Tom Tait observed, numerous full-time workers at Disney are homeless. In the Bay Area, meantime, Google and other tech firms have fueled the growth of "car people," who live in their vehicles because it's too expensive to rent even a tiny apartment in the region. Many tech workers live hours away from their jobs, increasing the vehicle miles that alarm environmental bureaucrats.

It's unclear whether a new labor movement could gain momentum in one-party California. Working-class Democrats must pressure the party, with the support of the building trades and other private-sector unions. They'll need help confronting San Francisco oligarchs like Progressive activist Tom Steyer and virtue-signaling CEOs at Apple, Salesforce, LinkedIn, and Hollywood studios, who mandate allegiance to the party's intersectional platform of environmental, racial, and gender equity.

Moderate Democrats have become rare—witness Colorado governor John Hickenlooper getting booed at the state Democratic convention for daring to reject socialism—and once-centrist politicians are tacking further left. California's Republicans, to paraphrase the late comedian Rodney Dangerfield, are no bargain, either. Their alienation of Latino voters, along with a tone-deaf approach to economic issues, has left them with a small, and shrinking, public presence.

How long can working- and middle-class Californians endure such conditions while being hectored by billionaires and celebrities? An alternative may exist: the development of a pragmatic, solutions-oriented new party, as proposed by former GOP congressman Tom Campbell. This would constitute what the late historian Kevin Starr called "the party of California"—one that doesn't adhere to a green religion or do the bidding of tech mavens but instead seeks to restore the promise that attracted so many to this peculiarly blessed state.

Stopping California's Downward Spiral Into Progressivism Madness

This article is from the Summer 2010 *City Journal* article "The Golden State's War on Itself" by Joel Kotkin used in *California Madness*:

Today's California represents most everything wrong with today's Progressivism movement. In retrospect, California's Progressive mistakes provide an incubator and testing ground to show America and prove to the world, why it's not in the best interest of the overwhelming number of Californians and Americans.

In the 19th and 20th centuries, California was the destination for those seeking a better place to live. For most of its history, the state enacted sensible policies that created one of the wealthiest and most innovative economies in human history. California realized the American dream—but better—fostering a huge middle class that, for the most part, owned their homes, sent their kids to public schools, and found meaningful work connected to the state's amazingly diverse, innovative economy.

In the middle of the 20th century, the leadership of Governor Pat Brown and his practical Democrats made California, the Golden State, the envy of all others. These were the sapient leaders with old school Democrats values, ideas and policies that helped create the California dream.

However, since the dawn of the 21st century, the dream has been evaporating. Between 2003 and 2007, California state and local government spending grew 31 percent, even as the state's population grew just 5 percent. The overall tax burden as a percentage of state income, once middling among the states, has risen to the sixth-highest in the nation, says the Tax Foundation.

Since 1990, according to an analysis by California Lutheran University, the state's share of overall U.S. employment has dropped a remarkable 10 percent. When the state economy has done well, it has usually been the result of asset inflation—first during the dot-com bubble of the late 1990s, and then during the housing boom, which was responsible for nearly half of all jobs created earlier in this decade, and big tech most recently.

Guiding the agenda of California's Democrats are a ruling elite, small in number, but wielding incredible power. Among these elites are government union leaders, liberal billionaires from Hollywood to Silicon Valley, extreme environmentalists, and the social justice vanguard. The money and influence these elites bring to California politics cannot possibly be matched by the opposition. But all the money in the world cannot make up for the fact that their policies have made life miserable for millions of ordinary Californians.

We've heard all this before. Much of what Californians face are challenges confronting everyone in America. But California, the biggest state, and the bluest state, is a powerful trendsetter. California is broken, hijacked by opportunists wielding overwhelming financial and political power. Just how bad are things in California? Consider these frightening state rankings as evidence of the destructive outcomes of so-called Progressivism polices.

With the exception of its fine weather, California is at the bottom of the heap when it comes to just about every measurable quality of life indicator. Here is a partial breakdown from *California Madness: A SAPIENT Being's Guide to the State's Recall, Leftist Policies & Progressive Downward Spiral*:

- Poverty rate: 50th

- Housing affordability: 49th

- Cost of living: 49th

- Inflation-adjusted household income: 27th

- Tax rate for top earners: 50th

- Sales tax rate: 50th

- Business taxes: 49th

- Overall tax burden: 40th

- Business climate: 47th, 48th, 50th

- Infrastructure quality: average grade of D+

- Traffic congestion: 47th

- K–12 learning outcomes: 42nd

- Homelessness rate: 50th

The ideological failure of California falls squarely on the shoulders of Progressive politicians and activists, social justice reformers, civil rights workers, cultural appropriation enforcers, diversity, and inclusion warriors and the like who have spread into the media, government, college campuses, neighborhood organizations and workplaces.

Undergirding all this is the assumption that a just society will be gained through the intervention of government. Only government can force the needed changes. This is achieved through a complex and extensive web of government mechanisms: civil rights laws; affirmative action programs; minimum wage laws; housing assistance; guaranteed income; income maintenance programs that seamlessly transfer wealth from haves to have nots; block grants to states; guaranteed health care for all; national disaster relief—and more.

In the Progressive view there is little tolerance for government that cannot deliver equal outcomes for all. However, every human being is unique and not standardized widgets, so ultimately, government is incapable of creating a society of equals (which is impossible) and will fail.

Fixing California: The Themes That Make Anything Possible

This section is from the June 2021 article "Fixing California—Part One: The Themes That Make Anything Possible" comes from the California Policy Center's Edward Ring:

For conservatives across America, California has become the cautionary tale for the rest of the country. Anyone who actually lives in the Golden State, and enjoys the best weather and the most beautiful, diverse scenery on earth, knows there are two sides to the story of this captivating place. Nevertheless, the story keeps getting worse.

For every essential—homes, rent, tuition, gasoline, electricity, and water—Californians pay the among the highest prices in the continental United States. Californians endure the most hostile business climate in America, and pay the highest taxes. The public schools are failing, crime is soaring, electricity is unreliable, water is rationed, and the mismanaged forests are burning like hell.

Yet all of this can be fixed. The solutions aren't mysteries and consist of the following:

- Deregulate housing permits.

- End the disastrous "housing-first" policies and instead give the homeless safe housing in inexpensive barracks where sobriety is a condition of entry.

- Repeal Proposition 47, which downgraded property and drug crimes.

- Build reservoirs, desalination, and wastewater recycling plants.

- Build nuclear power plants and develop California's abundant natural gas reserves.

- Recognize that the common road is the future of transportation, not the past, and widen California's freeways and highways.

- Let the timber companies harvest more lumber in exchange for maintaining the fire roads and power line corridors.

- Implement school choice and make public schools compete with private schools on the basis of excellence.

Done!

This isn't just about ideology. The politicians who governed California during what arguably were its greatest yesteryears were Democrats. Old-timers refer to them as the Pat Brown Democrats (not to be confused with his son Jerry Brown and his Progressive Democrat constituents), leaders whose approach to politics was pragmatic and focused on serving the people.

During that heyday, homes were affordable, and freeways weren't crowded. Public schools were good, and the University of California campuses offered the best public higher education in the country. The California Water Project, taking barely more than a decade to construct, remains the most successful feat of interbasin water transfers in the world.

The Coalition That Will Realign California

This section is from the December 2020 article "Fixing California–Part One: The Themes That Make Anything Possible" comes from the California Policy Center's Edward Ring:

Across several areas of policy, the Democratic party, led by Gavin Newsom, has not merely alienated, but enraged millions of Californians.

The key to political realignment in California is not only to offer these groups a political agenda that incorporates solutions to all their grievances, but does so in a manner so coherent, so practical, and so promising, that a common solidarity is generated which transcends all the ways California's ruling class has thus far divided them.

Hardcore populist support for Democrats in California comes primarily from millions of white liberals, living in inherited homes, who pay minimal property taxes and are hence immune from the consequences of an out-of-control public sector bureaucracy, along with the government employees that work in that bureaucracy.

The critical swing constituency, currently solidly in the Democratic camp, are black, Latino, and Asian voters—and the battle to turn back California's Progressive downward spiral is in the hands of these critical groups.

The Battle for California is the Battle for America

These sections below are from the October 2020 article "The Battle for California is the Battle for America" comes from the California Policy Center's Edward Ring:

By now, this is a familiar story. California is a failed state. Thanks to years of Progressive mismanagement and neglect, the cities are lawless, and the forests are burning. Residents pay the highest prices in America for unreliable electricity. Water is rationed. Homes are unaffordable. The public schools are a joke. Freeways are congested and crumbling. And if they're not still on lockdown or otherwise already destroyed by it, business owners contend with the most hostile regulatory climate in American history.

It is understandable that conservatives in the rest of the United States would be happy to write off California. But California is not writing off the rest of the United States, and therein lies grave danger to American prosperity and freedom.

What if California doesn't implode, a victim of its own political mismanagement? What if California instead completes its transformation into a successful plutocracy, run by a clique of multi-billionaires in a partnership of convenience with environmentalist extremists and backed by the power of a unionized state bureaucracy?

What if the people who would resist this tyranny leave, and the remaining population peacefully accepts universal basic income and subsidized housing? What if all it takes to be a feudal overlord in Progressive California is to proffer to the proletarians a pittance of alms, while reliably spouting incessant, blistering social justice and climate change rhetoric?

Why won't that work? After all, it's worked so far. It won't work because the Progressive policies have one fatal weakness: They're fundamentally wrong.

This has already been shown in the first part of this chapter and will become more apparent in the rest of the chapter. The fundamental premises Progressives use to justify their actions are flawed. Many maddingly—and a few idiotically.

Nonetheless, in total, they're only a small sampling and for a complete smorgasbord on everything that's wrong with Progressive California, dig deeper in the S.A.P.I.E.N.T. Being's *California Madness: A SAPIENT Being's Guide to the State's Recall, Leftist Policies & Progressive Downward Spiral* textbook.

Miami: "The Least Woke City in America"

As per the Oliver Wiseman "The Least Woke City in America" *City Journal* Winter 2022 in-depth report: They're still talking about the caravans: the miles-long lines of cars, their passengers waving American flags, Cuban flags, and Donald Trump banners, that painted streaks of red, white, and blue down Calle Ocho and around Little Havana, bringing much of Miami to a halt for hours at a time ahead of the 2020 election.

On a recent trip to the city, those I spoke with—Republican operatives and supporters, as well as more impartial observers of Miami's political scene—described these demonstrations vividly. The multinational, multilingual expressions of support for a Republican presidential candidate were unmistakably Miami. Miami's increasingly conservative political culture reflects the influence of immigrants fleeing socialist dystopias.

They displayed a flavor of GOP enthusiasm that couldn't happen anywhere else, at least not on this scale. The demonstrators took cues from the city's proud anti-Communist past. Some of the organizers of the events—officially known as the "Anti- Communist and Anti-Socialist Caravans for Freedom and Democracy"—included groups established to fight the Cuban dictatorship. The parades were a rejoinder to pollsters who warned not to read too much into enthusiastic displays of support for a given candidate. Miami was the site of major political change in 2020, and if you watched the car parades, you saw the indicators earlier than most.

Miami-Dade, Florida's largest county, is two-thirds Hispanic and shifted dramatically toward the Republicans in the last election. In 2016, Hillary Clinton won by 64 percent to Trump's 35 percent in the county. Four years later, Joe Biden triumphed, but in a much closer contest: 53 percent to 46 percent. That huge swing in such a big county was key to Trump's relatively straightforward Florida win. In raw numbers, Trump nearly doubled his vote count in Miami-Dade, from 333,000 in 2016 to 617,000 in 2020. His statewide margin of victory, under 120,000 in 2016, more than tripled, to 372,000 in 2020.

The changing habits of voters in Miami are perhaps the most important part of the story of why what was once the most coveted swing state in the Electoral College has taken on a reddish hue. What's true on a presidential level is true on a gubernatorial level. Ron DeSantis sneaked into office by just 30,000 votes in 2018. Since then, his stock has soared; his 2022 reelection seems likely. The swing in 2020 was also enough to flip two South Florida House seats from blue to red.

It soon became clear that the Miami results were indicative of a national story of Hispanic voters shifting rightward in 2020. Latino-heavy precincts everywhere from the Rio Grande Valley, Texas, and Clark County, Nevada, to Paterson, New Jersey, and Milwaukee saw a marked move to the right. According to a Pew survey of validated election voters, the nationwide Democratic margin of victory among Hispanic voters dropped from 38 points to 21 points from 2016 to 2020, with 38 percent of Hispanics voting for a second Trump term.

Florida's growing less white and more conservative offers Republicans nationwide a feel-good story.

Florida senator Marco Rubio, himself a Cuban-American from Miami, has argued that the lesson from 2020 is that his party must be built on a "multi-ethnic, multi-racial, working-class coalition." It's not hard to see the appeal of this vision, undercutting, as it would, Democratic assumptions about the party's rainbow coalition.

Adding to this demographic and electoral shift are the results that Republicans in power have delivered in recent years. DeSantis has overseen a practical approach to the pandemic that—at least according to the revealed preferences of exiles from Democratic states—is what many Americans wanted. According to the state's Office of Economic and Demographic Research, Florida grew by an estimated 329,717 new residents in the 12 months to April 2021.

Meantime, Miami's Republican mayor, Francis Suarez, has hustled his city onto the tech hub map, doing all he can to lure talent and capital from Silicon Valley and New York. (See "America's Tomorrow City.") Thanks to policymaking at a city and state level, Miami has become perhaps the most prominent counterexample to instances of Democratic dysfunction.

The Miami lesson is also about how much Republicans stand to gain if they don't neglect cities. The urban Republican has become something of an endangered species lately; at times, it can feel like the GOP has given up on serious attempts to win votes in the country's major cities. But Miami underscores the prominent role that cities can play in Republican victories. The party doesn't need to win majorities in densely populated areas for an improved urban performance to count: it just needs to pick some low-hanging electoral fruit, make inroads into large Democratic margins in metropolises, and then the path to statewide victory for Senate, gubernatorial, and presidential candidates suddenly looks clearer.

The question is whether Republicans in other cities can learn anything from South Florida. Is Miami a road map? Or do its idiosyncrasies—especially its Cuban population, a self-selecting group that fled Communism—make it a special case?

A 1930s guide to Florida, published as part of the Federal Writers' Project, notes the miracle of Miami: "In less than a quarter century, miles of rainbow-hued dwellings, bizarre estates, ornate hotels, and office buildings have grown from a mangrove swamp, jungle, coral rock, and sand dunes." Then a resort town, Miami, the guide reports, is, in the sporting season, "100 days of perpetual carnival." Of busy racetracks, the author writes, "the playboy and the plowboy, the dowager in pearls and the sylph in shorts, the banker on vacation and the grifter on the prowl keep turnstiles clicking and feed staggering sums into the pari-mutuels."

The city is 60 times more populous today—and no less miraculous. The same quality is still identifiable almost a century later: an ebullient cross-section of America chasing riches and the sun and having fun along the way.

For all this continuity, the biggest change in the last century has been demographic, which started with the influx that followed after Fidel Castro took control of Cuba in 1959. It transformed Miami, though what today is an essential feature initially seemed an aberration. "When a prince builds a palace, he does not intend a shelter for paupers. When men built Miami they did not see it as journey's end for a tide of empty-handed refugees," mused the *New York Times* in 1961. "There is perhaps no large city in the nation less suited by temperament and resources to take in the destitute." The new arrivals would soon rewrite that economic story and outperform gloomy accounts of their predicament.

"The Miami lesson is also about how much Republicans stand to gain if they don't neglect cities."

After a decade or so, Cuban-Americans had figured out how to flex their political muscles. By the early 1970s, they were a voting bloc that politicians couldn't ignore. Eventually, that political power took on national significance. When Ronald Reagan came to town in 1984 and promised that "someday, Cuba itself will be free," he was the first president since JFK to visit Miami and directly appeal to Cubans.

The late Joan Didion started her 1987 book-length account of Miami in a graveyard. "Havana vanities come to dust in Miami," she wrote. If you want to explain Miami's weirdness, Woodlawn Park Cemetery is still a good place to start. Among those buried there: Cuban presidents and senators, Nicaraguan leaders, Latin American first ladies, and Bay of Pigs veterans. The graves are a reminder that city politics and geopolitics cannot be separated in Miami. It was Miami's status as a stage on which Caribbean and Central American politics played out that made it, in Didion's words:

A settlement of considerable interest, not exactly an American city as American cities have until recently been understood but a tropical capital: long on rumor, short on memory, overbuilt on the chimera of runaway money and referring not to New York or Boston or Los Angeles or Atlanta but to Caracas and Mexico, to Havana and to Bogotá and to Paris and Madrid. Of American cities Miami has since 1959 connected only to Washington, which is the peculiarity of both places, and increasingly the warp.

Today, memory has displaced rumor. Once a site from which to launch invasions, coups, and counterrevolutions, Miami knows what other American cities have forgotten, or never properly understood. Anti-Communism is hard-wired into this town.

Florida Democrats have long bet on a new generation of Cuban-Americans letting bygones be bygones, and forgiving the party of Kennedy, a villain in Miami ever since he abandoned 1,500 Cuban exiles in the botched Bay of Pigs invasion. But it hasn't worked out that way. More than 60 years have passed since the exodus from Cuba to Miami, and Cuban-Americans remain a distinct—and conservative—electoral bloc.

It isn't just Cubans who are frustrating Democratic assumptions about Latino voting habits, however.

Today, Venezuelans and Nicaraguans, informed by political failures in their own countries of origin, are crucial parts of a bloc of Hispanic Republicans. Add to that smaller cohorts of Latin American–origin voters who also swung rightward in the last election, and something broader is happening.

When I met Suarez, the mayor of the City of Miami (the municipality covers only the downtown of what today is a sprawling city) in his waterfront office, I asked him whether such a thing existed as Miami Republicanism, a brand of politics unique to the city.

"I think there is," explained the trim 44-year-old over cafecito. "And I think it stems from the fact that a lot of us are exiles. We've seen firsthand the destructive power of Communism. And we know how it promises the world and delivers misery. So I think that is the base of how this Miami movement and formula is created. It is a rejection of an ideology that is probably one of the largest frauds perpetrated on humankind."

From that hard-earned anti-Communism flows much else. "We are a city that believes in capitalism," says Suarez. "That believes in innovation as a means of democratizing opportunities."

Last March, Suarez was maybe the first public official with any real national profile to catch the coronavirus. Nearly two years on, he has emerged as one of the big political winners from the pandemic. The son of Xavier Suarez, Miami's first Cuban-American mayor, Francis's first foray into city politics was at two years old, when he appeared in one of his father's campaign commercials. "Vote por Papi, por favor," was the toddler's polite request.

Suarez, a registered Republican, was elected to the nonpartisan mayoralty himself in 2017. Since 2020, he has been unapologetic about the opportunities that emerged for his city because of the coronavirus. At times, Suarez's techno-optimist hustle feels gimmicky—to demonstrate his determination to make Miami the crypto capital of America, he is planning to pay city employees in bitcoin. But as mayor, he doesn't enjoy as many executive powers as his counterparts in other U.S. cities, so boosterism is one of the few ways he can move the dial.

And the hype, Suarez argues, can be backed up by results. "All of these ingredients have now created a quantifiable narrative," he says. "Before we were talking about all the migration that was happening. Now we have a lot of statistics to back it up." He cites more than $1 trillion in total value in assets under management of companies that recently moved to the city. Many new businesses have launched, and a study of LinkedIn data found that Miami experienced the largest percentage increase in software and IT services workers of any American city.

Suarez was reelected in November with 79 percent of the vote. Away from the flashy tech hub sales pitch, he pushes an agenda that focuses on low taxes, combating homelessness, and encouraging school choice and a well-funded police department. In January, Suarez takes over as chairman of the Conference of Mayors, an organization of city leaders. From that position, he hopes to push his center-right brand of urban policy on a national stage.

Some of this, he concedes, is not replicable—palm trees wave outside his office, as if a reminder of the city's natural advantages were needed—but part of it is. "Miami has changed in the last ten years," says Suarez. "It's become the prototypical city, the city that you want to be like."

Miami Republicanism comes in many varieties.

Suarez is at one end of the spectrum: a centrist, business-friendly fixer who has frequent tussles with the more populist governor. Though not from Miami, DeSantis embodies a more raucous, brash Republicanism, as does the former president, who now lives 70 miles up the coast. But there seems to be an accommodation between the city's GOP factions often lacking in the rest of the country.

The Republicans I spoke with along this spectrum, whether red-hat wearers or metropolitan Suarez supporters, identified two binding agents that keep Miami Republicans pulling together: patriotism and a firmly held belief in freedom and opportunity.

"In the end, everyone wants the same thing, which is a home, opportunities for prosperity and growth, and freedom," says Ileana Garcia, the founder of Latinas for Trump and a state senator who flipped a central Miami district in the November 2020 election. "People are keen to stigmatize support for Trump and the Republican Party, including from Latinos, as a cult," says Garcia. "But we're not cultish at all. What motivates us is freedom: freedom to live your life according to your values, freedom to do what you want with your money and freedom to live in a country where you don't have to have government hovering over you and telling you what to do all the time."

Armando Ibarra, chairman of Miami Young Republicans, says that the lesson from Miami is a focus on enterprise, patriotism, and the American dream. "A lot of Latinos and Hispanics are very optimistic and we love this country," he says. "We believe in its ideals. When the Left and the Democratic Party attacks our country or attacks our ideals or presents this very pessimistic view of America as inherently racist and a place where you can't get ahead, we know all of these things not to be true."

Cuban-American writer Alex Perez, a Miami native who has written for *City Journal*, explained to me that the city is "old-school American," more so than much of the rest of the country these days. Another Miami native made a similar point. "This is the least woke city in America," she told me, referring to the city's boisterous, politically incorrect spirit.

Miami scrambles the Progressive Left's preferred racial classifications. Instead of a hierarchy of intersectional identities that pits "people of color" against whites, the city is a patchwork of national identities and often competing loyalties: Cubans, Haitians, Venezuelans, Nicaraguans, Dominicans, Colombians, Jamaicans, and others. The notion that American politics can be reduced to a coalition of people of color taking on white supremacy looks silly when viewed from Miami.

"Our heritage is always front and center," says Garcia. "But if you ask any non-English-speaking Hispanic in Miami what they are, they will tell you 'soy Americano.' I'm American." The frequent Progressive use of the term "Latinx"—a gender-ideology-compliant neologism that only 4 percent of Hispanics say they prefer—encapsulates how the Democrats' increasing adoption of identity politics turns off many nonwhite voters, especially among the working class.

It is a cliché in Washington to claim that Hispanic voters (or, for that matter, any demographic bloc) are "not a monolith"—but it rings particularly true in Miami GOP circles, where Republicans have actually acted on this insight. "A lot of people don't want to be a generic Latino," says Ibarra. "What we [Miami Young Republicans] did is embrace the customs, the parts of the culture that they enjoy, that they love. Because they are proud. If you're Cuban or any other national background, you're proud of your family's customs and heritage. I think our ability to connect with them on that basis was really key." In that sense, Miami's voting blocs resemble the white-ethnic voting groups that once dominated U.S. urban politics. And the party that treats them as such could gain the most at the ballot box.

Miami Republicanism is at ease with the populist style but more optimistic and forward-looking than recent populist currents.

(The "American carnage" theme of Donald Trump's inaugural speech, for example, would have little resonance in a city full of strivers like Miami.) It is infused with a patriotism that only a few years ago was uncontroversial in public life—and resolutely anti-woke. It has the instinctive libertarianism of the small-business owner and a confidence that can find expression in two kinds of Miami newcomer: the venture capitalist backing a fresh idea or the recent arrival to the U.S. betting his future on the American dream. It is not an angry cry from those on the "wrong side of history," nor is it shy about fighting the culture wars. It takes aim at a liberal political and cultural elite that describes a country that Miami denizens don't recognize.

Miami is a reminder that the rising support in 2020 for the GOP among nonwhite voters, and Hispanics in particular, cannot be disentangled from the party's performance in major cities. According to surveys, a Latino voter is roughly as likely as a white voter to describe himself as conservative. But for decades, traditional solidarities have trumped ideology, with conservative Hispanics reliably voting Democrat. That may be changing, with nonwhites starting to sort themselves more according to ideology. If that proves a real trend, it would create new opportunities for the GOP.

A recent Manhattan Institute report sketched the outlines of a "metropolitan majority": a cohort of voters in America's large and growing cities that is ethnically diverse (survey respondents were nearly one-quarter Hispanic or Latino) and politically moderate. Their biggest worries, the polling found, are the cost of housing, homelessness, the coronavirus, traffic, public safety and crime, and high taxes. And the survey finds a very limited appetite for some of the most prominent Progressive policies being pushed at a state and city level.

All this suggests that Miami may not be an aberration but a sign of a more competitive urban politics. Miami's various Latino blocs, drawing on a fervent anti-Communist tradition, swung rightward earlier and further than nonwhite voters in other cities, and the city's unique history meant that it had an active, engaged local Republican Party ready to capitalize on the opportunity. But brave is the Democrat who waves away Miami as a stand-alone case. And foolish is the Republican who believes that something similar couldn't happen elsewhere.

15 – Stopping America's Impending Destruction From Progressivism Madness

Credit: The S.A.P.I.E.N.T. Being.

As we've seen and discovered through the course of this textbook, attempting to find any semblance of sapience in today's Progressive arguments is as elusive as Big Foot, let alone facts, logic, and the truth. Furthermore, many Progressive policies are outright racist, unconstitutional, and Marxist based, at the very least. And finally, Progressives cannot admit they're wrong on so many issues, and continuously fail to produce logical arguments, provide proven results, and/or utilize unbiased data to back their ideology.

With so much going against today's Progressivism movement, the anti-Progressive long game must be focused on educational policies, legislation, and pedagogy that help wins the culture war by restoring conservative values, viewpoint diversity, and sapience to high school and college campuses—as well as enlighten their students, administrators, and faculty of the many blessings to humankind that are the direct result of Western European culture, American exceptionalism, and Judeo-Christian values.

This prudent approach, is a project of recapture and reinvention, enabling sapient beings, independents, libertarians, and conservatives the opportunity to finally to demonstrate an effective countermeasures against Progressivism's long march through the institutions. The Progressive Left's permanent bureaucracy will be dead-set against this gambit, but if it succeeds, a new era for higher education—and for the country—is possible.

This task will be monumental, yet critical, to America's survival and future, and this chapter, along with the others, provides the means and methods to enable the mission and vision of sapient beings to reverse the idiocracy and hypocrisy of the 'Regressivism' movement. Outlined in this final chapter are a number of successful strategies to help make this happen, like we showed in earlier chapters, particularly at the K12 parents and school board level and with college trustees and alumni intervention.

Shut Down Activist Academic Departments

For decades, conservatives have lamented the rise of activist academic departments that push left-wing ideology in the guise of dispassionate scholarship. In 1989, Claremont McKenna College scholar Harry Jaffa described the process of his university buckling, under threat of violence, to the establishment of a left-wing black studies department. In 1998, Roger Scruton scoffed at the same activist disciplines, which he called "mock subjects that will in time destroy our universities." In 2012, Bruce Bawer documented the "victim's revolution" that had laid waste to humanities departments in nearly every elite university.

Per the Christopher F. Rufo "Shut Down Activist Academic Departments" *City Journal* March 2023 article: All these writers decried the rise of the new departments but seem to have accepted them as part of an inevitable process of decline. But the conservative position has been too fatalistic. The activist disciplines are not inevitable, and decline is always, in part, a choice—one that can be reversed with sufficient courage, insight, and will.

For conservatives, the first step in reforming the universities is to expose the abuse of "academic freedom," which has been used as a defense of intellectual license, and to propose a clear policy that any academic departments that pursue activism instead of scholarship will lose their taxpayer funding. Administrators, faculty, and students can advance left-wing ideology in their private capacity, but the First Amendment is not an entitlement to state support and taxpayer subsidies. Lawmakers are well within their rights to demand that public universities focus on rigorous academic work over partisan polemics with a scholarly veneer. Any program that violates this compact will be abolished.

What would shutting down activist academic departments look like in practice? Here, we don't need to speculate; we can look to the past as a guide. Some of America's most prestigious universities have shut down academic departments that strayed too far from their mission. Two case studies are particularly notable: the decision by the University of California, Berkeley, to shut down its criminology department in 1974 and the University of Chicago's decision to close its education department in 1998.

At Berkeley, the story is familiar. In the late 1960s, university officials capitulated to activist faculty associated with the Black Panther Party and left-wing revolutionary movements. They assented to the transformation of the criminology school, which had previously trained law-enforcement officials in the latest management techniques, into a hub for "radical criminology," which advocated defunding traditional police departments and fomenting left-wing "prison action."

As the department grew more radical, Berkeley administrators pushed back. First, they fired four activist assistant professors who had undermined the university's mission. Then, in 1974, Chancellor Albert Bowker shut down the entire School of Criminology, ignoring large-scale student demonstrations, which supporters described as "militant and spirited."

Bowker justified the closure by citing the need to make budget cuts due to an economic recession, but the political subtext was clear: the radical criminologists had degraded the university's scholarly mission. After the chancellor's announcement, students occupied an administrative building, but Bowker sent in law enforcement, armed with shotguns and grenade launchers, and the students were removed.

The process of shutting down the education department at University of Chicago was more orderly. The department's pedigree was impressive: it was founded by reformer John Dewey and had been home to prominent scholars such as Bruno Bettelheim and William S. Gray, creator of the "Dick and Jane" reading series. But in the 1970s, the department turned away from educational practice and focused more on left-wing educational theory. Over time, the quality of academic work declined, and external funding began to dwindle. Finally, in 1996, after a formal review, the dean of the social science division, Richard Saller, recommended that the university close down the department, citing "uneven" research and "low expectations." It was officially shuttered soon afterward.

These examples establish an important precedent: it is not a violation of "academic freedom" to close down ideologically captured or poor-performing academic departments; it is, to the contrary, part of the normal course of business. Legislators in states such as Florida and Texas, which will both be considering higher education reform , should propose the abolition of academic departments that have abandoned their missions in pursuit of shoddy scholarship and ideological activism.

It is time for the "victim's revolution" to be met with a meaningful counter-revolution. Legislators have an opportunity to abolish academic programs, such as critical race theory, ethnic studies, queer theory, gender studies, and intersectionality, that do not contribute to the production of scholarly knowledge but serve as taxpayer-funded sinecures for activists who despise the values of the public whom they are supposed to serve.

Enough is enough. It is time for principled action, not fatalism and defeat. Conservatives have an opportunity to move beyond critique and enact meaningful reforms that will restore the pursuit of truth as the telos of America's public universities.

Woke Schooling: A Toolkit for Concerned Parents

The June 17, 2021 Manhattan Institute report offers an excellent "Woke Schooling: A Toolkit for Concerned Parents" toolkit that provides most everything concerned parents need to know about every aspect of defeating the Progressivism agenda at their woke schools. For a link to this toolkit, please check out the Appendix.

The following advice is based on conversations with a number of activists, journalists, and others who have spent the past several years pushing back on critical pedagogy in their children's and others' schools. It is not meant to be comprehensive but rather a starting point—a way for you to begin thinking about how you can take an active hand in making your child's school a better place for him or her to learn.

What follows are a few principles to keep in mind before taking action.

Proportionality

We are all probably aware of the most controversial instances of critical pedagogy in classrooms: the Buffalo, New York, school district that told students that they must become "activists for antiracism" instead of focusing on their failing test scores, or the California model "ethnic studies" curriculum that speaks approvingly of Aztec human sacrifice, to name just two cases. That these incidents made it into the national news means that they are rarefied examples of critical pedagogy at its most expansive.

By contrast, maybe the problem you are dealing with is a single assignment that your child's teacher has handed out—something that might have been hastily scraped from a seemingly reliable website. You could respond by calling down the school board or launching a boycott—but doing so may induce the board to circle the wagons and force a conflict where a few simple words would have made the problem evaporate.

But at times, you do need to prepare for an extended fight. When resolving any problem—including the problem of dangerous falsehoods in your child's classroom—it's important to make your response proportional to the scale of the issue. Throughout the rest of this section of the guide, we'll cover solutions ranging from a polite conversation to total parent boycott. Remember: start small and think about the scale of the problem before you go nuclear.

The Minority Rule

There is rarely such a thing as a truly popular movement, and the spread of critical pedagogy is no exception. Most diversity initiatives at major schools are spearheaded by administrators, often in a specifically designated department of diversity, equity, and inclusion (DEI); social media protests are often instigated by a small group of students or alumni, not a spontaneous and uncoordinated mass action.

The point is not about the legitimacy of these movements but about how they operate. A small group of people who demand something will generally get the compliance of the majority who are indifferent. This is what mathematician, investor, and social critic Nassim Taleb calls the "minority rule": the insight that majorities will follow minorities' preferences if the latter are intransigent and the former are "flexible."

This is a useful principle to understand not only because it allows you to focus on the minority of actors who are driving the change to which you object; it also makes you aware that you and other parents like you can together become an intransigent minority. If you're more stubborn than the most stubborn proponent of critical pedagogy in your school, you may win through intransigence alone.

Effective Persuasion

In every step of the process, it's important to keep in mind how you're communicating, which means keeping in mind with whom you're communicating. Your fundamental goal is a change at some level, whether it be in your child's classroom or across the whole school. To attain that change, you need to convince someone—a teacher, a principal, a school board—and therefore you need to think about effective persuasion.

In general, being polite and conciliatory is the correct first move—you catch more flies with honey than with vinegar. No one thinks of himself as a bad guy, including a teacher teaching your child something you don't want your child to learn. If you go in guns blazing, you are more likely to elicit a defensive response, which will move you further away from your goal. Do not allow politeness to make you a pushover—your goal should be calm and reasonable but firm.

That said, do not discount the effectiveness of getting angry, particularly if you find that you need to escalate past a one-on-one conversation. Advocates of critical pedagogy have wrung huge changes out of administrations through pressure campaigns built on assertions of "righteous rage" and "justified anger." The squeaky wheel, as it were, gets the grease, and you should not be afraid to match your opponents' level of being demanding—after all, it has been successful for them.

Another insight that can be gleaned from paying attention to critical pedagogy advocates: a story is worth a thousand arguments. The persuasiveness of so-called critical race stories comes from their pathos—anecdotes are a powerful tool for swaying public emotion, and you should actively strive to use them. You can outline why you think critical pedagogy is bad; but actual stories of how these practices are hurting kids are far more effective in changing the minds of administrators—never mind the community at large.

Solving the Problem Yourself

As mentioned, it's important to adapt your response to the scale of the problem. Before you do anything, assess the level at which the problem is happening. Although curricular guidelines may be set at the school district or even the state level, day-to-day decisions about what your children are reading and learning are still mostly in the hands of teachers. So start by consulting with their teachers: Is their use of a critical pedagogy resource a one-off, or is it part of a deliberate learning plan? Are they incorporating a variety of perspectives, or only offering one view? You may find that a simple conversation can get you further than you would have thought.

If the original teacher is recalcitrant, it's time to move up the administrative ladder. In a public school, that might mean the head of the division, the principal, and then the district superintendent's office. Be calm and polite but persistent—administrators should see you as someone who demands to be taken seriously. In a private school, that might mean going to the head of the division, followed by the head of the school.

While you're still prosecuting your issue on an individual level, here are a few tips to keep in mind:

Document everything. Make sure to save e-mails and take notes after meetings. Consider recording conversations—but be aware that this may be interpreted as hostile before you need to become hostile. If you do record conversations, be aware of the laws surrounding recording in your state.

Consider whether you want to press for your child to be able to opt out of the objectionable lesson/content. Such opt-outs have long existed—for example, for parents concerned about the content of sex education classes. Rather than asking your teacher/administrator to change the curriculum for everyone else, consider the pros and cons of keeping it away from your own child.

Don't let yourself be bullied. A major feature of critical pedagogy is the way that it dispatches critics through personal invective and guilt by association—dissenters are tarred as "racists," "white supremacists," and the like. You should recognize that these assertions are nothing more than an attempt to intimidate you; do not let these words have power over you. If you hold firm, the most ardent critical pedagogy advocates will quickly discover that they've run out of ammo.

Getting Organized

Maybe your efforts to address the problem one-on-one have gone nowhere, or maybe the problem was too big for a one-on-one solution. Some schools have implemented large-scale critical pedagogy programs, with the full endorsement of the administration and associated staff. In situations like that, your complaint about one teacher isn't going to cut it. What you need, then, is to move from solving the problem yourself to working in concert with other parents.

In fact, operating as a lone wolf may make it easier for the administration to dismiss your concerns. Be wary of techniques designed to mollify you without addressing the problem: for example, offering you a teacher's aide position, or a favored teacher for your child next year, or bringing in the PTA to outnumber you.

Your first step is to identify other parents who are sympathetic to your concerns and skeptical of the school's new direction. This is easier said than done—in a school that has fully leaned in to critical pedagogy, those who speak out critically may find themselves ostracized. You may need to be the first person to step forward by speaking out publicly, such as at a PTA meeting or over a parent e-mail list. Alternately, if you observe others expressing discontent or being reticent, approach them.

Another approach is to give parents an anonymous forum to vent, and then form connections. At Los Angeles's Harvard-Westlake school, an Instagram page called "Woke at Harvard-Westlake" has documented critical pedagogy excesses over the past year. It includes a public-facing e-mail address and form so that parents and students can contact its anonymous administrator(s). Such an anonymous venue could highlight absurdities in your school as well as help build connections.

A key reality of establishing a group of parents is that the bigger the group becomes, the easier it gets. That's because another parent you bring in might know two more sympathetic parents. But it's also because the bigger the group becomes, the easier it is to be comfortable affiliating with it—knowing that five other people are on your side is exponentially more comforting than knowing that only one person is.

After you have more than two or three parents on your side, it may make sense to create a central venue for coordination. An e-mail list works well, as does a group chat application like WhatsApp or Discord. For those who are particularly concerned about privacy, encrypted apps like Signal or Keybase may be a better option.

Being aware of other parents' privacy concerns is paramount to organizing a successful group. Particularly in private schools, where enrollment is at the discretion of the administration, parents might fear that dissenting from pedagogical practices will hurt their kids' educational future. Giving parents a variety of options to disclose information about themselves to you might be a useful way to build their confidence and trust—ultimately producing a more cohesive group. Encourage parents to engage anonymously in a text chat, and then encourage an in-person meeting when they seem comfortable doing so.

Responding as a Group

Once you've organized even a small group of parents, you want to think about how to make your voice heard at school. Consider a similar escalation strategy to the one outlined above in "Solving the Problem Yourself"—approach a problematic teacher, and if that proves futile, work your way up. In general, at this stage, you have two goals: the ultimate goal of correcting the problematic behavior; and the instrumental goal of attracting more parents to your cause.

You should consider the medium by which you and your group of parents communicate your displeasure. Parents at the Dalton School in New York, for example, penned an anonymous letter to the administration condemning the school's turn toward critical pedagogy; parents in the Southlake, Texas, public school district pushed through an entirely new school board. But you could also consider asking for a sit-down meeting before moving to that step. Remember the principle of proportionality: only escalate if your less aggressive response is not getting the desired results.

You should consider the trade-offs of anonymity. As mentioned, some parents will be uncomfortable attaching their names to any opposition to the school's "diversity" agenda, particularly if you are in a private school where your child has no formal right to attend. At the same time, anonymity is inherently delegitimizing: the Dalton letter gives no sense of how many or which parents are opposed to your school's critical pedagogy agenda. This gives opponents an opportunity to dismiss you as a small, irrelevant group—or as not confident enough of, or committed enough to, your views to defend them publicly. Be aware that at a certain point, anonymity will no longer be tenable.

Once you have tried direct conversation and accepted the need to go public, many responses become available. You could consider organizing your group to write letters to the editor of your local newspaper (more on this in the next section), attend your local PTA or school board meeting en masse, and even organize a real-life protest, as parents did after D.C.-area magnet high school Thomas Jefferson High School dumped its race-blind admissions test.

If you are a private school parent, now may also be a time to consider talking about annual contributions to the school, one of the few points of leverage that such parents have over their schools' administrations that advocates of critical pedagogy usually do not. A group of parents can inform their school that they will not be giving annual contributions if divisive material remains in the curriculum. Doing so connects the issue to the school's bottom line and may instigate change.

To the extent possible, it pays to be aware of the diversity of the people presenting criticism of an ideology that has framed itself, however dishonestly, as promoting diversity and inclusion. To the extent that parents from different racial/socioeconomic backgrounds are genuinely represented in your group, their public expression of criticism helps make the case that the group's concerns are not rooted in racism but in a genuine concern that "antiracism" may make discrimination worse, not better.

You also should consider offering a range of ways for parents to get involved, so that even those who don't want to do too much can do something. Make it easy to write a letter to your school board or principal by offering a form outlining the specific problem, alluding to more general objections to critical pedagogy (consult the Glossary for more details), and emphasizing your investment as a parent in your child's right to an education that is free from racial and ethnic discrimination. Similarly, if you write a letter to the editor of your local paper (see the next section on working with the media), you can then ask fellow parents to sign it, which is relatively easy for them but helps make their support for your project public.

Offering a Positive Vision

Pushing back against critical pedagogy is a worthwhile and noble project, but it is also important and helpful to be positive. Some people who support (or believe they support) critical pedagogy in schools have strange beliefs about critics, thinking, for example, that skeptical parents do not want their children to ever face hard historical truths, or that they support a whitewashing of American history. That's not the case: critics of critical pedagogy are concerned that it defines America in an exclusively and simplistically negative light, not that it offers any criticisms of America at all.

One solution to emphasize—particularly in history and social studies curricula at the middle-and high-school level—is the importance of presenting a variety of perspectives on an issue and trusting students to sort out right from wrong. Parents and administrators are likely to be far more open to adding thinkers to the curriculum than subtracting them—consider floating the works of moderate (and even left-leaning) academic critics of critical pedagogy like John McWhorter, Glenn Loury, Carol Swain, Erec Smith, Stephanie Deutsch, Peter Boghossian, and others.

A related strategy is to try to offset critical pedagogy's relentlessly negative account of ethnic relations with a more positive, affirmative story. Your student's school can use black history month to learn only about the "white supremacy" allegedly inherent in standardized tests or negative reactions to being called racist, or they can use it to celebrate great black Americans and try to respectfully build a better understanding of the many contributions of black people and black culture to America. Critical pedagogy's fixation on the negative can turn minority students into tokens of oppression—a more positive approach can help them celebrate who they are in school without dividing students into friend and foe.

Lastly, it is important to take seriously individual acts of bias and intolerance in schools. Regardless of critical pedagogy's claims, it's still the case that kids can be and often are cruel to each other—and parents should want an environment that minimizes and condemns bigoted bullying. Adopting critical pedagogy training and "antiracist statements" actually lets school administrators avoid the much harder work of treating acts of bigotry as a disciplinary problem.

If you want to push back on these practices, make clear that you agree that racism should not be tolerated in your school—but critical pedagogy is the wrong way to go about reducing it.

Working With the Media

If your parent-group actions aren't working, or even if they are, you might consider bringing public attention to the problem. Even if your child's school is united behind the idea of critical pedagogy, much of the nation is not. Bringing your story into the spotlight can apply much needed pressure, highlighting unreasonable behavior in a way that can fix it.

If you've been carefully documenting your activities until this point, those details will be invaluable. Other parents should have been doing so, as well. You may want to organize those details in a common Google Doc or other online file-sharing service.

If your child is enrolled in a public school, you might want to familiarize yourself with your state's freedom of information laws. As government entities, public schools are generally subject to such laws, and administrators can be compelled to release everything from internal documents to the texts of their e-mails. For a guide to your state's public records law, consult a group such as the National Freedom of Information Coalition.

Note that compelling the release of, say, a principal's e-mails is a very aggressive action—so do so only if you're prepared to burn bridges. But if your child is a public school student, freedom of information laws exist to help hold public employees accountable, so don't be afraid to use them. For example, investigative journalist Asra Nomani (whose son attends Virginia's public Thomas Jefferson High School) used her state's freedom of information law to reveal a $20,000 contract (for a one-hour video presentation) between Virginia's Fairfax County Public School district and critical race theorist Ibram Kendi.

Whether you want to publish your personal story, the details of other parents' struggles against the administration, or something that you've uncovered through a public records request, you need to think about the platform on which you do it. Self-publishing allows you to spread your message quickly without relying on others, but it also limits your reach (unless you already have a large social media following). By contrast, working with local—or national—outlets gives you a bigger platform but also reduces your control over the story.

If you'd like to self-publish, a wide variety of platforms are now available that are easy to set up and use. Blogging services like Medium or WordPress allow you to set up a public-facing blog in minutes, while newsletter services like Substack enable you to produce similar output for a select list of subscribers. You might also consider using social media platforms like Twitter and Facebook to get the message out.

You can do only so much with such platforms, however, so you might want to approach the media. A good place to start is local media—your local paper or TV station—which are eager for local stories and, in general, less likely to be ideologically sympathetic to critical pedagogy than many large national outlets.

Before choosing to approach local media, consider whom you want to approach—a local television station, a local paper, etc. Take partisan slant into account—a right-leaning outlet will likely be more sympathetic but may give your opponents the opportunity to tar you as partisan yourself.

If you're not having success with the local media, or if you think that your message needs a broader audience, you might consider a news source with wider reach. A particularly clear-cut story of critical pedagogy–motivated wrongdoing may get traction at a national, left-leaning paper like the *New York Times* or *Washington Post*, but such outlets have evinced sympathy toward the goals of "antiracism," and thus might be less interested than you would hope.

Explicitly right-leaning outlets have the challenge of partisan tilt but are likely to be more sympathetic: consider sites like the Manhattan Institute's *City Journal*, *National Review*, the *Washington Free Beacon*, or the Daily Signal. Working with such sites will be more likely to connect you to a journalist interested in your story but may also make it harder for your story to have an impact with other parents skeptical of these outlets. Last, consider particular angles of your story: if, for example, you are dealing with critical pedagogy–inspired antisemitism, a site like Tablet, which focuses on Jewish issues, may be interested.

Before you approach anyone in the media, organize the information you want to present—a PDF of the most salacious documents you can share, a list of other parents with whom they can talk, for example. Giving a journalist something to work with makes him or her much more likely to take your story.

When talking to a reporter, be aware of journalistic norms around quoting and attribution. Unless you have explicitly stipulated that the conversation is "off the record," and your interlocutor has agreed, assume that everything that you are saying can and will appear on the front page of your local newspaper tomorrow, and conduct yourself accordingly. Be courteous and avoid personal criticisms of your opponents—your problem is with a failure of teaching, not with the people you may be butting heads with.

The trade-off of going to the media is that while your story will get a wider audience, it also becomes no longer your story to control. The journalist with whom you are working is free to quote you however he or she sees fit and is indeed professionally obligated to get the opinion of the "other side." This doesn't mean that you shouldn't approach the media, but you should be aware that your interlocutor's work product may not perfectly line up with how you imagined it.

While this guide advises speaking to the media only after you've tried internal recourse and sought to build connections to other parents, it's worth noting that a public story may have the effect of jump-starting those connections. Schools trying to push critical pedagogy over and above parents' objections have every reason to keep them in the dark and separated from each other, as many parents have experienced. A story about something crazy happening at your school can change the conversation, giving parents a concrete concern to discuss and coalesce around, and making the airing of thoughts socially permissible in a way that it previously was not.

Taking Legal Action

Critical pedagogy is not merely counterproductive and divisive, critics increasingly argue—it may also be illegal. The Fourteenth Amendment to the U.S. Constitution and the 1964 Civil Rights Act spell out certain rights to not be discriminated against on the basis of race, as well as certain guarantees of the right to free speech, even (in some cases) by students in public schools. Training and activities in public schools (and, potentially, private schools that have accepted federal funding) that divide students by race demean certain students as "oppressors" or inherently evil, or they compel students to profess certain beliefs that may run afoul of their state and federal rights.

These are the grounds for a number of lawsuits designed to fight back against critical pedagogy across the country. Although they are still in the early stages at the time of this guide's publication, they offer a promising approach for protecting students from discrimination, as well as a tool for you to consider when no other option is available.

Interested groups have, for example, sued the Santa Barbara Unified School District, the Democracy Prep Public Schools of Las Vegas, and Virginia's Thomas Jefferson High School. In these cases, plaintiffs have alleged that implicit bias training violates nondiscrimination rules, that compelled "antiracist" speech in the classroom is constitutionally impermissible, and that moves to end merit-based admissions to selective public high schools unconstitutionally discriminate against Asian-Americans.

Whether these arguments will be palatable to the courts remains to be seen. But parents should keep abreast of developments and consider whether their own situation could serve as a test case.

Whom Can I Ask for Help?

This guide is meant to be a starting point for parents looking to fight back against critical pedagogy in their school, but it's far from the only resource. Many national organizations—many brand-new—are interested in fighting various manifestations of critical pedagogy at every level of education, from kindergarten through college. They can help you connect to other parents, give you advice on organizing in your school, offer tips on talking to the media, and even help with lawsuits. Here are a few organizations:

Foundation Against Intolerance and Racism (see Appendix for link), a nonpartisan, centrist organization focused on responding to radicalism with a "compassionate anti-racism" dedicated to equal dignity and equality under the law. FAIR runs a membership organization, including local chapters, to help connect people from all parts of society skeptical of "woke" approaches that they term "neo-racism." It can also help connect parents like you to other parents and to professional and legal aid.

Parents Defending Education (see Appendix for link), a "national grassroots organization working to reclaim our schools from activists promoting harmful agendas," PDE is a school-focused group working to connect parents and provide resources to respond to critical pedagogy. It can help you find other parents in your local area and offer resources on how to respond effectively to your administration's agenda.

Foundation for Individual Rights in Education (see Appendix for link), has historically focused on repressive speech policing at the college level, however, FIRE has been expanding its work to K–

12 education. Its high school network offers a free-speech curriculum, as well as resources for parents and students concerned about their voices being silenced.

Pacific Legal Foundation (see Appendix for link), a national nonprofit public-interest law firm focusing on civil rights issues. It has recently taken an interest in critical pedagogy discrimination in public schools, organizing the lawsuit against Thomas Jefferson High School. If you are considering legal action, or if you believe that you have a test case, this organization may be a useful resource.

Republicans Revive Counter-CRT Bills in Congress

While the battles over critical race theory have, for the most part, occurred at the state and local levels, two conservative lawmakers are taking up the fight in Congress. Per the Nate Hochman "Exclusive: Republicans Revive Counter-CRT Bills in Congress" *National Review* February 2023 article:

Representative Dan Bishop (R., N.C.) and Senator Tom Cotton (R., Ark.) are set to reintroduce two anti-CRT bills, both of which were originally introduced by the Republican lawmakers in the last legislative session: the Stop CRT Act, which would prohibit federal funding for schools and universities that promote CRT-based concepts, and the Combating Racist Training in the Military Act, which would bar the use of similar ideas in military institutions, including service academies.

The two bills reenter the fray with a deep bench of support in the Republican caucus, with each boasting dozens of co-sponsors. "Critical race theory (CRT) is a poisonous ideology that seeks to divide Americans based on their skin color, and it must be ripped out, root and branch, from our institutions," Bishop told NR in a statement. "The Biden administration and radical Left's relentless promotion of these racist, anti-American ideologies is toxic to our country and culture. These bills are one crucial part of our fight against the insidious effort from the Left to fundamentally transform society based on their designs."

The Stop CRT Act, as Education Week reported in 2021, "would prohibit federal funds from going to schools that teach students that one race is inherently inferior or superior to another, that someone is inherently oppressive or racist because of his or her racial identity, that America is a fundamentally racist country, or that promote critical race theory in general," as well as codifying Trump's executive order barring CRT-inspired trainings for federal-government employees and contractors.

The Combating Racist Training in the Military Act would bar the military from including similar concepts "in trainings or other professional settings, if their inclusion would reasonably appear as an endorsement," and prohibit "hiring consultants to teach such theories, compelling individuals to profess belief in such theories, or segregating individuals on the basis of race in any setting," according to a 2021 press release from Cotton's office.

Conservatives should welcome the concerted anti-CRT push from federal lawmakers such as Bishop and Cotton. Thus far, state-level Republicans have generally served as the vanguard in the fight against the left-wing education bureaucracy. With their direct control of state universities and public schools, and a relative lack of bureaucratic barriers and competing national interests to navigate, Republican majorities at the state level have begun to target radical pedagogies with a slate of anti-CRT laws, restrictions on ideas derived from gender ideology, and even efforts to defund social-justice programs, gender-studies departments, and the "diversity, equity, and inclusion" (DEI) bureaucracy.

But to dismantle the sprawling apparatus that produced CRT, conservatives will have to confront the system at the source. The federal bureaucracy's ubiquitous presence in modern American life has made it the primary benefactor of radical programs under both Republican and Democratic presidencies and congressional majorities, often slipping under the radar with euphemistic titles that conceal their real function.

Today, an astonishing quantity of government programs end up lining the pockets of left-wing activists, from targeted education grants and Covid-relief funds to the National Science Foundation and the Department of Defense. A tally from the Claremont Institute estimates that over $4.3 billion in federal funding has been lavished on Progressive causes—CRT and gender-studies education grants, DEI or "culturally responsive" reeducation boot camps, LGBT advocacy groups, and so on—since 2016.

This Subsidization of Progressivism

This subsidization of Progressivism, as Congressman Jim Banks (R., Ind.) noted in the American Mind, "is spent not only to spread anti-American doctrines which will tear the nation apart; it also funds a class of activists, paying their salaries so they can be a perpetual revolutionary class." And "astonishingly," Banks added, "Congress sent more funding to woke institutions and activities in 2017 and 2018, when Republicans controlled both chambers, than it did in 2019 and 2020 with Nancy Pelosi in the Speaker's chair. This Congress, we should aim to eliminate all such funding."

In a refreshingly simple way, that's what the Stop CRT Act and the Combating Racist Training in the Military Act aim to do: cut off CRT's lifeline at the national level by ending its access to the gravy train of federal dollars, routing the ideology from influential government institutions such as the Department of Defense and the broader military bureaucracy, and applying restrictions to the concepts that CRT espouses rather than the narrow definition of CRT itself.

With a Democratic Senate majority, to say nothing of an octogenarian president whose administration has a bottomless appetite for anti-American racialism, the odds of the aforementioned Republican bills passing this session are about as good as those of a blizzard slamming Death Valley. But with only a one-chamber Republican majority, conservative statecraft in the 118th Congress is going to have to mean something other than just passing laws. In a moment when the GOP appears to have very little idea of who it is and what it stands for, so-called messaging bills such as the pair introduced by Bishop and Cotton have a two-pronged disciplining and consensus-making function: First, they rally a disorganized and internally divided Republican Party around a specific set of priorities; and second, they forge the outlines of a new Republican agenda, legitimating the policy proposals with the popular support of the caucus.

They also set the tone. Legacy media have consistently sounded the alarm about the "chilling effect" that state-level anti-CRT laws inflict on teachers. But that's a feature, rather than a bug, of these efforts—a "chilling effect" on the proliferation of CRT means that the bans are having their intended effect. Republicans at every level of government should be seeking to put the CRT regime on notice. Gone are the days when taxpayer-funded Progressive activism can persist without meaningful resistance from the Right. One way or another, this country is headed for a reckoning over the corruption of its education system.

How to Run For a School Board Seat Against Progressives and Win

The Joseph U. Oswald Patriot Online School Board Training Program from The Leadership Institute allows anyone to acquire the skills needed to wage and win your campaign for school board to put a stop to Progressivism madness.

In every community, school boards have an important role. They make sure students receive the education they deserve to prepare them for higher education, trade school, or the workforce. Sadly, many school boards are used as social engineering tools or are captured by labor union officials trying to control both sides of the collective bargaining table.

Conservative leaders must engage in school boards from coast to coast to ensure schools focus on their educational mission for our children's future success. Political technology determines political success. Get the skills for a successful campaign—it's essential. Learn from successful, experienced leaders who have served on school boards.

The Joseph U. Oswald Patriot Online School Board Training Program features presentations from seasoned conservatives who have served on school boards, plus campaign professionals experienced in local campaigns.

You'll learn how to design, wage, and raise funds for a successful school board campaign. In addition, you'll receive briefings and background information you'll need to be well informed and articulate your own experiences and issue positions to voters in your community.

Specifically, you will learn to: develop a campaign and communications strategies specifically for school board elections; communicate effectively with voters through highly effective voter contact techniques, scalable to highly localized elections; raise funds and build a volunteer team.

Laying Siege to the Institutions

The lesson we've drawn from reporting on institutions that promote ideologies such as critical race theory and radical gender theory is that they have been captured at the structural level and can't be reformed from within. So the solution is not a long counter-march through the institutions. You can't replace bad directors of diversity, equity, and inclusion with good ones. The ideology is baked in. That's why we call for a siege strategy.

As laid out by Christopher F. Rufo's "Laying Siege to the Institutions" *Imprimis* April/May 2022 Volume 51, Issue 4/5 report:

This means, first, that you have to be aggressive. You have to fight on terms that you define. In responding to opponents of the Florida bill, for instance, don't argue against "teaching diversity and inclusion," but against sexualizing young children. And don't pull your punches. We will never win if we play by the rules set by the elites who are undermining our country. We can be polite and lose every battle or we can be impolite and actually deliver results for the great majority of Americans who are fighting for their small businesses, fighting for their jobs, fighting for their families.

Second, you have to mobilize popular support. This requires ripping the veil off of what our institutions are doing through real investigation and reporting so that Americans can make informed choices. We live in an information society, and if we don't get the truth out, we will never gain traction against the narratives being constantly refashioned and pushed by the Left.

Less than two years ago, an infinitesimal number of Americans knew about critical race theory. Through investigation and reporting, we've brought that number up to 75 percent. The public now opposes critical race theory by a two-to-one margin, and it is being hounded out of schools and other places. This kind of action is a model for dealing with every ideology and institution that is undermining the public good and America's future.

Remember that institutions don't choose these ideologies democratically—they don't ask people or employees to vote for them. They impose them by fiat, through bureaucratic, not democratic rule. So it isn't surprising that the institutions lose big when we force their agendas into the political arena. What politician or campaign manager in their right mind would ignore an issue that is supported by a two-to-one margin? So-called conservative politicians who do ignore such issues—or who oppose bringing them up out of a false sense of decorum—aren't on the people's and the country's side.

With public institutions like K-12 education, another crucial step is to decentralize them. It is centralization and bureaucratization that makes it possible for a minority of activists to take control and impose their ideologies. Decentralizing means reducing federal and state controls in favor of local control—and it ultimately means something like universal school choice, placing power in parents' hands. Too many parents today have no escape mechanism from substandard schools controlled by leftist ideologues. Universal school choice—meaning that public education funding goes directly to parents rather than schools—would fix that.

Progressive Left: Overwhelmingly Democratic and nearly unanimous in their support for Joe Biden in 2020

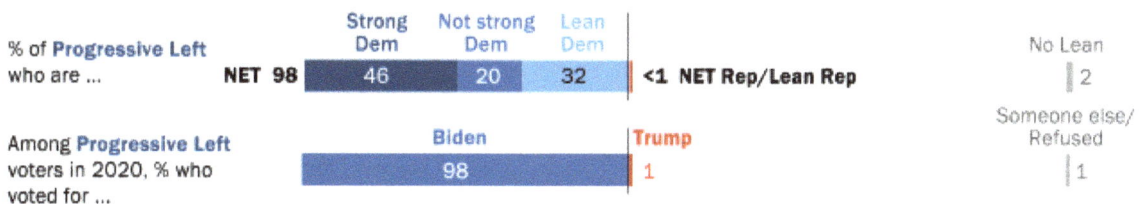

Note: Voter figures based on validated voters, those citizens who said they voted in a post-election survey and were found to have voted in commercial voter files.
Source: Surveys of U.S. adults conducted Nov. 12-17, 2020, July 8-18, 2021, and July 26-Aug. 8, 2021.

PEW RESEARCH CENTER

Conservatives have for too long been resistant to attacking the credibility of our institutions. Trust in institutions is a natural conservative tendency. But conservatives need to stop focusing on abstract concepts and open their eyes. Our institutions are dragging our country in a disastrous direction, actively undermining all that makes America great.

To some extent, the institutions are now destroying their own credibility. Look at the public health bureaucracy and teachers' unions, which acted in concert to shut down schools and keep children needlessly masked—and for far too long. As a result, there has been an explosion in homeschooling, as well as in the number of alternative K-12 schools such as the ones Hillsdale College is helping to launch around the country. What is needed is to build alternative or parallel institutions and businesses in all areas. There is no reason, for example, why plenty of high production value children's entertainment can't be produced outside the ideological confines of the Walt Disney Company.

Conclusion

In conclusion, we make a mistake in thinking about politics simply in terms of a Left versus Right dynamic. That dynamic is significant, but where the opportunity really lies today is focusing on a top versus bottom dynamic. An elite class, representing a small number of people with influence in the knowledge-based institutions, are acting in their own interest and against the interest of the vast majority of the American people—those who are still attached to the idea that America is a force for good and who think, to take just one example, that young children should be protected from the imposition of radical gender ideology.

In terms of the top versus bottom dynamic, the choice today is between the American Revolution of 1776 and the leftist revolution of the 1960s. The first offers a continued unfolding of America's founding principles of freedom and equality. The second ends up in nihilism and demoralization, just as the Weather Underground ended up in a bombed-out basement in Greenwich Village in the 1970s.

Even those of us who are temperamentally predisposed to defense must recognize that offense—laying siege to the institutions—is what is now demanded. Now is the time to become involved and get to work, saving America's destiny from Progressivism madness.

Appendix

40 *MADNESS* Textbook Titles Published to Date: https://www.fratirepublishing.com/madnessbooks

- *Fake News Madness*
- *Crime Rate Madness*
- *Voting Madness*
- *California Madness*
- *Free Speech Madness*
- *Democratic Party Madness*
- *Education Madness*

Complete List of Woke Companies: https://daveseminara.com/complete-list-of-woke-companies-condemning-so-called-racist-voting-laws/

Critical Race Theory Briefing Book: https://cplaction.com/wp-content/uploads/CRT-Briefing-Book-Rufo.pdf

Foundation Against Intolerance and Racism: https://www.fairforall.org

Foundation for Individual Rights in Education: https://www.thefire.org

Heterodox Academy Guide to Colleges: https://heterodoxacademy.org/blog/the-heterodox-academy-guide-to-colleges-starting-a-methodological-discussion/

New Group Equips Parents With 7 Tools to Combat Wokeness in K-12 Education: https://www.dailysignal.com/2021/10/08/new-group-equips-parents-with-7-tools-to-combat-wokeness-in-k-12-education/

Pacific Legal Foundation: https://www.pacificlegal.org

Parents Defending Education: https://www.defendinged.org

President Biden Issues Executive Order Creating National DEI Bureaucracy (Video): https://www.youtube.com/watch?v=WH2RWBgg9jk

SAPIENT BEING PROGRAMS: https://www.sapientbeing.org/programs

- **Sapient Conservative Textbooks (SCT) Program**
- **Free Speech Alumni Ambassador (FSAA) Program**
- **Make Free Speech Again On Campus (MFSAOC) Program**
- **Journalism Code of Ethics, Practical Logic & Sapience Standards:**

https://editor.wix.com/html/editor/web/renderer/edit/06d69a20-d6db-4ae0-a458-a22723ff3e41?metaSiteId=d68a3b84-6415-475d-818c-ab8cdd34b311

- **Program Handbooks:** https://www.sapientbeing.org/resources

The Critical Classroom – The Heritage Foundation: https://www.heritage.org/the-critical-classroom

The Joy of Being Wrong – Video by the John Templeton Foundation: https://youtu.be/mRXNUx4cua0

The S.A.P.I.E.N.T. Being: https://www.fratirepublishing.com/books

Woke Schooling: A Toolkit for Concerned Parents – Manhattan Institute: https://www.manhattan-institute.org/woke-schooling-toolkit-for-concerned-parents

Glossary

Affinity Group – Is meant to be safe spaces for educators or students who share an identity, such as a common race or heritage, to discuss mutual concerns.

American Dream – Is a national ethos of the United States, the set of ideals in which freedom includes the opportunity for prosperity and success, as well as an upward social mobility for the family and children, achieved through hard work in a society with few barriers.

Antiracism – An illiberal term by Ibram X Kendi who argues unsapiently that the opposite of racist is anti-racist rather than simply non-racist, and that there is no middle ground in the struggle against racism; one is either actively confronting racial inequality or allowing it to exist through action or inaction.

Cancel Culture – An intolerance of opposing views, a vogue for public shaming and ostracism, and the tendency to dissolve complex policy issues in a blinding moral certainty.

Civil Rights Act of 1964 – Outlawed discrimination on the basis of race, color, religion, sex, or national origin, required equal access to public places and employment, and enforced desegregation of schools and the right to vote.

Colorblindness – Is a term that has been used by justices of the United States Supreme Court in several opinions relating to racial equality and social equity, particularly in public education.

Confirmation Bias – Happens when a person gives more weight to evidence that confirms their beliefs and undervalues evidence that could disprove it.

Constructive Disagreement – Occurs when people who don't see eye-to-eye are committed to exploring an issue together, alive to their own fallibility and the limits of their knowledge—and open to learning something from others who see things differently than they do.

Critical Legal Theory (CLT) – A Progressive movement that challenges and seeks to overturn accepted norms and standards in legal theory and practice.

Critical Pedagogy – Is a teaching approach inspired by critical theory and other radical philosophies, which attempts to help students question and challenge posited "domination," and to undermine the beliefs and practices that are alleged to dominate.

Critical Race Theory (CRT) – Programs, based on a neo-Marxist ideology that originated in law schools a generation ago, purport to expose and correct "unconscious racial bias" and "white privilege" among their employees. Critical race theory treats "whiteness" as a moral blight and maligns all members of that racial group as complicit in oppression.

Critical Theory (CT) – A Marxist-inspired movement in social and political philosophy originally associated with the work of the Frankfurt School.

Deconstruction – Doesn't actually mean "demolition;" instead it means "breaking down" or analyzing something (especially the words in a work of fiction or nonfiction) to discover its true significance, which is supposedly almost never exactly what the author subconsciously intended.

DEI – Diversity, equity, and inclusion; a conceptual framework that promotes the fair treatment and full participation of all people, especially in the workplace, including populations who have historically been underrepresented or subject to discrimination because of their background, identity, disability, etc. However, 21st century Progressive regressive DEI programs have returned us to the days of Jim Crow, with some races seen as virtuous and others as evil, the only difference being the colors have changed.

Disparate impact – Also called adverse impact, occurs when a decision, practice or policy has a disproportionately negative effect on a protected group, even though the impact may be unintentional.

Diversity – In today's Progressive regressive ideology, "diversity" is defined not by opinion, such as viewpoint diversity and heterodox thinking, but instead by race, ethnicity, or gender identity.

Dystopia – An imagined state or society in which there is great suffering or injustice, typically one that is totalitarian or post-apocalyptic.

Equality of Outcomes – It means that given the same opportunity and privileges two people should end up in the same position or at least equal position. But equality of "opportunity" does not promise equality in the "outcome." People have different levels of skill and put different amounts of effort into whatever they do. Only a totalitarian state can enforce equal outcomes, creating a state of dystopia.

Equity – In today's Progressive regressive ideology, "equity" is no longer the laudable goal of equality of opportunity, but the insistence on equality of outcome, meaning the statistical equivalence of races and genders. This in practice means more of the preferred and fewer of the despised (i.e., institutionalized racism and discrimination), a desirable goal by Progressives, as long as their preferred categories benefit.

First Amendment – States that "Congress shall make no law respecting an establishment of religion, or prohibiting the free exercise thereof; or abridging the freedom of speech, or of the press; or the right of the people peaceably to assemble, and to petition the government for a redress of grievances" and applies to every American citizen.

Frankfurt School – The Frankfurt School's biggest intellectual creation was Critical Theory, an approach to cultural analysis that focuses on criticizing existing social structures. It's founding members included Max Horkheimer, Theodor Adorno, Erich Fromm, Walter Benjamin, Jürgen Habermas, and Herbert Marcuse.

Groupthink – A phenomenon that occurs when a group of individuals reaches a consensus without critical reasoning or evaluation of the consequences or alternatives. Groupthink is based on a common desire not to upset the balance of a group of people.

Hypocrisy – Is the practice of engaging in the same behavior or activity for which one criticizes another or the practice of claiming to have moral standards or beliefs to which one's own behavior does not conform.

Identity Politics – Is a political approach wherein people of a particular gender, religion, race, social background, social class or other identifying factors, develop political agendas that are based upon these identities.

Idiocracy – An idiocracy is a disparaging term for a society run by or made up of idiots (or people perceived as such). Idiocracy is also the title of a 2006 satirical film that depicts a future in which humanity has become dumb.

Illiberalism – The 21st century term is used to describe an attitude that is close-minded, intolerant, bigoted and is a key attribute of the 21st century Progressivism movement.

Implicit Bias Training – Are programs purport to expose people to their implicit biases, provide tools to adjust automatic patterns of thinking, and ultimately eliminate discriminatory behaviors.

Inclusion – In today's Progressive regressive ideology, "inclusion" means including preferred races and genders, and excluding others, as we see in hiring, college admissions, funding, promotions, and awards.

Intersectionality – A term that refers to the "multiple social forces, social identities, and ideological instruments through which power and disadvantage are expressed and legitimized."

Jim Crow – Racial segregation laws up to 1965, that were enacted and enforced in the South in the late 19th and early 20th centuries by white Southern Democrat-dominated state legislatures to disenfranchise and remove political and economic gains made by blacks during the Reconstruction period.

Liberating Tolerance – Herbert Marcuse propounded this Orwellian and illiberal oxymoron in the 1960s that would involve "the withdrawal of toleration of speech and assembly from groups and movements" on the Right, as opposed to the aggressive partisan promotion of speech, groups, and Progressive movements on the Left.

Libertarian – An advocate of the doctrine of free will; a person who upholds the principles of individual liberty especially of thought and action; a member of a political party advocating libertarian principles.

Marxism – The political, economic, and social principles and policies advocated by Marx and a theory and practice of socialism including the labor theory of value, dialectical materialism, the class struggle, and dictatorship of the proletariat until the establishment of a classless society.

Meliorism – Is the doctrine that the federal government should intervene in the market economy to improve the economic condition of citizens

Meritocracy – Is the only way a free people can create an efficient, prosperous, opportunity society. Without it, nobody has any incentive to innovate or work hard. The capable and hard-working become cynical and resentful, while the incompetent and the indolent know they don't have to step up, because they can live for free. This is the inherent flaw of Marxism, Communism, and Socialism.

Microaggression – It has entered the national conversation to mean brief, subtle verbal or nonverbal exchanges—often unintended—that send denigrating messages because of the recipient's group membership.

Multiculturalism – The view that cultures, races, and ethnicities, particularly those of minority groups, deserve special acknowledgement of their differences within a dominant political culture.

Nihilism – Is a philosophy, or family of views within philosophy, that rejects generally accepted or fundamental aspects of human existence, such as objective truth, knowledge, morality, values, or meaning.

Political Correctness – A term used to describe language, policies, or measures that are intended to avoid offense or disadvantage to members of particular groups in society.

Postmodernism – Is an intellectual stance or a mode of discourse that rejects the possibility of reliable knowledge, denies the existence of a universal, stable reality, and frames aesthetics and beauty as arbitrary and subjective.

Progressivism – A political philosophy, in prior 19th and 20th centuries' periods, in support of social reform based on the idea of progress in which advancements in science, technology, economic development, and social organization are vital to improve the human condition. However, today's 21st century Progressivism has now devolved into a neo-Marxist and racist ideology founded on illiberal DEI principles.

Sapience – Also known as wisdom, is the ability to think and act using knowledge, experience, understanding, common sense and insight. Sapience is associated with attributes such as intelligence, enlightenment, unbiased judgment, compassion, experiential self-knowledge, self-actualization, and virtues such as ethics, benevolence, and critical thinking.

Social Justice – A political and philosophical theory which asserts that there are dimensions to the concept of justice beyond those embodied in the principles of civil or criminal law, economic supply and demand, or traditional moral frameworks.

Telos – Its purpose, end, or goal.

White Privilege – The set of social and economic advantages that white people have by virtue of their race in a culture characterized by racial inequality.

White Supremacy – The term "white supremacy" can be confusing because it can mean an actual belief in the superiority of white people, in which case it is despicable. However, it is nearly always employed to mean something much larger—anything from classical philosophers to Enlightenment thinkers to the Industrial Revolution.

Woke – Or wokeism, is a left-wing racialist ideology of attempting to achieve "critical consciousness," which is a neo-Marxist term, meaning awakening the subject to their own oppression, then recruiting them into left-wing revolution. In reality, per Progressive regressive ideology, if we use "woke" as a stand-in for an illiberal concept such as critical race theory, it literally means subverting the United States into an oppressor nation that divides classes along the lines of race and then endorses active discrimination in order to create racial equity or equality of group outcomes. Being woke is the opposite to being sapient.

References

Arnn, Larry P. "Orwell's *1984* and Today." *Imprimis.* December 2020. Volume 49, Issue 12. https://imprimis.hillsdale.edu/orwells-1984-today/.

Beyond Red vs. Blue: The Political Typology-11. Progressive Left. Pew Research Center. November 9, 2021. https://www.pewresearch.org/politics/2021/11/09/progressive-left/.

Burke, Lindsey M. "DeSantis Tackles Divisive 'Diversity, Equity, and Inclusion' Programs on College Campuses." The Heritage Foundation. January 11, 2023. https://www.heritage.org/education/commentary/desantis-tackles-divisive-diversity-equity-and-inclusion-programs-college.

Concha, Joe. "Joe Biden's 'Ministry of Truth.'" The Hill. 05/01/22. https://thehill.com/opinion/white-house/3472878-joe-bidens-ministry-of-truth/.

Concha, Joe. "Ron DeSantis is winning the culture wars." The Hill. 03/27/23. https://thehill.com/opinion/campaign/599871-ron-desantis-is-winning-the-culture-wars /.

Connor, Bill. "The increasing intolerance of the left must stop." *Charleston Mercury*. March 25, 2023. https://www.charlestonmercury.com/single-post/the-increasing-intolerance-of-the-left-must-stop.

Continetti, Matthew. "From Woke to Broke." *National Review.* October 26, 2019. https://www.nationalreview.com/2019/10/from-woke-to-broke/.

Copland, James R., John Ketcham and Christopher F. Rufo. "Next Step for the Parents' Movement: Curriculum Transparency." *City Journal.* December 1, 2021. https://www.city-journal.org/how-to-achieve-transparency-in-schools.

Daniel, Grace. "My Woke Employees Tried to Cancel Me: Here's How I Fought Back and Saved My Nonprofit." The Daily Signal. June 07, 2021. https://www.dailysignal.com/2021/06/07/my-woke-employees-tried-to-cancel-me-heres-how-i-fought-back-and-saved-my-nonprofit/.

Feehery, John. "Feehery: On the ballot this year: progressives' embrace of the 'Brave New World.'" The Hill. 05/10/22. https://thehill.com/opinion/3482368-feehery-on-the-ballot-this-year-progressives-embrace-of-the-brave-new-world/.

Flaherty, Peter. "Where Is the BLM $60 Million?" Real Clear Politics. February 9, 2022. https://www.realclearpolitics.com/articles/2022/02/09/where_is_the_blm_60_million_147160.html#!.

Gold, Howard. "Opinion: At America's most 'woke' colleges, extreme liberal politics fails students and free speech." Market Watch. Jan. 27, 2020. https://www.marketwatch.com/story/at-americas-most-woke-colleges-extreme-liberal-politics-fails-students-and-free-speech-2020-01-27.

Goldberg, Zachary and Eric Kaufmann. "Yes, Critical Race Theory Is Being Taught in Schools." *City Journal.* October 20, 2022. https://www.city-journal.org/article/yes-critical-race-theory-is-being-taught-in-schools.

Gonzalez, Pedro L. "The Progressive Call for Compassion at the Border Is a Political Prop." *Newsweek*. 3/22/21. https://www.newsweek.com/progressive-call-compassion-border-political-prop-opinion-1577896.

Graber, Richard. "Woke Foundations Use Dollars Acquired Through Capitalism to Undermine Free Market Principles." The Daily Signal. May 18, 2021. https://www.dailysignal.com/2021/05/18/woke-foundations-use-dollars-acquired-through-capitalism-to-undermine-free-market-principles/.

Groothuis, Douglas. "Critical Race Theory in Six Logical Fallacies." National Association of Scholars. Summer 2022. https://www.nas.org/academic-questions/35/2/critical-race-theory-in-six-logical-fallacies.

Haidt, Jonathan. "Why Universities Must Choose One Telos: Truth or Social Justice." Heterodox Academy. October 21, 2017. https://heterodoxacademy.org/blog/one-telos-truth-or-social-justice-2/.

Hanson, Victor Davis. "A Country We No Longer Recognize, a Coup We Never Knew." *Epoch Times*. January 9, 2023. https://www.theepochtimes.com/the-coup-we-never-knew_4964793.html?utm_source=Opinion&src_src=Opinion&utm_campaign=opinion-2023-01-09&src_cmp=opinion-2023-01-09&utm_medium=email&est=OzVL4iho43ZC2QWnyxSN5OH0%2BLcGQr13rLz1BDrqC3207KNptBn7dWOs5FzFEncEbw%3D%3D.

Hanson, Victor Davis. "Anatomy of the Woke Madness." Independent Institute. June 16, 2021. https://www.independent.org/news/article.asp?id=13622.

Hanson, Victor Davis. "Why Are Progressives So Illiberal?." Independent Institute. February 1, 2021. https://www.independent.org/news/article.asp?id=13400.

Hartney, Michael. "Ron DeSantis's Big Night." *National Review*. August 26, 2022. https://www.nationalreview.com/2022/08/ron-desantiss-big-night/.

Hartney, Michael. "Schooled by DeSantis." *City Journal*. November 15, 2022. https://www.city-journal.org/ron-desantis-school-board-candidates-vs-teachers-unions.

Hendrickson, Mark. "The Three Meta-Errors That Pervade Progressivism." *Epoch Times*. April 16, 2019. https://www.theepochtimes.com/the-three-meta-errors-that-pervade-progressivism_2879139.html?utm_source=ai&utm_medium=search.

Hochman, Nate. 'Gavin Newsom's Real Constituents." *National Review*. March 4, 2023. https://www.nationalreview.com/2023/03/gavin-newsoms-real-constituents/.

Hochman, Nate. "Exclusive: Republicans Revive Counter-CRT Bills in Congress." *National Review*. February 28, 2023. https://www.nationalreview.com/2023/02/exclusive-republicans-revive-counter-crt-bills-in-congress/.

Hogan, Thomas. "A Litany of Failure." *City Journal*. August 30, 2022. https://www.city-journal.org/the-failure-of-progressive-criminal-justice-reforms.

Humphrey Clifford. "The Myth of Change as Progress in Progressivism." *Epoch Times*. February 20, 2019. Updated: February 20, 2019 https://www.theepochtimes.com/the-myth-of-change-as-progress-in-progressivism_2800152.html?utm_source=ai&utm_medium=search.

Joyce, Tom. "Companies are going woke, but consumers aren't." *Washington Examiner.* January 12, 2023 https://www.washingtonexaminer.com/restoring-america/community-family/companies-are-going-woke-but-consumers-arent.

Kirchoff, Courtney. "Here Are 8 Stupid Things You Need to Know About the Idiotic Green New Deal. Louder With Crowder. February 07, 2019. https://www.louderwithcrowder.com/herere-8-things-you-need-to-know-about-the-idiotic-green-new-deal.

Kotkin, Joel. "California's Progressive Betrayal *City Journal."* June 11, 2019. https://www.city-journal.org/california-progressive-policies-hurt-working-and-middle-class.

Kotkin, Joel. "California's Woke Hypocrisy." *City Journal.* July 29, 2020. https://www.city-journal.org/california-woke-hypocrisy.

Kotkin, Joel. "The Regression of America's Big Progressive Cities." August 6, 2019 https://joelkotkin.com/the-regression-of-americas-big-progressive-cities/.

Leef, George. "A Racially 'Woke' Agenda Is Now Hardwired in Public Schools." Minding the Campus. November 4, 2019. https://www.mindingthecampus.org/2019/11/04/a-racially-woke-agenda-is-now-hardwired-in-public-schools/.

Lowry, Rich. "Joe Biden Is the Brezhnev of DEI." *National Review.* February 20, 2023. https://www.nationalreview.com/2023/02/joe-biden-is-the-brezhnev-of-dei/?bypass_key=cFhieFFSTHh0ZTcxaU1TdnhTeW5IQT09OjpNRFV2UWxZM1prSmtSbVZKV2tWNGVsTk9RM2xZVVQwOQ%3D%3D&utm_source=Sailthru&utm_medium=email&utm_campaign=NR%20Daily%20Monday%20through%20Friday%202023-02-20&utm_term=NRDaily-Smart.

Lucci, Michael. "Not a National Model—a National Warning." *City Journal.* July 28, 2022. https://www.city-journal.org/gavin-newsoms-california-is-a-warning-not-a-model.

Mangual, Rafael A. "What George Soros Gets Wrong." *City Journal.* August 1, 2022. https://www.city-journal.org/what-george-soros-gets-wrong-on-criminal-justice.

Mansfield, Erin and Kayla Jimenez. "These PACS are funding 'parents' rights advocates' running for local school board positions." USA Today. Oct. 24, 2022. https://www.usatoday.com/in-depth/news/politics/2022/10/23/super-pacs-spending-local-school-board-races/8125668001/.

Morris, Kathy. "The Most Woke States (and the Least)." Zippia. Aug. 22, 2022. https://www.zippia.com/advice/most-woke-states/.

Mukherjee, Renu. "Without a 'Diversity' Leg to Stand On." *City Journal.* October 12, 2022. https://www.city-journal.org/affirmative-action-and-viewpoint-diversity-at-harvard.

Nickels, Thom. "No Cause for Controversy." *City Journal.* May 6, 2022. https://www.city-journal.org/florida-parental-rights-law-should-be-no-cause-for-controversy.

Oswald, Joseph U. "Patriot Online School Board Training Program." The Leadership Institute. https://www.leadershipinstitute.training/enrollments.

Owens, Ernest. "Here's the Real Takeaway From Black Lives Matter's Sketchy Finances." Daily Beast. May. 20, 2022. https://www.thedailybeast.com/heres-the-real-takeaway-from-black-lives-matters-sketchy-finances.

Peterson, Jordan. "Who Is Teaching Your Kids?" Prager U Video. https://www.prageru.com/video/who-is-teaching-your-kids?gclid=CjwKCAiAqaWdBhAvEiwAGAQltp9fPSnUTfV7LNKBQnJBtl0vroG3F_pOIqW_YaZkaAXUYHd-t58OvBoCXLkQAvD_BwE.

Philipp, Joshua. "Orwell Explains How Socialists Alter Language to Alter History." *Epoch Times.* August 28, 2019. https://www.theepochtimes.com/mkt_app/orwell-explains-how-socialists-alter-language-to-alter-history_2962515.html.

Price, Harley. "From Mao to Now: A 'Progress' Report on the New Millennium." *Epoch Times.* December 29, 2020. https://www.theepochtimes.com/from-mao-to-now-a-progress-report-on-the-new-millennium_3634981.html?utm_source=ai&utm_medium=search.

Rascius, Brendan. "What does it mean to be 'woke?' Majority in the US have positive view, study finds." *Kansas City Star* March 8, 2023. https://www.kansascity.com/news/nation-world/national/article272907550.html.

Reilly, Wilfred. "The Whiteness of Wokeness." Prager U Video. April 11, 2022. https://www.prageru.com/video/the-whiteness-of-wokeness?gclid=CjwKCAjw586hBhBrEiwAQYEnHbveXGCrWn2UzLhbD1h8USaquy7Hutf8ua3vgiGi7M4EuN_JbCDMrRoCoXMQAvD_BwE.

Rufo, Christopher F. "'Antiracism' Comes to the Heartland." *City Journal.* January 19, 2021. https://www.city-journal.org/antiracism-comes-to-the-heartland.

Rufo, Christopher F. "Anarchy in Seattle." *City Journal.* June 10, 2020. https://www.city-journal.org/seattle-capitol-hill-autonomous-zone.

Rufo, Christopher F. "Bad Education." *City Journal.* February 11, 2021. https://www.city-journal.org/philadelphia-fifth-graders-forced-to-celebrate-black-communism.

Rufo, Christopher F. "Biden Nationalizes the DEI Bureaucracy." Substack Email. Feb. 23, 2023.

Rufo, Christopher F. "Critical Race Theory's Chief Marketing Officer." *City Journal.* July 23, 2021. https://www.city-journal.org/ibram-x-kendi-master-marketer.

Rufo, Christopher F. "Cult Programming in Seattle." *City Journal.* July 8, 2020. https://www.city-journal.org/seattle-interrupting-whiteness-training.

Rufo, Christopher F. "DEI Cult." *City Journal.* February 9, 2023. https://www.city-journal.org/the-university-of-south-floridas-diversity-cult.

Rufo, Christopher F. "Florida v. Critical Race Theory." *City Journal.* December 16, 2021. https://www.city-journal.org/florida-v-critical-race-theory.

Rufo, Christopher F. "Gone Crazy." *City Journal.* February 18, 2021. https://www.city-journal.org/east-side-community-school-tells-parents-to-become-white-traitors.

Rufo, Christopher F. "Laying Siege to the Institutions." *Imprimis.* April/May 2022 Volume 51, Issue 4/5. https://imprimis.hillsdale.edu/laying-siege-to-the-institutions/.

Rufo, Christopher F. "Man in the Arena." *City Journal.* November 16, 2022. https://www.city-journal.org/how-did-ron-desantis-outperform-the-gop.

Rufo, Christopher F. "Racism in the Name of 'Anti-Racism.'" Substack Email. Feb. 17, 2023. https://rufo.substack.com/p/racism-in-the-name-of-anti-racism?utm_source=post-email-title&publication_id=1248321&post_id=103110646&isFreemail=true&utm_medium=email.

Rufo, Christopher F. "Recapturing Higher Education." *City Journal.* January 12, 2023. https://www.city-journal.org/recapturing-higher-education.

Rufo, Christopher F. "Senator Cotton's Stand." *City Journal.* March 24, 2021. https://www.city-journal.org/tom-cotton-senate-bill-on-critical-race-theory.

Rufo, Christopher F. "Shut Down Activist Academic Departments." *City Journal.* March 15, 2023. https://www.city-journal.org/shut-down-activist-academic-departments.

Rufo, Christopher F. "Subversive Education." *City Journal.* March 17, 2021. https://www.city-journal.org/critical-race-theory-in-wake-county-nc-schools.

Rufo, Christopher F. "Teaching Hate." *City Journal.* December 18, 2020. https://www.city-journal.org/racial-equity-programs-seattle-schools.

Rufo, Christopher F. "The Commissars Will See You Now." *City Journal.* March 1, 2023. https://www.city-journal.org/florida-international-university-dei-bureaucracy.

Rufo, Christopher F. "The Courage of Our Convictions." *City Journal.* April 22, 2021. https://www.city-journal.org/how-to-fight-critical-race-theory.

Rufo, Christopher F. "The Dismantlers." *City Journal.* August 3, 2022. https://www.city-journal.org/san-diego-schools-gender-extremism.

Rufo, Christopher F. "The Enablers." *City Journal.* July 10, 2021. https://www.city-journal.org/the-enablers-of-critical-race-theory.

Rufo, Christopher F. "The Fight for Curriculum Transparency." *City Journal.* February 23, 2022. https://www.city-journal.org/the-fight-for-curriculum-transparency.

Rufo, Christopher F. "The Highest Principle." *City Journal.* February 2, 2023. https://www.city-journal.org/florida-state-university-adopts-dei-programming.

Rufo, Christopher F. "The New Segregation." *City Journal.* October 19, 2020. https://www.city-journal.org/seattle-race-segregated-diversity-trainings.

Sailer, John D. and Ray M. Sanchez. "An Overt Political Litmus Test." *City Journal.* May 16, 2022. https://www.city-journal.org/california-community-colleges-impose-political-litmus-test.

Salzman, Philip Carl. "Free Speech in Peril: SJW's Are Changing America Word by Word." Minding the Campus. May 21, 2019. https://docslib.org/doc/3588643/free-speech-in-peril.

Salzman, Philip Carl. "Hate and Fear Are Now Major Motivators on Campus." *Epoch Times.* October 11, 2022. https://www.theepochtimes.com/hate-and-fear-are-now-major-motivators-on-campus_4785439.html?utm_medium=search&utm_source=ai.

Salzman, Philip Carl. "How Progressives Are Retrogressive." *Epoch Times.* January 6, 2022. https://www.theepochtimes.com/how-progressives-are-retrogressive_4193422.html?utm_source=ai&utm_medium=search.

Salzman, Philip Carl. "National Suicide by Education." Minding the Campus. September 23, 2022. https://www.mindingthecampus.org/author/philip-carl-salzman/.

Salzman, Philip Carl. "Safeguarding Our Republic From Progressivism Madness." *Epoch Times*. October 11, 2022. https://www.theepochtimes.com/hate-and-fear-are-now-major-motivators-on-campus_4785439.html?utm_medium=search&utm_source=ai.

Schneider, Elena. "Soros caps off midterm spending with $50M super PAC contribution." Politico. 12/07/2022. https://www.politico.com/news/2022/12/07/george-soros-midterm-super-pac-00072797.

Seminara, Dave. "The Bogeyman." *City Journal*. May 6, 2022. https://www.city-journal.org/ron-desantis-media-bogeyman.

Sinha, Sohil. "Alexandria Ocasio-Cortez: The Dumbest Democrat and the Most Underperforming Congresswoman." TFI Global News. April 5, 2021. https://tfiglobalnews.com/2021/04/05/alexandria-ocasio-cortez-the-dumbest-democrat-and-the-most-underperforming-congresswoman/.

Stimson, Charles "Cully" and Zack Smith. "Meet Marilyn Mosby, the Rogue Prosecutor Wreaking Havoc in Baltimore." The Heritage Foundation. October 27, 2020. https://www.heritage.org/crime-and-justice/commentary/meet-marilyn-mosby-the-rogue-prosecutor-wreaking-havoc-baltimore.

Stimson, Charles "Cully" and Zack Smith. "Soros' Claim About Leftist Prosecutors Is Big Lie." The Heritage Foundation. August 18, 2022. https://www.heritage.org/crime-and-justice/commentary/soros-claim-about-leftist-prosecutors-big-lie.

Thayer, Bradley A. "Our 1776 Moment: Either a Liberal or Progressive America." *Epoch Times*. January 26, 2022. https://www.theepochtimes.com/our-1776-moment-either-a-liberal-or-progressive-america_4231197.html?utm_source=ai&utm_medium=search.

The 3 Big Differences Between Conservatives and Progressives. The Heritage Foundation. https://www.heritage.org/conservatism/heritage-explains/the-3-big-differences-between-conservatives-and-progressives.

Thomas, Bradley. "Statistical Disparities Among Groups Are Not Proof of Discrimination." Foundation for Economic Education (FEE). May 21, 2019. https://fee.org/articles/statistical-disparities-among-groups-are-not-proof-of-discrimination/?itm_source=parsely-api.

Traldi, Oliver. "Peak Woke?" *City Journal*. July 6, 2022. https://www.city-journal.org/have-we-reached-peak-woke.

Ursúa, Soledad. "San Francisco's Heart of Darkness." *City Journal*. February 14, 2022. https://www.city-journal.org/san-franciscos-harm-reduction-policies-a-nightmare.

Wiseman, Oliver. "The Least Woke City in America." *City Journal*. Winter 2022. https://www.city-journal.org/miami-the-least-woke-city-in-america.

Woke Schooling: A Toolkit for Concerned Parents. Manhattan Institute. June 17, 2021. https://www.manhattan-institute.org/woke-schooling-toolkit-for-concerned-parents.

Index

F

T

Author Bio

Author: Corey Lee Wilson.

Corey Lee Wilson was raised an atheist by his liberal *Playboy* Bunny mother, has three Anglo-Hispanic siblings, a bi-racial daughter, a brother who died of AIDS, baptized a Protestant by his conservative grandparents, attended temple with his Jewish foster parents, baptized again as a Catholic for his first Filipina wife, attends Buddhist ceremonies with his second Thai wife, became an agnostic on his own free will for most of his life, and is a lifetime independent voter.

Corey felt the sting of intellectual humility by repeating the 4th grade and attended eighteen different schools before putting himself through college (without parents) at Mt. San Antonio College and Cal Poly Pomona University (while on triple secret probation). Named Who's Who of American College Students in 1984, he received a BS in Economics (summa cum laude) and won his fraternity's most prestigious undergraduate honor, the Phi Kappa Tau Fraternity's Shideler Award, both in 1985. In 2020, he became a member of the Heterodox Academy and in 2021 a member of the National Association of Scholars and 1776 Unites.

As a satirist and fraternity man, Corey started Fratire Publishing in 2012 and transformed the fiction "fratire" genre to a respectable and viewpoint diverse non-fiction genre promoting practical knowledge and wisdom to help everyday people navigate safely through the many hazards of life. In 2019, he founded the SAPIENT Being to help promote freedom of speech, viewpoint diversity, intellectual humility and most importantly advance sapience in America's students and campuses.

The SAPIENT Being has three programs: Make Free Speech Again On Campus (MFSAOC) Program, Free Speech Alumni Ambassador (FSAA) Program, and the Sapient Conservative Textbooks (SCT) Program—all working together to promote its mission and vision of sapience.

If you're interested in the MFSAOC Program and starting a S.A.P.I.E.N.T. Being club, chapter, or alliance on or off campus, please go to https://www.SapientBeing.org/start-a-chapter, e-mail SapientBeing@att.net, or call (951) 638-5562 for more information.

If you're interested in becoming a conservative campus advisor or free speech champion for right-leaning campus organizations as part of the FSAA Program from the S.A.P.I.E.N.T. Being, please e-mail at SapientBeing@att.net, or call (951) 638-5562 for more information.

If you're interested as an educator, administrator, or student in the SCT Program and their 40 MADNESS series of textbooks from the S.A.P.I.E.N.T. Being, please check them out at the Fratire Publishing website at https://www.FratirePublishing.com/madnessbooks, for more information.

Hopefully, this textbook was enlightening and your journey through it—along with mine—made you aware of the issues and challenges ahead of us. If it has, your quest and mine towards becoming a sapient being has begun. If it hasn't, there's no better time to start than now. Come join us in creating a society advancing personal intelligence and enlightenment now together (S.A.P.I.E.N.T.) and become a sapient being.